Jesús Padilla-Gálvez (ed.)

Wittgenstein, from a New Point of View

PETER LANG
Europäischer Verlag der Wissenschaften

Bibliographic Information published by Die Deutsche Bibliothek
Die Deutsche Bibliothek lists this publication in the Deutsche Nationalbibliografie; detailed bibliographic data is available in the internet at <http://dnb.ddb.de>.

With financial support by
Alexander von Humboldt-Stiftung.

ISSN 1439-7668
ISBN 3-631-50623-6
US-ISBN 0-8204-6407-4
© Peter Lang GmbH
Europäischer Verlag der Wissenschaften
Frankfurt am Main 2003
All rights reserved.

All parts of this publication are protected by copyright. Any utilisation outside the strict limits of the copyright law, without the permission of the publisher, is forbidden and liable to prosecution. This applies in particular to reproductions, translations, microfilming, and storage and processing in electronic retrieval systems.

Printed in Germany 1 2 3 4 6 7

www.peterlang.de

Contents

Jesús Padilla-Gálvez
Introduction 7

Norberto Abreu e Silva Neto
Wittgenstein's Philosophy throughout the Corners of Brazil:
Data for the Study of Its Reception 13

Axel Arturo Barceló Aspeitia
Grammatical Necessity in Wittgenstein's Middle Period 47

Jesús Padilla-Gálvez
"Metamathematics Does Not Exist" – Wittgenstein's Criticism of
Metamathematics 67

Francisco Rodríguez-Consuegra
Wittgenstein and Russell on Propositions and Forms 79

Josep-Maria Terricabras
(Theology as Grammar) – Wittgenstein in Brackets 111

Alejandro Tomasini Bassols
Wittgensteinian Considerations about Time 125

Jesús Padilla-Gálvez
Spanish Wittgenstein Bibliography (1986 - 2001) 145

Authors and Editors 159

JESÚS PADILLA-GÁLVEZ

Introduction

Undoubtedly, Ludwig Wittgenstein (1889 – 1951) is considered one of the most famous philosophers in many areas such as logic, philosophy of languages, philosophy of mathematics and philosophy of psychology. In contrast to other 20th century philosophers, who arranged to have their complete works published while still alive or after their deaths, Wittgenstein's works are still incompletely published with only part of them being in print. He wasn't concerned with the issue of notoriety nor was he concerned with fame. However, his lectures and publications would very early be recognized by his Spanish colleagues and were reviewed as early as in 1933.

The aim of this introduction is to briefly examine the reception of Wittgenstein's works by Spanish and Latin-American philosophers. The following section contains papers written by contemporary philosophers about Wittgenstein's works and its reception in Latin America.[1]

One of the earliest references about the *Tractatus* goes back to J. David García Baca, who wrote an article about the foundations of mathematics in Catalan language.[2] The *Tractatus* was characterized as a general introduction to symbolic logic. Some years later, he would publish his '*Introduction to Modern Logic*', in which he made several remarks about Wittgenstein's "logic of schema".[3]

Needless to say, that these have had a significant impact on early discussions on logic and mathematical questions. From that point of time onwards, the academic philosophy had embraced Wittgenstein's works which gained popularity some years later, and was further expounded when J. David García Baca published several studies about the relationship between the logic of schema and Hilbert's axiomatic logic.[4]

---

[1] You will find details about the reception of Ludwig Wittgenstein in Brazil in the article of Norberto Abreu e Silva Neto in this volume.

[2] J. David García [Baca], *Assaigs Moderns per a la fondamentació de les matemàtiques*. Societat Catalana de Ciènces Fisiques, Químiques i Matemàtiques, Barcelona 1933.

[3] J. David García Baca, *Introducción a la lógica moderna*, Barcelona 1936, 49.

[4] J. David García Baca, "Sobre las relaciones entre la lógica esquemática de Wittgenstein y la lógica axiomática de Hilbert", *Acta Científica Venezolana*, 2, 1951, 56-61, 103-105,144-147. J. David García Baca, "Wittgenstein: Philosophical Investigations", *Revista Nacional de Cultura*, mayo-junio, 1954, 157-158.

During the Spanish Civil War many scientists and academics emigrated to the Americas where they continued with their research. One of these well-known philosophers is José Ferrater Mora, who carried out a sound investigation of the main thoughts and ideas of the Viennese philosopher.[5] The end of the Spanish Civil War signaled a period of restriction in scientific research and thought. This it was hoped would end with the death of the Dictator. Unfortunately it turned out, that some (questionable) forms of academic style had had an impact on the way of doing research even after 1975. Traditional schools of philosophy imposed their right to give admission only to certain scholars, which as a consequence, lead to very specific and often restricted points of view within the lines of investigation and research. Over the long period of the twentieth century, many attempts were made to break down these barriers. One of the first attempts to include Wittgenstein's works into the philosophical discussion is therefore closely connected to the publication of the philosophical journal *Theoria* in Madrid (1952-1956).

Thirty-three years later, the editor Miguel Sánchez-Mazas would characterize the intellectual climate of the previous years as culturally deficient and obscure, or in his own words "[...] un clima culturalmente difícil y oscuro."[6] Within this short period of time, contributions from Raimundo Drudis Baldrich,[7] José Ferrater Mora[8] and Miguel Sánchez-Mazas[9] would be published in *Theoria*. These articles contained general overviews and were hardly ever reviewed or cited by later colleagues.

In 1972 a monography about the *Tractatus logico-philosophicus* was published in Valencia. This contained contributions from researchers who stood in contact with the journal *Teorema*. The most famous of them was Alfonso García Suárez, who worked about private languages and was dealing with the reception of private languages within the English-speaking world.[10] His thesis was published as

---

[5] José Ferrater Mora, "Wittgenstein o la destrucción", *Realidad*, 13, 1949, 1-2; 14, 1949, 129-140. José Ferrater Mora, "Wittgenstein oder die Destruktion", *Der Monat*, 4, 1952, 41, 489-495. José Ferrater Mora, "Wittgenstein, a Symbol of Troubled Times", *Philosophy and Phenomenological Research*, 14, 1953, 89-96.

[6] Miguel Sánchez-Mazas, "Eadem mutata resurgo", *Theoria – Segunda época*, 1, 1985, 1-11, 1.

[7] Raimundo Drudis Baldrich, "Ludwig Wittgenstein y su obra filosófica", *Theoria*, 2, 1952, 57-61.

[8] José Ferrater Mora, Wittgenstein, "símbolo de una época angustiada", *Theoria*, 7/8, 1954, 33-38.

[9] Miguel Sánchez-Mazas, "La ciencia, el lenguaje y el mundo según Wittgenstein", *Theoria*, 7/8, 1954, 127-130.

[10] A. García Suárez, "Cartesianismo fuerte y cartesianismo débil: A propósito de David Pears: Wittgenstein", *Teorema*, 8, 1972, 99-103. A. García Suárez, "Es el lenguaje del *Tractatus* un lenguaje privado?", *Teorema*, Número monográfico sobre el Tractatus logico-

a monograph and deals with the philosophical proposition which led to the idea of the private languages and thus reflects the development of Wittgenstein's works. Then he concentrated on the criticism of grammatical illusions and the egocentric perspective. Finally he analyzed the functioning of propositions about feelings in the first person perspective with a special focus on the knowledge of one's own experience and other people's propositions about experience. In this context he investigated the notion of criteria.

A majority of the studies since the 1970s had one aspect in common: many Spanish-speaking authors didn't read the original text sources. They tend to wait for the English translations of the texts which are then the basis for further translations into Spanish. This led to two obvious consequences: firstly, the research studies turn out to be fairly delayed compared to the new editions. Secondly, as most authors use translated text versions, hardly any of the authors quotes the Wittgenstein Archives in Cambridge.

At the beginning of the 1980s we were confronted with numerous publications on Wittgenstein's works.[11] These studies can be characterized as follows:

(1) they tend to reflect primarily the discussion going on in the English-speaking countries,[12]

(2) they don't promote discussion among Spanish researchers with the effect that authors hardly ever cite their colleagues,[13]

(3) rather than following specific lines of investigation, the discussion concentrates on what has already been said about Wittgenstein,[14]

(4) there is a tendency of writing rather general introductions which reflect only some parts of Wittgenstein's work,[15]

---

philosophicus, 1972, 117-130. A. García Súarez, "Solipsismo y 'experiencia privada'", *Teorema*, IV/1, 1974, 91-106. A. García Súarez, *La lógica de la experiencia. Wittgenstein y el problema del lenguaje privado*, Madrid 1976.

[11] J. L. Prades / V. Sanfélix, *Wittgenstein: Mundo y lenguaje*, Madrid, 1990. María Cerezo, *Lógica y lenguaje en el* Tractatus *de Wittgenstein. Crítica interna y problemas de interpretación*, Pamplona 1998.

[12] "Aspectos de la filosofía de L. Wittgenstein", *Daimon*, 2, 1990, 5-41; 43-70; 87-98; 217-227.

[13] It is interesting to realize that Spanish authors do not quote their colleagues in the majority of the publications.

[14] Most of the monographs are simplified versions copied from other investigations rather than new thoughts. J.L. Gil Pareja, *La filosofía de la psicología de Ludwig Wittgenstein*, Barcelona 1992.

[15] J. Sadaba, *Conocer a Wittgenstein y su obra*, Barcelona, 1980. P. López de Santamaría, *Introducción a Wittgenstein*, Barcelona 1986. R. Drudis Baldrich, *Wittgenstein*, Madrid 1998.

(5) they contain formal and methodological mistakes in the sense that some authors simply copy the translated Spanish texts without quoting the source. There doesn't seem to exist a clear distinction between plagiarism and a quotation,[16]

(6) Wittgenstein's works are sometimes referred to the form of an essay, which leads to a kind of diminution of a logically stringent thinker.[17]

There are only few authors who have established a specific line of investigation and if they have managed to do so, they tend to publish in other languages than Spanish.[18] A social history of the reception of a philosopher like Wittgenstein or a group of authors has already been written. One can also easily trace back the groups of researchers who follow a certain topic. One can easily analyze those investigations where certain authors are referred to and others are not. It is important to ask why specific references were never made and why certain questions were never addressed. This way of doing research shows that the present methods of investigation are still restricted and full of problems. The research papers seem to be repetitive and the ideas and hypothesis are primarily duplicated.

This volume is designed to present new ideas and approaches to analysis in order to open up a new perspective in the reception of Wittgenstein's works. The authors have worked outside the above mentioned tradition in Spain and have published most of their contributions in international journals. They are willing to present their results to debate and would welcome constructive feedback. Hopefully, the following years will motivate other researchers to come up with new ideas on the topics mentioned. However, recent reforms in the academic organizations suggest, that there might be a setback in the other direction.

---

[16] Parts of the original text of Wittgenstein's works are included in some articles and books without being quoted. One such example is the work of J. J. Acero, *Lenguaje y filosofía*, Barcelona 1993.

[17] Manuel Cruz, "Cincuenta años en la estela de Wittgenstein", *El País, Opinión*, 28. 4. 2001, 12. Isidoro Reguera, "El destino de un genio: El filósofo Ludwig Wittgenstein", *El País, Babelia*, 28. 4. 2001, 4-5. Jaime de Salas, "El judío errante", *ABC, Cultura*, 29-4-2001, 44. José Manuel Costa, "Wittgenstein, cincuenta años de silencio", *ABC, Cultura*, 29-4-2001, 44.

[18] Jesús Padilla-Gálvez, "Die spanische Rezeption des Wiener Kreises" en: *Nachrichten der FDÖP*. 5, 1994, pp. 7-24. Jesús Padilla-Gálvez, "Filosofía austriaca. Investigación y documentación" *LLULL*, 1995, Vol. 18 (Nr. 34), 300-302. Jesús Padilla-Gálvez, "El Círculo de Viena, reconsiderado", *Arbor*, CLV, 612, 1996, 9-13. Jesús Padilla-Gálvez, "Wittgenstein y el Círculo de Viena. Wittgenstein und der Wiener Kreis", en: *Wittgenstein und der Wiener Kreis* (ed. Jesús Padilla-Gálvez, Raimundo Drudis-Baldrich), Cuenca, 1998, 11-12.

Norberto Abreu e Silva Neto presents a short history of the reception of Ludwig Wittgenstein's work in Brazil. Norberto Abreu e Silva Neto is Professor at the University of Brasilia (Brazil). He is the author of numerous articles and books.

An interest in grammar initially led Wittgenstein from language to philosophy. Almost half of his work during the middle period is in this area. Whereas his discussions in the transition period include highly technical details, he later concentrates on questions which can be illustrated by reference to philosophy of language. Axel Arturo Barceló Aspeitia evaluated Wittgenstein's contribution to grammar from a different point of view. Axel Arturo Barceló Aspeitia is research fellow at the Instituto de Investigaciones Filosóficas at the Universidad Nacional Autónoma de México (Mexico). He published *Mathematics as Grammar. 'Grammar' in Wittgenstein's Philosophy of Mathematics during the Middle Period* (2000).

One wonders how Wittgenstein obtained his views about metamathematics? This seems to me more than merely a historical question, as I wished to know how the basic concepts were differentiated and how could one establish their adequacy. One possible approach which suggests itself is to take typical definitions, and examine case by case what assumptions and concepts are involved. The obstacle in such study, apart from the obvious demand of excessive time, is the lack of conclusiveness in both result and justification. The attempt to find an answer to this question led me to some interesting fragments of history of metamathematics. Jesús Padilla-Gálvez is Professor at the University of Castilla – La Mancha in Toledo (Spain). He is the author of numerous articles and books including *Referenz und Theorie der möglichen Welten* (1989), *Tratado metateórico de las teorías científicas* (2000) and the editor of *El Círculo de Viena, reconsiderado* (1996), and *Wittgenstein und der Wiener Kreis* (1998), among others.

Francisco Rodríguez Consuegra reinvestigated the relationship between Bertrand Russell and Ludwig Wittgenstein, both defined logic in relation to a particular logical language. The fundamental characteristic of logic, obviously, is that which is indicated when we say that logical propositions are true in virtue of their form. The question of argumentation cannot be easily displayed, which is in one system, deduced from the premises, might in another system, be itself taken as a premise. The author explains the most important differences between the two philosophers. Francisco Rodríguez Consuegra is Professor of Philosophy at the University of Valencia (Spain). He is the author of numerous articles including books such as *El método en la filosofía de Bertrand Russell* (1988), *The mathematical philosophy of Bertrand Russell: origins and development* (1991), *Ensayos inéditos / Kurt Gödel* (1994), *Kurt Gödel: unpublished philosophical essays; with a historico-philosophical introduction* (1995), *Análisis filosófico / Bertrand Russell; introducción y traducción* (1999).

It is known that Ludwig Wittgenstein was very interested in the problem of religion. He takes a new point of view in looking into the philosophical perspective. This has lead to a new form of discussion which has consequences for theology. Josep-María Terricabras is Professor at the University of Gerona (Spain). He is the author of *Ludwig Wittgenstein. Kommentar und Interpretation* (1978), and editor in Catalan of the *Tractatus logico-philosophicus* (1981), *A Wittgenstein Symposium: Girona*, (1989), *Teoría del coneixement* (1998), *Atrévete a pensar: la utilidad del pensamiento riguroso en la vida cotidiana* (1999), among others.

Considerations of the concept of time are surely to be found taking the first place amongst the problems that have marked the 20th century philosophical discussion. In Tomasini's essay, he would like to address the same issues by considering what Ludwig Wittgenstein had to say about the philosophy of time. In particular, he looked at his solution to Augustine's paradox about the 'evanescence' of the present. Alejandro Tomasini Bassols is researcher at the Instituto de Investigaciones Filosóficas at the Universidad Nacional Autónoma de México (Mexico). He is the author of *Los atomismos lógicos de Russell y Wittgenstein* (1986), *El pensamiento del último Wittgenstein* (1988), *Lenguaje y Anti-Metafísica. Cavilaciones wittgensteinianas* (1994), and *Enigmas filosóficos y filosofía wittgensteniana* (1995), among others.

Finally, I would like to thank the Deutsche Ludwig Wittgenstein Gesellschaft e.V., and my special thanks go to the President, Prof. Dr. Lütterfelds who supported the publication of this monograph.

I am much indebted to Dr. Salehi, who has read earlier drafts with care and insight and has made many helpful suggestions. The publication was generously supported by the Alexander von Humboldt Stiftung (Germany).

NORBERTO ABREU E SILVA NETO

Wittgenstein's Philosophy throughout the Corners of Brazil: Data for the Study of Its Reception

The world is a common body to all men.
The changes that occur in it produces changes
in the soul of all men that face it.
(Lichtenberg)[1]

Introduction

This work, as far as I can know, deals for the first time extensively with the reception of Wittgenstein's philosophy in Brazil. Being a first approach I hope it will be understood as the description of a data survey that can suggest future research on the topic. In collecting the data, I did not take any particular problem as a guideline. The objective of the research was to identify works on Wittgenstein published by thinkers that have been dedicating themselves to the study of his life and philosophy in Brazil. For the final composition of the report, I took as orientation the presentation of the collected material in a simple chronological linear order of events detaching the pioneers, distinguished philosophers, and the main tendencies in the scene. This ordering lead me to the attempt of establishing a continuous thread and a framework of Brazilian history of science, philosophy and culture in which Wittgenstein's ideas have been inserted. The result is the present overwiew on Wittgenstein studies in Brazil.

The research showed that something like three historical introductions of Wittgenstein's philosophy in our country happened, and that they were preceded by the work of Brazilian neopositivists, which in the very beginning of the last century paved the way for the reception. So, at first, in this report, some precise roots of Neopositivismus in Brazil are traced down in the beginning of the 20th century. Afterwards, the focus is directed at the three historical presentations: first, the one that occurred by the end of the forties in the context of *Sociedade Brasileira de Filosofia*, national association founded in 1949 for the develop-

---

[1] "El mundo es un cuerpo comúm a todos los hombres. Los cambios que el él ocurren producen cambios en el alma de todos los hombres que lo encaran". Em: Georg Christoph Lichtenberg, *Aforismos*, (Juan Villoro, Trans.), México: Fondo de Cultura Económica, 1992, p. 263. (First edition in German, 1902-1908). The free translation of this aphorism to English in this work is mine.

ment of philosophy and that operates as a center in the movement of Brazilian philosophy since then; the second happened in the context of French philosophical tradition, orientation kept by the Departament of Philosophy of University of São Paulo, through the courses given by Giles Gaston Granger in the sixties and the appearance of *Tractatus* translation by his successor José Arthur Giannotti, 1968; and a third one in the nineties is connected to the translation of Rudolf Haller's book, *Questions on Wittgenstein*, 1990, and the two Brazilian visits he made, the first in 1990 as Visiting Professor of *Instituto de Estudos Avançados* of University of São Paulo, and the second in 1991, organized by the Austrian Embassy. And, finally, information about the present time situation is given, followed by some suggestions for future research. Two lists of publications complete the data, one of secondary literature produced by researchers working in the country (Brazilians or not), and another composed of secondary literature translations.

The Theory of Relativity and *Principia Mathematica*

The forerunners of Neopositivismus in Brazil made the work of rupture with the philosophy of Auguste Comte, the dominant orientation in the mathematical sciences since the beginning of XIX century. The first reference to this movement is the work of Otto de Alencar (1874-1912), engineer from the Polytechnics School of Rio de Janeiro, the very fountain of Positivism in Brazil. By mathematical reasons and because he accepted integrally the contemporary science, gradually he abandoned Comte's positivistic doctrine. In 1898, he published his studies on the errors of mathematics he found in the *Subjective Synthesis* of Auguste Comte, work with which he begins the criticism of the old positivism.[2] According to Paim (1971, 43), after the rupture, Alencar did not adhere or disseminate any other philosophy and kept an attitude of acting in accordance with the development of science itself, and this attitude created a favourable ground for "the aceptance of the new physics and non-Euclidian geometries." In the next two decades, a reduced group of his students and disciples: Amoroso Costa, Teodoro Tamos, Lélio Gama, Roberto Marinho e Felipe dos Santos Reis, continued the fight and reversed completely the situation. By the end of the twenties, the new conception of science or the conception of Neopositivismus was then the dominant trend.

---

[2] About Alencar and the very beginning of Neopositivismus in Brazil see Amoroso Costa, Manuel, "Conferência sobre Otto de Alencar", in Manuel Amoroso Costa, As Idéias Fundamentais da Matemática e Outros Ensaios, São Paulo: Editora da USP/Editorial Grijalbo, 1918/1971, 67-86; Paim, Antonio, "O neopositivismo no Brasil. Período de formação da corrente", in Manuel Amoroso Costa, idem anterior, 39-63.

The first most prominent student of Alencar to continue the movement for the new science was Manuel de Amoroso Costa (1885-1928). He made the movement to advance beyond the limits of scientific demonstrations and entered into the realm of philosophy of sciences (Paim, 1971, 43). He is described by his colleagues as a passionate cultivator of "Philosophia Mathematica" and a person endowed with an "aesthetic sense" (Ramos, 1933, 17-18), or as a "geometrician poet" (Gama, 1929/1971, 29). His philosophical work was considered by Professor Miguel Reale (1971) a dividing mark between two stages of Brazilian philosophy. The previous age in which science and philosophy were worlds kept apart and the new one in which philosophy asserts itself as theory of knowledge and acquire its own meaning. According to Reale, the hypothesis of considering philosophy as epistemology raised before by Tobias Barreto[3] was accomplished only with the work of Amoroso Costa.[4]

In 1924 Albert Einstein visited Brazil and gave two lectures: one at the Brazilian Academy of Sciences under the title, "Observações sobre a situação atual da teoria da luz" [Remarks on the actual situation of light theory], published in 1926 by the Journal of the Academy, and another at Polytechnics of Rio de Janeiro on "Theory of Relativity" (Paim, 1971, 58). The visit was organized by Amoroso Costa and Teodoro Ramos, and it represented the consolidation of Alencar's and his two disciples work for a new conception of science based on the theory of relativity and the ideas of Russell and Whitehead. In his book, *As idéias fundamentais da matemática* [The fundamental ideas of mathematics], at the end of the chapter dedicated to *Principia Mathematica*, Amoroso Costa (1929/1971, 216) declares that in a book like that we can found "the quintessence of mathematical knowledge" and that it can be considered as "a demonstration that science can be built as a rational whole."

---

[3] Tobias Barreto (1839-1889), distinguished Brazilian philosopher adherent of the Materialistic system and the perspective of the Evolucionist Monismus (Franca, 1918/1990, 286-313). About the intellectual education and the philosophy of Barreto, specially on the influence of XIX century German Philosophy see Newton Sucupira 2001.

[4] The basic reference for the work of Amoroso Costa is the edition of his book, *As idéias fundamentais da matemática* (1929) made in 1971 by *Instituto Brasileiro de Filosofia*. This book was published together with his lectures, essays and articles of 1918-1922. The ideas of Poincaré, Einstein, Borel and Bergson are in the center of them and comprises de first part. In the second part are the articles of the period 1923-1928 and the lecture for the Kant's Bicentennial Celebration in 1924, *Kant e as ciências exatas*. The third part is properly the book of 1929. In the Introduction there are three articles: a biographical one by Arthur Gerhardt Santos, an analysis of his work by Lélio Gama, his colleague in Polytechnics, and the above mentioned of Paim on the origins of Neopositivism in Brazil. In Paim's article we can find the bibliograpy of Otto de Alencar, the list of works he published on Mathematics, Astronomy and Physics, and the bibliography of Amoroso Costa on Philosophy of Sciences, Mathematics, Astronomy and Physics, and a list of studies dedicated to him.

Yes, Einstein visited Rio de Janeiro

The visit of Einstein is registered by Marcondes-César (1988, 55-56) as an opening moment of a period after the domination of Comte's positivistic philosophy in which through the establishment of the new way of making science is laid down the basis for the majority of philosophical tendencies developed in Brazil until today. According to her, the new perspective symbolized by Einstein's visit includes also as a consequence the Phenomenological Movement, and she holds the opinion that this movement is responsible for the basic orientations in philosophy of science in Brasil: the first, "Neopositivismus", which is exemplified by the work of Amoroso Costa, and is divided in two branches, one that approaches Humanism and science and another guided by Analytic Philosophy; and the second, dominated by the effort of many towards the restoration of metaphysics. On the side of metaphysics she points out "Heideggerian phenomenology" as the most influential philosophy in the 40s and 50s and Vicente Ferreira da Silva as its best interpreter in Brazil.

As a supplement to Marcondes-César's picture, we can say that since the thirties, the Phenomenological Movement and Existentialist Philosophy exerted a strong influence upon Brazilian philosophy and psychology, not only Husserlian and Heideggerian phenomenologies but also those of Jaspers, Sartre, Gabriel Marcel and Merleau-Ponty. It should be mentioned in this sense the philosophy of Ortega y Gasset, and the presence of Italian Existentialism in Brazil. It is remarkable that two of the main authors that dedicated themselves to the study of Wittgenstein's philosophy, Euríalo Cannabrava and José Arthur Giannotti, firstly were known as Husserlian phenomenologists. In this way, the reception of Wittgenstein in Brazil must be seen in this wider context. However, it is not my aim to cover here the history of Phenomenology in Brazil, in the same way as it is not possible to include the whole history of Neopositivismus in it but only to detach those who dealt with Wittgenstein's philosophy. Being so, I will return to our mathematicians and what they created.

Theodoro A. Ramos (1895-1935) and Amoroso Costa shared the legitimate desire of making "pure and disinterested science" in a culture where in their time researchers emphasized the "application of the sciences" rather than the investigation of foundations, as it happens until now in Brazil. They were defenders of the setting up of university studies in the country and the establishment of basic research. Amoroso Costa died very early by an aircraft accident and could not see the opening and functioning of universities during the thirties. Teodoro Ramos[5] also died early but he still could have a deep influence on Brazilian university teaching.

---

[5] In the "Necrológio" ("Obituary Notice") of Teodoro Ramos published in the *Anuário da Faculdade de Filosofia, Ciências e Letras: 1934-1935*, University of São Paulo (1937), there is a relation of his publications on Mathematics and Mechanics and a list of the technical works.

He worked as Professor at Polytechnics School of São Paulo and besides his scientific and didactic activities he was very active also as a professional of Engineering. He directed the construction of the waterworks of the City of Rio Claro, São Paulo, and of the large district of Santo Amaro in the periphery of São Paulo City. In the thirties, the building of this last one waterworks helped to solve the problem of watering in São Paulo. He was Secretary of Education and even for some time Major of São Paulo City.

He elaborated the project of reformation of Engineering teaching of São Paulo. And, he participated in the foundation of the University of São Paulo. He made the draft of its structure, the study of the necessary credits to its suitable initial installation and was particularly entrusted by the Government with the task of choosen the foreign professors for the composition of the first staff teaching. And during the years 1934-1935, he worked as the first Director of *Faculdade de Filosofia, Ciências e Letras* [Faculty of Philosophy, Sciences and Letters]. One of those he had chosen was Jean Maugüé, a young philosopher that became the first Professor of Philosophy and Psychology of the Faculty, and who lived in São Paulo from 1935-1944. But before focusing at Professor Maugüé there is another forerunner of the twenties to be introduced.

The Laboratory of Psychology of *Engenho de Dentro*

In 1923, the Polish psychologist Waclav Radecki (1887-1953) arrived in Brazil. Before coming to our country he studied at the University of Cracow, and then followed a period of studies first in Florence and after in Geneve where, in 1911, under the direction of Flournoy and Claparède, he obtained his doctorate defending a thesis on "psychoelectrical phenomena". When he returned to Poland he first organized and directed the Laboratory of Psychology of Cracow University and after the laboratory of Free University of Poland until 1923. In this year, by "ignored motives" he left Poland and moved to Paraná, in South Brazil, where he had some relatives. Soon after his arrival he gave some lectures in São Paulo and, in 1924, was invited to organize and take the direction of the "Laboratório de Psicologia da Colônia de Alienados Mentais do Engenho de Dentro", Rio de Janeiro [Psychology Laboratory of the Mental Insanes Colony of *Engenho de Dentro*]. In the course of its evolution this laboratory will become later the Institute of Psychology of Federal University of Rio de Janeiro, formerly named University of Brazil. No one can dispute his influence on Brazilian psychology. He lived in Rio de Janeiro for ten years, founded a school of psychology but in 1933 by political motives he emigrated to Uruguay, living there till his death (Centofanti, 1982).

Radecki published a *Tratado de Psicologia* in which he declares to be a follower of Brentano's psychology. In this book he discusses his ideas and of those connected to his school: Husserl, Külpe, Meinong, Stumpf, Twardowski and Witasek. The history of his formation in Europe is a research to be made. It is possible that he had been trained by one of the students of Twardowski and it is possible he had attended Brentano courses in Florence.

From another side, Radecki declared himself also a follower of Wilhelm Wundt, and that he was in search of a synthesis of empirical psychology and experimental psychology. In fact, the method he was searching there existed yet and was created by Alfred Binet (1857-1911), the famous French psychologist, who did not accept the experimentalism of Wundt and developed his experimental psychology based on the line of research he saw in the Laboratory of Würzburg. Binet's synthesis is made out of these three components: empirical psychology, the method of using "mental tests", and the categories developed by French psychiatric Humanism. He named his procedure "Psycho-clinic Method" and in this way inaugurated an alternative model of experimentalism, or, the French experimental psychology. Anyway, the School of Radecki produced some of the best researchers we have in Brazil until now. One of them was Euríalo Cannabrava, who in the fifthies will become the chief philosopher of Neopositivismus in Brazil.

Euríalo Cannabrava: "German phenomenology" and Neopositivismus

Euríalo Cannabrava (1908-1978) began his career in 1930 working at Radecki's Laboratory. In 1937, he became Diretor of *Instituto de Pesquisas Educacionais* [Institute of Educational Research] of the Ministery of Education and in 1951 Professor of Philosophy of the traditional *Colégio Pedro II*. Later, in the sixties, he became Professor of Aesthetics, Cibernetics and Mathematical logic at Federal University of Rio de Janeiro. Cannabrava's work is in close relation of continuity to that of Amoroso Costa, and he praised him because of his discussion about philosophical aspects of the changing equations problem (pure mathematics) into physical laws (applied mathematics) (Cannabrava,1956, 96). On the other side, he was situated opposite to Heideggerian philosophy of Vicente Ferreira da Silva, who former was a prominent philosopher of Brazilian Neopositivismus.

During the forties, Willard Van Orman Quine worked at *Escola de Sociologia de São Paulo* for a few years, and Vicente Ferreira da Silva (1916-1963) was his assistant. Ferreira da Silva had interest in Mathematical logic and published in 1940 his book, *Elementos de lógica matemática* [Elements of Mathematical Logic]. He also wrote the preface to the book of Quine published in São Paulo in

1942, *O sentido da nova lógica*.[6] However, after 1948, Ferreira da Silva changes his direction and enters the way of Heidegger's Existential analysis (*Daseinanalyse*). Ferreira's work is described by Vita (1958, 337) as the project of a Philosophical antropology and an Existencial ontology that would exclude any possibility of "a naturalistic presentation of the real" or of "a vitalist conception, like the Bergsonian", and that had the human freedom as the "sole foundation upon which the ultimate meaning of the real could be elucidated." It is enough about this philosopher for this work.

And, in what refers to the participation of Quine in the reception of Neopositivismus in Brazil is still a research to be made. Euríalo Cannabrava does not mention him in his works of the forties and fifties but in his book of 1977, *Teoria da Decisão Filosófica* [Theory of Philosophical Decision], Quine is throughout a presence.[7] And José Arthur Giannotti, in the "initial considerations" about his book, *Apresentação do mundo: considerações sobre o pensamento de Ludwig Wittgenstein* [Presentation of the World: Considerations on Ludwig Wittgenstein's Thought], 1994, tells that when he discovered the closeness of his "notion of operatory schemas to what Wittgenstein called non-verbal language games" he felt some strangeness because, "from the point of view of logic" he had his "implicit dialogue" with Quine, and from the phenomenological point of view with Merleau-Ponty (p. 13). And recently, Luis Milman (1999), as a result of his Ph.D. thesis dealing with questions of the contemporary analytical thought on language and mind defended at Federal University of Rio Grande do Sul (Department of Philosophy), published the book, *A Natureza dos Símbolos: explorações semântico-filosóficas*, which is mostly devoted to the development of Quine's criticism of Vienna Circle Verificationism.

Let us return then to Cannabrava, who as it was mentioned, began his work in a laboratory of experimental psychology. However, I could find only one work published by him from this initial period. It is an article on the psychoanalytic pedagogy of Anna Freud first published in *Arquivos de Pediatria* [Archives of Pediatrics], and that in 1934 served as an introduction to his translation of her book, *Einführung in die Technik der Kinderanalyse*, 1927. He is very critical of the possibility of this pedagogy because the fundamental contradiction between

---

[6] "The Meaning of the New Logic". In his book, *From a Logical Point of View*, Quine (1953/1963, 170) refers to this book as being in the origins of its Chapter VIII on "Reference and Modality". He says this chapter resulted from the fusion of two other articles published in 1943 and 1947 and that, in the main, "a translation in turn of portions of my book, *O Sentido da Nova Lógica* (São Paulo, Brazil, Livraria Martins, 1944) which embodied a course of lectures delivered at São Paulo in 1942."

[7] The works referrred by Cannabrava are: *Word and Object*, 1960; *Set theory and its logic*, 1963; *Epistemology naturalized*, 1968; and "Carnap and logical thruth", in *Logic and Language*, 1962.

the psychoanalytical view of the child as an adult in miniature and the conceptions of modern pedagogy that defends the opposite view, the specificities of childhood. This and any other work of this kind is mentioned by him when he describes his self-development in one book he published in the fifties, *Ensaios Filosóficos* (1957).

Cannabrava (1957) reports that he began his investigations by experimenting "Husserlian phenomenology and German existentialism" but with an attitude of trying to keep himself "in a certain way independent of the two speculative movements". This attitude he maintained during the thirties and part of the forties. After the war, he spent a period in the United States as Visiting Professor at the Columbia University. During this time, he received the influence of the Neopositivist group of Chicago and defined his philosophy as a "way of language criticism" that was given to him by Carnap and Morris. He reports that at the end of the forties he had the opportunity of handle manuscripts of Wittgenstein on the problem of induction. And in a work of 1952, Cannabrava tells he bought in Columbia one of the *Wittgenstein's Dictations*, "paying for its weight in gold".

In 1941, Cannabrava published *Seis temas do espírito humano* [Six Themes of the Human Spirit], and, in 1943, *Descartes e Bergson*. In the first book, he adopted an existentialist position, and because of it he was announced as the introductor of Existential philosophy in Brasil (Martins, 1994). The one on Descartes and Bergson was more a book of transition from this dogmatic anti-rationalistic moment to an attitude free of dogmatism. In the anti-rationalistic stage, his "technique of critical reflection" ascribes to psychology the most important role, and in the anti-dogmatic attitude logic takes this role from psychology. So, Cannabrava (1957, 23) describes that this attitude lead him to try "to reduce the speculative activity to the method and this one to language". During 1948-1949, very impressed by Wittgenstein's philosophy he wrote a series of texts about the "mechanism of inductive prediction". These texts composed his thesis for the Contest to Philosophy's Professorship at *Colégio Pedro II*, Rio de Janeiro, which he won in 1951. The thesis became a book, *Elementos de metodologia filosófica* [Elements of Philosophical Methodology], that was published having another as complement, *Introdução à filosofia científica* [Introduction to Scientific Philosophy], both issued in 1956. "Scientific philosophy" is the concept that gives unity to his work and the one he will defend along his life.

In 1952 Cannabrava published an article were he exposed ideas of Wittgenstein and the impressions and doubts he had about his philosophy. He published also the essay *Introdução ao objetivismo crítico* [Introduction to Critical Objetivism], that deals with Russell and Wittgenstein ideas, and a brief article named "Ludwig Wittgenstein", a kind of "official" introduction of the philosopher.

Both articles were published in *Revista Brasileira de Filosofia* [Brazilian Journal of Philosophy],[8] Volume II, fasc. 1 and 3, respectively. What is remarkable is that in the same volume of the Journal, fasc. 4, a report and comments on the "Visit of Professor Herbert Feigl" to the *Instituto Brasileiro de Filosofia* [Brazilian Institute of Philosophy] in São Paulo appeared, when he discussed with a group of philosophers fundamental points of contemporary logical empiricism and the criticism it wakes up. The report makes clear that Wittgenstein's *Tractatus* was in the center of the debate. It is possible to say *Revista Brasileira de Filosofia* was making in this volume a kind of formal introduction of Wittgenstein in Brazilian philosophy.

When Cannabrava describes in his "Ludwig Wittgenstein" (1952) what he found in the "Dictations", his words are quite impressive. So we read that:[9]

> Nessas páginas dispersas, o pensamento do filósofo está vivo: é como se ouvisse a sua própria voz. Em primeiro lugar, Wittgenstein não obedece a método algum de exposição. As suas aulas não tinham tema certo e definido. Ele indaga, inicialmente, o sentido da palavra. Estuda, depois, a natureza do pensamento que se considera, geralmente, como o veículo do sentido da palavra, conceito ou proposição. Ora, a palavra é mero sinal, mas seria êrro grosseiro considerar o pensamento como a sua própria vida. Os processos mentais não vivificam o conceito ou proposição, porque aquilo que denominamos pensamento se reduz à atividade de operar com sinais (592-593).

Cannabrava's most stimulating book is *Ensaios filosóficos* [Philosophical Essays], published in 1957, but containing, in fact, essays from the end of the 30s. till the beginning of the 50s. He presented it as a sort of intellectual autobiography in which he criticized his Existential phenomenological stage and introduced his scientific philosophy. So, he analyzed Existential philosophy from the declared point of view of logic and the concept of scientific philosophy of the-Vienna Circle. These essays were written with the aim of showing how possible is to give a scientific basis for philosophy. In this sense, the eight first chapters were dedicated to the criticism of Existencial philosophy, that seems to serve

---

[8] This Journal began to be published in 1951 and is still regularly in circulation. It is a publication of *Instituto Brasileiro de Filosofia*, a national entity founded, in 1949, in São Paulo, by Professor Miguel Reale, philosopher of the Faculty of Law – University of São Paulo.

[9] "In these scattered pages, the philosopher's thought is alive: it is as if I could hear his own voice. Firstly, Wittgenstein does not obey any method of exposition. His classes had not exact and defined themes. He investigates, initially, the meaning of the word."
"After, he studies the nature of the thought in which, generally, we consider it as the vehicle of the meaning of the world, concept or proposition. But, the word is mere sign, and it would be a coarse error to consider thinking as its own life. The mental processes do not enliven the concept or proposition, because that thing we name thinking is reduced to the activity of operating with signs".

him as the best example of anti-philosophic and anti-scientific literature. The other essays were dedicated to Russell (5 chapters), Ayer (2 chapters), Whitehead (one essay in which he reports his visit to him in Cambridge). There are chapters on Logic and Dialectics; a very creative dialogue along four chapters between Socrates and a Marxist. So discussing the ideas of these philosophers he was elaborating his new "scientific philosophy". During the sixties, he published two books on Aesthetics, *Estética da crítica* [Aesthetics of the Criticism], 1963, and, *Crítica literária e estética* [Literary and Aesthetic Criticism], 1969. His last book, *Teoria da decisão filosófica*, was published in 1977, and what is exposed in it is a synthesis of his whole work through the presentation of his "System Logos-Psiquê", that means, his concrete scientific philosophy. The book has a sub-title and it expresses clearly that at this moment of his life, the scientific psychologist and not the philosopher took the leading role. Through the theory of philosophical decision, the aim of this book was to settle "the psychological basis of Mathematics, Linguistics and Theory of Knowledge."

His contribution to Brazilian philosophy was acknowledged by historians of Brazilian philosophy. The sections referring to philosophy of science of his "Philosophical essays", 1957, were seen by Hegenberg (1978, 147) as an act of innovation because he introduced "ideas of authors almost unknown in the country: Russell, Ayer, Tarski, Nagel and Goodman" and who also acknowledged him the merit of introducing "some notions of modern logic – e.g., the notions of material implication, model, calculation and logical structure [...] and alluded to the strict implication of Lewin and, indirectly by extension to modal logic." From another side, Cannabrava'a aesthetics was classified by Nunes (1978) as one of the main positions in Brazilian aesthetic thought. And Vaz (1990, 353), stressing the actuality of Cannabrava's work, points out that he made clear the distinction between philosophy as speculative construction and philosophy as an elaboration of an "appropriate metalanguage with which to consider scientific knowledge as an object-language."[10]

Cannabrava did not live short as happened to the mathematicians Amoroso Costa and Teodoro Ramos but like these two, apparently, he did not leave disciples. Except by his appearance in the books of history, I could not find researchers continuing his work. To many his name sounds unknown. His work is disap-

---

[10] Almost all good books on the history of philosophy in Brazil dedicate some space to Euríalo Cannabrava. Beyond those here quoted we can find comments and references in the following works: Acerboni, Lídia, A filosofia contemporânea no Brasil, São Paulo: Grijalbo,1969; Amoroso Lima, Alceu, Meditação sobre o mundo moderno, Rio de Janeiro: José Olympio, 1942; Chisholm, Roderick M., "Anais do Primeiro Congresso Brasileiro de Filosofia" (Review), Philosophy and Phenomenological Research, XII (Republished in Revista Brasileira de Filosofia, II, 1952, 594-595); Martins, Wilson, História da Inteligência Brasileira, Vol. VII, São Paulo: T.A. Queiroz, 1996.

pearing and there is no information about his personal life. His bibliography is bigger than the one I could have access.[11] He is an author to be rescued. During the forties and fifties Cannabrava kept the tradition of Neopositivism, the connections with Analytic Philosophy and with the works of the Vienna Circle. For some time he lectured in London invited by Professor Ayer, that also visited Brazil many times. If not the first, Cannabrava was one of the first introductors of Wittgenstein's work in Brazil. But he was not the only channel.

University of São Paulo: The French Department of Philosophy

The Univertity of São Paulo was founded and installed in 1934, and is considered by Lévi-Strauss (1955/1996) the great lifework of George Dumas (1866-1946), who organized the French Mission and chose the staff for the Faculty of Philosophy, Sciences and Literary Arts, which was under direction of Theodoro Ramos, its first director. Dumas is described by Maugüé (1982) as a wise character composed of two halves: the psychiatrist and the philosopher, who was seduced by the works and passions of Auguste Comte. Dumas maintained close relations with the elite of Brazilian farmers and planned with them the University. Since there happened in the past a marriage between Brazil and Auguste

---

[11] The works of Euríalo Cannabrava: "À margem da pedagogia psicanalítica", in Anna Freud, Introdução à técnica da análise infantil, Rio de Janeiro: Marisa Editora, 1934, 5-37; Seis temas do espírito humano, São Paulo: Panorama, 1941; Descartes e Bergson, São Paulo: Amigos do Livro, 1943; "Present tendencies in Latin America Philosophy", The Journal of Philosophy, XLV(5), 1949, 113-119; Convention, Nature and Art", Philosophy and Phenomenological Review, IV(3), 1949; "Juizos analíticos e juízos sintéticos", Anais do I Congresso Brasileiro de Filosofia, II, 1950, 367-375; "Dois aspectos da teoria do conhecimento", Anais do I Congresso Brasileiro de Filosofia, II, 1950, 377-388; "Filosofia como síntese reflexiva", Revista Brasileira de Filosofia, II, 1950, 36-61; "Introdução ao objetivismo crítico", Revista Brasileira de Filosofia, II, 1952, 48-76; "Ludwig Wittgenstein", Revista Brasileira de Filosofia, II, 1952, 592-593; "Philosophical analysis, causality and space-time", Actes du XIème Congrès International de Philosophie, VI, 1953, 168-174; "Logica modal e dedução", Revista Brasileira de Filosofia, V, 1955, 60-68; A cultura brasileira e seus equívocos, Rio de Janeiro: Ministério de Educação e Cultura, 1955; "Estrutura e teoria científica", Anais do Congresso Internacional de Filosofia de São Paulo, Vol III, 1956, 799-806; Elementos de metodologia filosófica, São Paulo: Companhia Editora Nacional, 1956; Introdução à filosofia científica, São Paulo: Companhia Editora Nacional, 1956; Ensaios Filosóficos, Rio de Janeiro: Ministério de Educação e Cultura, 1957; "Estrutura lógica do argumento matemático", Anais do III Congresso Nacional de Filosofia, 1959, 295-298; "Teoria da decisão e matemática qualitativa", Anais do IV Congresso Nacional de Filosofia, 1962, 476-484; Estética da Crítica, Rio de Janeiro: Ministério de Educação e Cultura, 1963; Crítica Literária e Estética, Rio de Janeiro: Gernasa, 1969; Teoria da Decisão Filosófica: bases psicológicas da matemática, da linguística e da teoria do conhecimento, Rio de Janeiro: Forense-Universitária, 1977.

Comte it is clear for Maugüé the strong connection hold by Dumas and his role in the foundation of the university. "In a complete natural way this marriage became that of Brazil and George Dumas". However, it is of worth to note that in Maugüé's view the marriage of Brazil and Comte must be explained as a result of a situation in which there was no doubt that for Brazilians it was "a way of liberating from catholicism and from a very African fetichism" (77). And of course Maugüé was not a Comteam. It is also interesting to observe that the first director of the Faculty, Theodoro Ramos, was fighting against Comtean positivism, too.

Maugüé was a young philosopher who studied at the *École Normale Supérieure*, where he entered in 1926. There, he had as colleagues Sartre, Aron, Nizan, and Lagache among others. In 1935, he was appointed by George Dumas for the position and integrated the French Mission sent to São Paulo. Claude Levy Strauss (1996, 18), who was part of the Mission, reports that he, the anthropologist, Fernand Braudel, the historian, Pierre Monbeig, the geographer, and Maugüé, the philosopher, formed in the midst of the Mission a very coherent team. Maugüé lived long in São Paulo, from 1935 to 1944, when he engaged himself in the *Forces Françaises Libres*. After the war, he worked for ten years as diplomat, in Buenos Aires, Salonika and Toronto and then he was sent back to the university where he ended his career teaching human sciences for students of the *Grandes Écoles Comerciales*.

Maugüé published almost nothing: only one book of memories, *Les dents agacées* (1982), two articles and some other pieces I could find in São Paulo.[12] In his recollections he mentions the very faithful notes of his classes made by one of his students, Édeline, that comprise six books of 819 pages containing his course, and that he did not allow the publication despite the protest of the student (213-214). His book was reviewed by Fernand Braudel *(Le Monde,* december 31st., 1982), and reports and comments about Maugüé can be found in Braudel's biography written by Pierre Daix (1995). In São Paulo, his philosophy was analyzed by Paulo Arantes in his book, *Um departamento francês de ultramar* (1994) and that tells the history of "the French Department of Philosophy from Overseas". This book contains precious reports about him and his classes and lectures by his former students, today some of the most distinguished personalities of Brazilian cultural life.

---

[12] I could handle only four pieces Maugüé left in Brazil: Maugüé, Jean, "O ensino da filosofia - suas diretrizes", Anuário da Faculdade de Filosofia, Ciências e Letras: 1934-1935, São Paulo: Editora "Revista dos Tribunais", 1937, 25-42; "Programas de 1934-35 - 1a. Secção - Filosofia", idem anterior, 255; "Curriculum Vitae do Corpo Docente – Professor Jean Maugüé", ibidem, p. 295; and, "A pintura moderna", Revista do Arquivo Municipal, V, 1938, 41-46.

The fact that he did not publish his work is explained by him in his book of recollections as a consequence of his relation with written language. He declares his high respect for it and also the consciousness he had that writing demands the withdrawal from life. The speech, on the contrary, to which he dedicated the essential of his time, in the classes or in lectures and after during the time he spent in war and in diplomacy, never asked him for similar giving up. But to start writing, he says, "was to accept firstly, for some time, the idea that the games were signed, sealed and delivered" (9-10). Besides praising written language he had also an attitude of disbelief regarding university institutional practices that was an hindrance for him to conclude his Ph.D. thesis. He did not publish very much despite the fact he was an admirable writer as we can see through his book and the few articles. So, according to Arantes (1994, 65), there was another reason which he brings up for explaining this lack of publications. He says, it is due to Maugüé's philosophic-theatrical devotion to the 'alive word', which consisted in carrying out a kind of Socratic teaching by means of 'dialetic conversations', and that because of this he could be viewed "as representative of a modern blossoming of the Attic spirit".

In the history of the Philosophy Department told by Arantes (1994), Maugüé began the series of French philosophers that developed in São Paulo the tradition of philosophy inaugurated by Sartre and the French phenomenological philosophy during the 20s. and 30s. This tradition, says Arantes, is one that "widens de usual spectrum of the so called philosophical matters". After Maugüé the importation continues and in the fifties were brought to teach and fix the French tradition, first, Martial Gueroult, that mainly taught the philosophy of Leibniz, and second, Giles-Gaston Granger. The French philosopher of the sixties was Professor Gérard Lebrun, a former student of Michel Foucault. In 1960 Lebrun arrived in São Paulo, stayed long and came again many times until recently. In 1965, invited by Lebrun, for the first time Foucault visited Brazil and also like his student came again many other times.

A new presentation of Wittgenstein's philosophy was made by Granger. According to Arantes (1994), Granger taught Logic and Philosophy of Sciences and his teaching consisted of exposing an Epistemology of Human Sciences. He made changes in the text of his classes and turned his notes into a two volumes book, *Pensée Formelle et Sciences de l'homme* [Formal Thinking and Human Sciences] published in France in 1960, and which Arantes considered "one classic of the Department". The Brazilian translation of the book appeared only in 1974. Arantes reports that it was flagrant in his classes Granger's unwilling to whatever referred to Phenomenology. Through him, he says, the students could learn that what was necessary to epistemology was not a "philosophy of consciousness" but a "philosophy of the concept". By his teaching, Arates asserts, he surpassed Husserl and Merleau-Ponty, "without mention the *démi-philosophe*

Sartre". As a consequence the students learnt "to doubt about the lived meanings and to refuse, on principle, the supposed continuity between perception and scientific knowledge" (188).

Granger has been a presence in Brazilian philosophy. During the 60s he did not teach only at the University of São Paulo but also at the University of Campinas. He came again as Visiting Professor many times during the last thirty years. His most recent visit was in 1999 at the University of Campinas. In fact the relation of Granger with Brazil began before he came for teaching in the sixties. He has been a regular visitor to Brazil since the forties. In 1948, appeared in *Boletim da Faculdade de Filosofia da Universidade de São Paulo* his first work translated into Portuguese. In 1955, it was published his book, *Lógica e Filosofia das Ciências*, and after he published an article with a title that reminds Maugüé, "A arte e a interpretação do mundo atual", in *Boletim de Psicologia*, University of São Paulo, 1958. During the sixties, he published a long essay as an introduction to a collection of Descartes selected works for university students, and an article in *Kriterion*, Belo Horizonte, Minas Gerais, both in 1962. In the seventies, two of his books appeared in Brazilian editions: *Filosofia do estilo*, and *Pensamento formal e ciências do homem*, above mentioned. And, Marcelo Dascal (1987b) refers to a volume published By Granger, in 1975, under the title, *Teoria e Prática: notas de aula de um curso ministrado na Universidade Estadual the Campinas*. During the last twenty years Granger published 5 articles in Brazil: three in *Manuscrito*, one in *Ciência e Filosofia*, São Paulo, and one in *Cadernos de Estudos Lingüísticos*, Campinas. A measure of Granger's influence upon Brazilian philosophers can be seen in the special number Revista *Manuscrito* dedicated to his philosophy in 1987, edited by Marcelo Dascal.

In his editorial note to this celebration of Granger's philosophy, Marcelo Dascal (1987a), summarizes the importance of his work in Brazil by declaring that he considered highly appropriated to commemorate the tenth anniversary of the journal with a special issue devoted to his philosophy, because Granger, who had been at that time recently elected for a chair in the College de France, taught in São Paulo and in Campinas. And also because, he continues, "many of those who practice philosophy in Brazil were also his students in Aix-en-Provence". Dascal concludes by pointing out the intimate connection between the journal and Granger's style of making philosophy: "His clear, rigorous and stimulating thought has contributed in a decisive way to the formation of a style of philosophizing which is exactly the one we favour in this journal".

This special issue of *Manuscrito* is considered by Marcelo Dascal (1987b) "a modest step" for an assessment of Granger's work as a whole, a task for the future. It has articles published in four languages: French, English, Portuguese, and Spanish, and contributions of: Jules Vullemin, Andrés Raggio, David Braybrooke, Joelle Proust, Kuno Lorenz, José Arthur Giannotti, Arley R. Moreno, Sérgio Cremaschi, Ora Gruengard, Elizabeth Schwartz, Marcelo Dascal, and Giles Gaston Granger. The issue contains also a list of Granger's publications from 1947 up to 1985.

After his first staying at the University of São Paulo Granger left Brazil in 1959, and the course of Logic and Philosophy of Science was taken in charge by the young Brazilian philosopher, José Arthur Giannotti (1930-) that continued his teaching. But, Paulo Arantes (1994) reports that Giannoti gradually introduced changes in the course turning it into "a more ambitious meditation of philosophical stamp about the origins of contemporary Logic," in particular, the works of Frege, Russell and Wittgenstein, that had "as a classical counterpoint Aristotle, Leibniz and Husserl," and the emphasis was on "the semantic problem of denotation". In 1961, in order to conquest his doctorship Giannotti defended a thesis against the psychological foundation of logic.[13] And, in 1968, he published his translation of the *Tractatus* with an introduction where he makes a report about his program of logic developed in the course of Logic and Philosophy of Science (246).

According to Arantes (1994), the essencial topic of Granger's epistemology, the problem of the gap between perception and science or the rupture between the "experienced" and the "objective" is not explored by Giannotti in the transcendental framework of the question. Working the problem of the immediate meaning of social phenomena, not trying the elevation from the lived meanings to objective meanings and not using the operatory models but taken the marxist categories, because he clearly saw them not as models or a typology but as "meaning schemes"or "meaning systems" (254-256), Giannotti developed his own philosophy from the sixties till the eighties in this direction and not published very much about Wittgenstein until 1993 when after more than ten years of deep excavation and dialogue with some friends and students, he offered us his book classic born, *Apresentação do Mundo*.[14] However, although Giannotti did not publish very much, he stimulated his students to produce works on Wittgenstein. So, he had (and has) various disciples that orientated by him developed their own work on Wittgenstein's philosophy, in particular Arley R. Moreno, José Carlos Bruni, Luiz Henrique Lopes dos Santos, and João Virgilio Cuter.

---

[13] The title of Giannotti's thesis is "John Stuart Mill: o Psicologismo e a Fundamentação da Lógica", and it was published in *Boletim n. 269 da Faculdade de Filosofia, Ciências e Letras*, University of São Paulo, 1963.

[14] Other of his main works are: "Introduction", in Ludwig Wittgenstein, Tractatus lógico-filosófico, São Paulo: Cia Editora Nacional/Editora da USP, 1968; "Apresentação", in Ludwig Wittgenstein, Estética, Psicologia e Religião, São Paulo: Cultrix, 1972; Trabalho e Reflexão, São Paulo: Brasiliense, 1983; "Breves considerações sobre o método de Wittgenstein, Manuscrito, X (2), 1987, 77-90; "A sociedade travada", Novos Estudos, 28.

Thanks to him we have the translation José Carlos Bruni made of the *Philosophical Investigations*, published in 1979, and also a new translation of *Tractatus* made by Luiz Henrique Lopes dos Santos and published in 1994.

Also in the sixties and preceding Giannotti's translation of *Tractatus*, appeared in *Revista Brasileira de Filosofia*, first, in 1962, a short review of the *Philosophical Investigations* by Leonidas Hegenberg (Vol. XII, 45, 134), and later, in 1966, the review Vilém Flusser made of Ludwig Wittgenstein's *Schriften, Band 2 - Philosophische Bemerkungen*, (Vol. 16, 129-132). Flusser lived and worked long in Brazil till the end of the seventies when he returned to Europe and began a very sucessfull career in Germany. His article reflects the sixties: he discusses the book having Wittgenstein arguing in opposition to Hegel's philosophy and bringing Wittgenstein's thought near to Existentialism, especially the one of Albert Camus.

The Generation of the Seventies

During this decade, the new generation of philosophers that would have the leadership in the future work was studying in Europe. So, Arley Moreno, after obtaining his Master degree, in 1971, under the direction of Professor Giannotti, by defending the dissertation, *O problema da significação em Wittgenstein: uma introdução ao estudo do Tractatus* [The Problem of Meaning in Wittgenstein: An Introduction to the Study of the Tractatus], lived many years in France where, in 1975, orientated by Professor Granger he defended the thesis, *Recherches sur le "Tractatus logico-philosophicus" de Wittgenstein*, at the University of Provence, Aix-en-Provence, where he also worked as *"assistant associé"* at *Faculté des Lettres*.

At the same time, other Brazilian philosophers were also studying in Europe. So, in 1975, Werner Spaniol, of the Federal University of Minas Gerais, defended at Gregorian University, Rome, his doctoral thesis, *Ein Kampf gegen die 'Verhexung des Verstandes'; Philosophie und Methode bei Ludwig Wittgenstein*, that later, in 1989, became his book, *Filosofia e método no segundo Wittgenstein* [Philosophy and Method in the Second Wittgenstein]. Of the same year are the doctoral thesis of Balthazar Barbosa Filho, *La notion de signification dans les 'Investigations philosophiques' de Wittgenstein*, 1975, and of Raul Landim Filho, both in Louvain. The list includes Danilo Marcondes de Souza Filho, who after becoming Master of Philosophy in 1977, by Catholic University-Rio de Janeiro, studied in Great Britain, where, in 1980, he defended his Ph.D. thesis, *Language and Action: A Reassessment of Speech Act Theory*, at St. Andrews University . And also Nelson Gonçalves Gomes, who studied from 1970 to 1975 at the University of Munich under the direction of Professor Wolfgang Röd and received his Ph.D. by defending a thesis on the development of the ideas of Moritz Schlick on ethics and epistemology.

Two books of Witgenstein were translated in the seventies: *Lectures and Conversations on Aesthetics, Psychology and Religious Belief*, by José Paulo Paes, under the title, *Estética, Psicologia e Religião* (1972) and with a didactic, affect moving and critical introductions by Professor Giannotti; it was a publication by the State of São Paulo Culture Council. The other book is the first translation of *Philosophical Investigations*, by José Carlos Bruni, from the Department of Philosophy-University of São Paulo. It appeared in a volume of the Collection *Os Pensadores*, named *Wittgenstein: vida e obra* (1975), and it is supplemented with an anonymous and general introduction written after consultation with Armando Mora D'Oliveira, also logician from Philosophy Department (USP). There are two variations of the issue, in hardback and in paperback; it is destined to a large audience and books of the Collection as a whole are sold also by newsagents. It should be mentioned yet the translation of a selected essays by Frege named *Lógica e Filosofia da Linguagem* (1978), by Paulo Alcoforado, professor at Federal University of Rio de Janeiro.

The number of secondary literature translations is very small for the sixties and seventies. Nothing but a chapter in a book of Marcuse (1967) is the only one I could find published in the 60s. In the next decade the situation is better. There appeared the books of the inspired Susanne Langer (1971) announcing the new key in philosophy; the chapter in the book of Norman Brown connecting Wittgenstein and Freud; the clear and didactic Chisholm's *Theory of Knowledge* (1974); the substantial book of Wolfgang Stegmüller, *A Filosofia Contemporânea* (1977), in which the chapter "Ludwig Wittgenstein" was translated by L. A. Marcuschi and Leonidas Hegenberg, the chapter on empiricism and the Vienna Circle by Nelson Gonçalves Gomes, and the chapter on Analytic Philosophy by Leonidas Hegenberg. The list includes also Warren Shibles, *Wittgenstein, language and philosophy* (1974), by Leonidas Hegenberg and Octanny Silveira da Motta, and Granger's *Filosofia do estilo* (1974) by Scarlett Marton.

The publication of articles in this decade is almost inexistent. I could register only two articles published by Arley R. Moreno, one in Brazil and another in France, one by Balthazar Barbosa Filho, a review Leonidas Hegenberg made of Shibles's book, and the translation of an article of G. Hallet.

Friends at New Corners

By the end of the seventies other centers than Rio de Janeiro and São Paulo had their production more in evidence. So, since the eighties till now, the number of thesis and dissertations has increased, and differently from the seventies, with a few exceptions they were defended in the country. From 1980 until today, I could list 20 works (13 dissertations, and 7 thesis) that were approved in many universtities.At the Federal University of Minas Gerais (UFMG): Célio M. Cardoso (1980), Paulo Roberto Margutti Pinto (1980), Renato Machado (1989), Lívia M. Guimarães (1989), Mauro L. L. Conde (1993). At the Federal University of Rio Grande do Sul (UFRGS): Paulo F. E. Faria (1989 and 1994), Darley Dall'Agnoll (1993), Luís Milman (1998), Mauro Luiz Engelmann (2000). At the State University of Campinas, São Paulo (UNICAMP): Marco Antonio Ruffino(1990), Claudio Eduardo Müller Banzato (1994), Horácio Martinez (1996), Reinaldo Furlan (1998) João Carlos Salles Pires da Silva (1999). At the University of São Paulo (USP): Norberto Abreu e Silva Neto (1991), Sílvia F. A. Saes (1992), João Vergílio Cuter (1993). At the University of Brasília (UnB): Arilson Benedito Corrêa da Costa (1997), Luiz Eduardo de Lacerda Abreu (2000), Felipe Santiago do Amaral (2001), and Jorge Luiz Pennafort Palma (2001).

From these universities, the State University of Campinas is the most active regarding Wittgenstein studies, that are conducted in both, the Department of Philosophy and the *Centro de Lógica, Epistemologia e História da Ciência* [Center of Logic, Epistemology and History of Science] of the University. The library of this Center has a complete collection of *Wittgenstein Papers*, photocopies made of the existing one in Cornell University Library (Ithaca, N. Y.), and which is available to researchers. And, this Center publishes, since 1978, an international journal of philosophy, *Manuscrito*, having as founding editor, Marcelo Dascal (University of Jerusalem), a former student of Professor Giannotti and of Granger in the sixties. The actual Editor is Michael Wrigley, who studied philosophy in Oxford and holds a Ph. D. in Philosophy from the University of California at Berkeley. Since the eighties Wrigley has been Professor of Philosophy at the State of São Paulo University of Campinas and member of the Center for Logic, Epistemology and History of Science above mentioned. His current work is on the logicist philosophy of mathematics, and on the development of Wittgenstein's philosophy of mathematics. His publications are in English.

Revista *Manuscrito* plays an important role in the diffusion of Wittgenstein's philosophy by regularly publishing papers on it. In 1985 this Journal published a special issue on Wittgenstein. This number of 268 pages contains one article of Arley Moreno in Portuguese, one of Enrique Villanueva in Spanish, one in English by Mercy Helen and Morris Lazerowitz, and six articles in French by J. N. Kaufmann, François Latraverse, Jean-Claude Dumoncel, Bernard Stevens, Richard Vallée and Jean Laberge. In 1995, another special issue edited by Michael Wrigley was dedicated to Wittgenstein. The number is very large (470 pages), and contains twelve articles in Portuguese, three in Spanish, only two in French and three in English. In it Granger reviews Arley Moreno's book, *Wittgenstein: através das imagens* [Wittgenstein: Through the Images], Michael

Wrigley reviews the book of Rudolf Haller, *Wittgenstein e a filosofia austríaca: questões* [Questions on Wittgenstein]. There are articles of Arley Moreno, Antonio Zilhão, Nicolas Kaufmann, Colin Radford and Rudolf Haller. The number brings out the translation of Wittgenstein's essay, *Philosophy*, by Antonio Zilhão, Professor of Logic and Modern Philosophy at the University of Lisbon; the translation of the article Wittgenstein rejected, "Some Remarks on Logical Form", by Darley Dall'Agnol, Professor at Federal University of Rio Grande do Sul and that also, in 1995, published his translation of *A Lecture on Ethics*. And it is also presented by Norberto Abreu-e-Silva Neto a bibliography on secondary literature in Portuguese containing a relation of about a 100 works (thesis, articles, books, translations, and chapters of books).

Before the eighties, I could not find any book published by a Brazilian philosopher dedicated exclusively to the study of Wittgenstein's philosophy and not to some sort of work that uses philosophical clarity as a mean to the building of scientific conceptual pyramids, which is the case of Euríalo Cannabrava's last book published in 1977, where he takes philosophical clarity in the sense of Wittgenstein as a point of departure for the construction of a theory about "the psychological basis of mathematics, language and theory of knowledge". But the situation after 1980 is much better and the production increased highly in numbers, as it can be viewed in the two lists of publications annexed at the end of this work. The first list includes pieces of Brazilian researchers working in Brazil or abroad and publishing either in Portuguese or in another language, and items of researchers from other nationalities that live and work in Brazil, and that publish in their own native language or in Portuguese or another language. The second one is a list of secondary literature translations. Of course they are not exhaustive and should be taken as a first step for the organization of the existing bibliography.

So, compared with the meagre publication of books by Brazilians until the end of the sixties the production of the last twenty years is considerably high in numbers. I could include in the list eleven books issued after 1980. Among them appeared the outstanding essays of Professor Giannotti, *Apresentação do Mundo*, 1994, and the books of Arley Moreno, *Wittgenstein: através da imagens*, 1993, and, *Wittgenstein: labirintos da linguagem*, 2000. In the review Granger (1995) made of Moreno's book (1993), he concludes his paper by classifying (and I agree with him) this "elegant little book" as "one of the best examples of remarkable Wittgenstein studies recently developed by the Brazilian philosophers" (443). Another work is the long and deep essay of Luiz Henrique Lopes dos Santos, "A essência da proposição e a essência do mundo" [The Essence of the Proposition and the Essence of the World] which appeared as an introduction to his translation of *Tractatus* in1994. In addition, it should be mentioned the book of Plínio Margutti-Pinto, *Iniciação ao Silêncio: Análise do*

'Tractatus' de Wittgenstein [Initiation into Silence: Wittgenstein' Tractatus Analysis], 1989; in 1995, the books of Sílvia Faustino, *Wittgenstein: o eu e sua gramática* [Wittgenstein: The I and its Grammar], and of Cláudio Banzato, *Luzes de Babel: Wittgenstein e a crítica à linguística freudiana* [Babel Lights: Wittgenstein and the Criticism to Freudian Linguistics]; the book of Mauro Lúcio Leitão-Condé, *Wittgenstein: linguagem e mundo* [Wittgenstein: Language and World], 1998; and the collection of essays organized by Adriano Naves de Brito, 1998, *Filosofia lingüística, informática: language aspects* [Philosophy, Linguistics, Informatics: Language Aspects].

In 1990, Brazilian philosophers saw the appearance of Rudolf Haller's book, *Wittgenstein e a Filosofia Austríaca: questões*, translated by Norberto Abreu-e-Silva Neto. During this year, Haller stayed in São Paulo as Visiting Professor of Institute for Advanced Studies of the University of São Paulo. In the next year he came again for a series of lectures all over Brazil, organized by the Austrian Embassy and various universitites. During the first visit, Haller published a short article in a newspaper, *Jornal da Tarde*, and gave an interview for *Rádio USP*. In 1991, he published an article in the journal of the Institute, *Estudos Avançados*, and in 1995, an article in the special issue dedicated to Wittgenstein by *Manuscrito*, translated also by Norberto Abreu-e-Silva Neto, who has been developing his work under his influence. The impact of Haller's visits and work is something yet to be assessed. Since its appearance, his book has received three reviews by Brazilian philosophers and became an obligatory and constant reference for Wittgensteinian studies in Brazil. It is possible to say that the whole Wittgenstein he showed us changed in a not reversible way the former dominant vision that divided the philosopher in two.

Also in the nineties other few translations appeared that became quickly often referred in the production. The list includes the biography of Wittgenstein by Ray Monk and the Vienna of Janik and Toulmin. For the psychoanalysts interested in the study of Wittgenstein's philosophy it appeared the interpretation Paul-Laurent Assoun gave to the relation Freud-Wittgenstein, to my view more inclined to the the first than to Wittgenstein.We saw also the appearance of Christine Chauviré's, *Wittgenstein*. Besides, it was issued the substantive contribution brough to Wittgensteinian studies in Brazil by the translation of Hintikka and Hintikka, *Investigating Wittgenstein*, today considered a basic reference book. Recently were translated Glock's Dictionary, and P. M. S. Hacker's little introductory book, *Wittgenstein: sobre a natureza humana*, by João Vergílio Cuter. And finally, the wellcomed Brazilian issue of Cavell's *This New Yet Unapproachable America*. Cavell is presented in the blurb of the book by Claude Imbert (1997) as the philosopher that better than no one else "understood a culture having the age of cinema and photograph", and one whose work aims at putting our ears in tune with the style of thinking this culture produced. Imbert views Cavell's essays as guided by Wittgenstein's saying that what was important in his work was to change the style of thinking in order to understand the "new culture".

In what refers to the production of articles, in opposition to the incipient numbers we have for the period before the eighties (not much more than twenty articles published in thirty years), I could list about eighty articles published during the last twenty years, the majority of them (n = 60) in the 90s. Very representative of this production is the special issue of *Manuscrito*, 1995, above mentioned. The Brazilian authors that most published articles on Wittgenstein's work during the nineties attended the invitation to participate in this special number edited by Michael Wrigley: Arley Ramos Moreno, Paulo Roberto Margutti-Pinto, João Vergílio Cuter, José Oscar de Almeida Marques, Plínio Junqueira Smith, and Norberto Abreu-e-Silva Neto. It should be mentioned also the articles published in other journals or books by Danilo Marcondes; the "textual note" on the translation of *Bemerkungen über die Farben* by Anscombe presented by João Carlos Salles Pires da Silva in *Manuscrito* (1999); Nelson Gomes published his review of Haller's, *Neopositivismus*, 2000, in *Disputatio*. And, finally, part of these articles resulted from the participation of Brazilians in the Annual Wittgenstein Symposium of Kirchberg, which also increased in the last ten years.

To conclude this part two observations seem to be necessary for me. First, a few words about secondary literature produced in Portugal, and then some others about the translations of authors of Analytic Philosophy.

Despite Portugal and Brazil speak the same language, the historical context in which the secondary literature of both countries was produced is different, and I could not find any connection between Brazilian and Portuguese philosophers to be detached. Additionally, there is the problem of the spreading of Portuguese books and journals in Brazil which is not so intense as the diffusion of the editions in French, English, and specially Spanish, so that the preference of the researchers goes to what is more available, and they do not use very much what comes from Portugal. By these reasons they were not included in the lists. A relation of works published by Portuguese authors can be found in the bibliographies of Raymundo Drudys-Baldrich (1992), and of Peter Philipp (1996).

Notwithstanding, an exception should be made in order to include in the annexed lists Portuguese editions. Firstly, the books of Antonio Zilhão (1993) and of Manuel S. Lourenço (1993), today well known inside Brazilian philosophical movement. Antonio Zilhão has also published in the special issue *Manuscrito* (1995) dedicated to Wittgenstein his translation of Wittgenstein's essay "Philosophy" of the *Big Typescript*, and an article. And secondly, the list of translations of secondary literature will include the "Wittgenstein" of Algo Gargani (1982), the investigations of J. Ferrater-Mora (1982) on the change of meaning in philosophy, and the renowned book of Richard Rorty, *Philosophy and the Mirror of Nature*. Since the appearance of his book in Portuguese, in 1988, Rorty became one of the most frequent references not only in philosophical works but also in those of psychologists, sociologists, psychoanalysts, anthropologists, and literary and culture critics.

From another side, a word should be said about not including in the list of secondary literature translations the works of authors like Ryle, Austin, Wisdom, Searle, Strawson and Davidson among others, despite their relation to the philosophy of Wittgenstein. They exert an influence upon Brazilian philosophy and psychology that deserves an specific research.

Last Word

As mentioned in the introduction of this work, I did not intend to have presented here more than a description of what I have collected through a data survey of books and other works on Wittgenstein that were produced in Brazil. To my view, the result of it is nothing but a general map to enter the situation of Wittgenstein studies in our country; a map with references for the study of many themes in need of being explored and that I would like to suggest here for those interested in the genealogies and characteristics of our philosophers that try to practice and develop their philosophy having anchorage in Wittgenstein's ideas.

Being so, it could be illuminating for the knowledge of our style of thinking the deepening in the relation of Wittgenstein studies in Brazil with the Movement of Existential Phenomenology, the background in which he was thrown fifty years ago. From another side, the work of Euríalo Cannabrava taken as a whole is waiting for an assessment; and the historical and worthy figure of Jean Maugüé, this fine philosopher should be rescued and have his whole work known and published. The old relation of Granger with Brazilian philosophy, his ideas and influence is a theme for many essays. The impact of Rudolf Haller's book and his two visits on the actual development is another topic. And finally, more research is necessary for a better description of the present time situation of Wittgenstein studies in Brazil: on the questions discussed by the authors and the references they use, on the main themes of interest, and about the perspectives and affiliations of groups and centers of study.

References

Abreu-e-Silva, Norberto N. (1995), "Bibliografias sobre Wittgenstein e Literatura Secundária em Português", *Manuscrito*, XVIII (2), 407-435.

Amoroso Costa, Manuel (1929/1971), *As Idéias Fundamentais da Matemática e Outros Ensaios*, São Paulo: Editora da USP/Editorial Grijalbo.

Arantes, Paulo (1994), *Um Departamento Francês de Ultramar*, Rio de Janeiro: Paz e Terra.

Cannabrava, Euríalo (1952), "Ludwig Wittgenstein", *Revista Brasileira de Filosofia*, II, 48-76.

Cannabrava, Euríalo (1957), *Ensaios Filsoóficos*, Rio de Janeiro, Ministério da Educação e Cultura.

Cannabrava, Euríalo (1977), *Teoria da Decisão Filosófica*, Rio de Janeiro: Ministério de Educação e Cultura.

Centofanti, Rogério (1982), "Radecki e a Psicologia no Brasil", *Psicologia: Ciência e Profissão*, Ano 3(1), 2-50.

Daix, Pierre (1999), *Fernand Braudel: uma biografia*, Rio de Janeiro, Editora Record.

Dascal, Marcelo (1987a), "Editorial", *Manuscrito*, 10(2).

Dascal, Marcelo (1987b), "Observações sobre o programa epistemológico de Granger", *Manuscrito*, 10(2), 185-194.

Drudis-Baldrich, Raymundo (1992), *Bibliografia sobre Ludwig Wittgenstein – Literatura Secundária (1921-1985)*, Madrid: Aporia.

Faculdade de Filosofia (1937), *Ciências e Letras da USP, Anuário da Faculdade de Filosofia, Ciências e Letras: 1934-1935*, São Paulo: Editora "Revista dos Tribunais".

Franca, Pe. Leonel (1918/1990), *Noções de História da Psicologia* (24a. Ed.), Rio de Janeiro: Agir.

Gama, Lélio (1929/1971), "A obra de Amoroso Costa", in: Manuel Amoroso Costa, *As Idéias Fundamentais da Matemática e Outros Ensaios*, São Paulo: Editora da USP/ Editorial Grijalbo, 27-37.

Hegenberg, Leonidas (1978), "A lógica e a filosofia da ciência no Brasil", in: Adolpho Crippa (Org.), *As Idéias Filosóficas no Brasil*, São Paulo: Convívio, 143-201.

Imbert, Claude (1997), "Sinopse", in: Stanley Cavell, *Esta América Nova, Ainda Inabordável – Palestras a partir de Emerson e Wittgenstein*, São Paulo, Editora 34.

Lévi-Strauss (1996), Claude, *Saudades de São Paulo*, São Paulo, Companhia das Letras.

Lévi-Strauss, Claude (1996), *Tristes Trópicos*, São Paulo, Companhia das Letras (originally published in 1955).

Maugüé, Jean (1982), *Les dents agacées*, Paris: Buchet/Chastel.

Marcondes César, Constança (1988), *Filosofia na América Latina*, São Paulo: Paulinas.

Martins, Wilson (1976/1994), *História da Inteligência Brasileira*, Vol VII, São Paulo: T. A. Queiroz.

Milman, Luís (1999), *A Natureza dos Símbolos: explorações semântico filosóficas*, Porto Alegre, Editora da Universidade Federal do Rio Grande do Sul.

Nunes, Benedito (1978), "O pensamento Estético no Brasil", in: Adolpho Crippa (Org.), *As Idéias Filosóficas no Brasil*, São Paulo: Convívio, 85-142.

Paim, Antonio (1971), "O Neopositivismo no Brasil, Período de formação da corrente", in: Manuel Amoroso Costa, *As Idéias Fundamentais da matemática e Outros Ensaios*, São Paulo: Editora da USP/Editorial Grijalbo, 39-63.

Philipp, Peter (1996), *Bibliographie zur Wittgenstein-Literatur*, Bergen: The Wittgenstein Archives at the University of Bergen.

Quine, Willard Van Orman (1953/1963), *From a Logical Point of View*, New York: Harper Torchbooks.

Ramos, Teodoro (1933), *Estudos (Ensino, Sciencias Physicas e Mathematicas)*, São Paulo: Escolas Profissionais do Liceu Coração de Jesus.

Reale, Miguel (1971), "Apresentação", in: Manuel Amoroso Costa, *As idéias Fundamentais da Matemática e Outros Ensaios*, São Paulo: Editora da USP/Editorial Grijalbo, 9-11.

Severino, Antonio Joaquim (1999), *A Filosofia Contemporânea no Brasil*, Petrópolis: Vozes.

Sucupira, Newton (2001), *Tobias Barreto e a filosofia alemã*, Rio de Janeiro: Editora Gama Filho.

Vaz, Pe. Henrique (1990), "O pensamento filosófico no Brasil de hoje", in: Leonel Franca, *Noções de História da Filosofia* (24a. ed.), Rio de Janeiro: Agir, 343-377.

Vita, Luís Washington (1958), "A filosofia atual no Brasil", *Revista Brasileira de Filosofia*, VIII, 331-340.

Wrigley, Michael (ed.) (1995), "Wittgenstein", *Manuscrito*, 18(2).

Bibliography on Wittgenstein
(Secondary Literature by Brazilian Researchers)

Abreu, Luiz E. (2001), "Wittgenstein's Lecture on Ethics and French Anthropological Tradition", in: Rudolf Haller/Klaus Puhl (eds.), *Wittgenstein and the Future of Philosophy. A Reassessment after 50 Years*, Kirchberg am Wechsel: Austrian Ludwig Wittgenstein Society, 29-35.

Abreu-e-Silva, Norberto N. (1990), "O Centro de Pesquisa e Documentação de Filosofia Austríaca (Parte I)", *Revista Psicologia – USP*, 1(2), 177-190.

Abreu-e-Silva, Norberto N. (1991), *Anotações para um Curso de Psicologia Descritiva: Brentano e Wittgenstein* (Tese Livre Docência), Instituto de Psicologia da Universidade de São Paulo.

Abreu-e-Silva, Norberto N. (1991), "Mito e Psicanálise", in: Zélia de Almeida (ed.), *Mito, Religião e Sociedade*, São Paulo: Sociedade Brasileira de Estudos Clássicos, 347-353.

Abreu-e-Silva, Norberto N. (1992), "O Centro de Pesquisa e Documentação em Filosofia Austríaca Parte II), *Revista Psicologia – USP*, 3(1/2), 143-149.

Abreu-e-Silva, Norberto N. (1994), "Wittgenstein and John Wisdom: What is the place of psychoanalysis in philosophy?", in: Jaako Hintikka/Klaus Puhl (eds.), *The British Tradition in 20th. Century Philosophy*, Kirchberg am Wechsel: The Austrian Ludwig Wittgenstein Society, 1-7.

Abreu-e-Silva, Norberto N. (1995), "Resignations of feelings and will", in: Kjell S. Johannessen/Tore Nordenstam (eds.), *Culture and Value – Philosophy and the Cultural Sciences*, Kirchberg am Wechsel: The Austrian Ludwig Wittgenstein Society, 453-458.

Abreu-e-Silva, Norberto N. (1995), "Bibliografias sobre Wittgenstein e literatura secundária em português", *Manuscrito*, 18(2), 407-435.

Abreu-e-Silva, Norberto N. (1997), "Drury and Wittgenstein: Practical difficulties and philosophical perplexities", in: Paul Weingartner/Gerhard Schurz/Georg Dorn (eds.), *The Role of Pragmatics in Contemporary Philosophy* (2 Vols.), Kirchberg am Wechsel: Austrian Ludwig Wittgenstein Society, 715-720.

Abreu-e-Silva, Norberto N. (1998), "Afinidades analíticas: anotações sobre o parentesco entre Wittgenstein e Freud e o lugar da psicanálise na filosofia", *Psicologia em Estudo*, 3 (1), 13-20.

Abreu-e-Silva, Norberto N. (1998), "The knowledge of other minds: Wittgenstein and Carnap", in: Jesús Padilla-Gálvez/Raimundo Drudys Baldrich (eds.), *Wittgenstein y el Círculo de Viena / Wittgenstein und der Wiener Kreis*, Cuenca, Ed. UCLM, 49-60.

Abreu-e-Silva, Norberto N. (1998), "Maurice Drury and the psychiatric vocabulary", in: Peter Kampits/Karoly Kokai/ Anja Weiberg (eds.), *Applied Ethics* (2 Vols.), Kirchberg am Wechsel: Austrian Ludwig Wittgenstein Society, 13-20.

Abreu-e-Silva, Norberto N. (2000), "Ética", in: Ernesto Santos/Norberto Abreu e Silva Neto, *A ética no uso dos testes psicológicos, na informatização e na pesquisa*, São Paulo: Casa do Psicólogo, 99-121.

Abreu-e-Silva, Norberto N. (2001), "Facing the unavoidable metaphysics: Notes on the work of Maurice Drury", *Wittgenstein-Jahrbuch 2000*, Frankfurt am Main: Peter Lang, 63-87.

Abreu-e-Silva, Norberto N. (2001), "Ludwig Wittgenstein, professor de escola primária", *Boletim do Centro de Documentação e Pesquisa Helena Antipoff*, 15, 33-40. (Universidade Federal de Minas Gerais).

Abreu-e-Silva, Norberto N. (2001), "Wittgenstein throughout the corners of Brazil: shortened version", in: Rudolf Haller/Klaus Puhl (eds.), *Wittgenstein and the future of philosophy. A reassessment after 50 years* (2 Vols), Kirchberg am Wechsel: Austrian Ludwig Wittgenstein Society, 36-42.

Almeida, Claudio de (1992), "Russell on meaning and denotation: The argument of 'On denoting'" (Ph.D. Thesis), McMaster University.

Almeida, Claudio de (1995), "Russell: o argumento de 'On denoting'", in: Maria Cecília M. de Carvalho (Org.), *A Filosofia Analítica no Brasil*, Campinas, São Paulo, Papirus.

Almeida Marques, José O. (1991), "A ontologia do Tractatus e o problema dos Sachverhalte não-subsistente", O Que Nos Faz Pensar: Cadenos do Departamento de Filosofia da PUC-RJ, 5, 51-66.

Almeida Marques, José O. (1992), "Waismann, Ramsey, Wittgenstein e o axioma da redutibilidade", *Cadernos de História e Filosofia da Ciência*, Série e, 2(1), 6-48.

Almeida Marques, José O. (1995), "Pensar o sentido de uma proposição", *Manuscrito*, 18(2), 185-197.

Almeida Marques, José O. (1995), "Espaço e tempo no Tractatus", in F. Évora (Org.), *Espaço e Tempo: Anais do VIII Colóquio do CLE*, Universidade de Campinas.

Almeida Marques, José O. (1995), "Tractatus Logico-Philosophicus; Tradução de Luiz Henrique Lopes dos Santos" (Resenha), *Manuscrito*, 18(2), 1995, 445-463.

Alvim Júnior, Fausto, "Wittgenstein: sobre a explicação estética e a explicação científico causal", *Crítica* (Mex.), 5(13), 21-55.

Amaral, Felipe S. (2001), *Causação mental e redução*, (M.A. Dissertation), University of Brasília.

Bagolini, Luigi (1952), "A visita do Professor Herbert Feigl", *Revista Brasileira de Filosofia*, 2, 750-752.

Banzato, Claudio E.M. (1994), "A concepção lingüística freudiana e algumas de suas implicações filosóficas: ensaio inspirado nas críticas de Wittgenstein a Freud" (M.A. Dissertation), Universidade Estadual de Campinas, São Paulo.

Banzato, Claudio E.M. (1995), *Luzes de Babel: Wittgenstein e a crítica à lingüística freudiana*, Rio de Janeiro: Relume-Dumará Editores.

Barbosa Filho, Balthazar (1973), "Nota sobre o conceito de jogo-de-linguagem nas 'Investigações' de Wittgenstein", *ITA Humanidades* (São José dos Campos, São Paulo), 9, 75-104.

Barbosa Filho, Balthazar (1975), "La notion de signification dans les 'Investigations Philosophiques' de Wittgenstein" (Ph.D. Thesis), Louvain.

Barbosa Filho, Balthazar (1981-1982), "Sobre o positivismo de Wittgenstein", *Manuscrito*, 5(1), 17-32.

Brito, Adriano N. (1997), "Bedeutung, Gebrauch und Eigennamen: ein Kommentar zur Searles und Kripkes Auffassungen", in: Paul Weingarter/Gerhard Schurz/Georg Dorn (eds.), *The Role of Pragmatics in Contemporary Philosophy* (2 Vols), 694-699.

Brito, Adriano N. /Vale, Oto A. (eds.) (1998), *Filosofia lingüística, informática: aspectos da linguagem*, Goiania: Ed. da UFG.

Cannabrava, Euríalo (1952), "Introdução ao objetivismo crítico", *Revista Brasileira de Filosofia*, II, 48-76.

Cannabrava, Euríalo (1952), "Ludwig Wittgenstein", *Revista Brasileira de Filosofia*, II, 592-593.

Cannabrava, Euríalo (1955), "Lógica modal e dedução", *Revista Brasileira de Filosofia*, V, 60-68.

Cannabrava, Euríalo (1956), "Estrutura e teoria científica", *Anais do Congresso Internacional de Filosofia de São Paulo*, Vol. III, 799-806.

Cannabrava, Euríalo (1956), *Elementos de metodologia filosófica*, São Paulo: Nacional.

Cannabrava, Euríalo (1956), *Introdução à filosofia científica*, São Paulo: Nacional.

Cannabrava, Euríalo (1957), *Ensaios Filosóficos*, Rio de Janeiro: Ministério da Educação e Cultura.

Cannabrava, Euríalo (1959), "Estrutura lógica do argumento matemático", *Anais do III Congresso Nacional de Filosofia*, 295-298.

Cannabrava, Euríalo (1962), "Teoria da decisão e matemática qualitativa", *Anais do IV Congresso Nacional de Filosofia*, 476-484.

Cannabrava, Euríalo (1963), *Estética da Crítica*, Rio de Janeiro: Ministério de Educação e Cultura.

Cannabrava, Euríalo (1997), *Teoria da Decisão Filosófica: bases psicológicas da matemática, da lingüística e da teoria do conhecimento*, Rio de Janeiro, Forense-Universitária.

Cardoso, Célio M. (1980), "Wittgenstein: a filosofia da liguagem como primeira e paradigma" (M.A. Dissertation), Universidade Federal de Minas Gerais.

Carvalho, Edgar de A. (1995), "Descaminhos da linguagem antropológica: Wittgenstein e O Ramo de Ouro", *Manuscrito*, 18(2), 89-107.

Carvalho, Maria Cecília M. (Org.) (1995), *A Filosofia Analítica no Brasil*, São Paulo: Campinas.

Conde, Mauro L. L. (1993), "O problema da relação entre linguagem e mundo em L. Wittgenstein" (M.A. Dissertation), Universidade Federal de Minas Gerais.

Costa, Arilson B.C. (1997), "Delírio e Linguagem: três ensaios sobre psicose e referência" (M.A. Dissertation), Universidade de Brasília.

Costa, Claudio F. (1991), "A semântica implícita", O Que Nos Faz Pensar. Cadernos do Departamento de Filosofia da PUC-RJ, 5, 31-50.

Cuter, João V. (1993), "A teoria da figuração e a teoria dos tipos: o 'Tractatus' no contexto do projeto logicista" (Ph.D. Thesis), Universidade de São Paulo.

Cuter, João V. (1994), "Wittgenstein e o domínio da gramática: a ruptura com o Tractatus", *Educ. Filos.*, (8), 16, 173-181.

Cuter, João V. (1995), "Aritmética no 'Tractatus'", *Manuscrito*, 18(2), 109-139.

Cuter, João V. (2001), "Time and language in the transitional period", in: Rudolf Haller/Klaus Puhl (eds.), *Wittgenstein and the Future of Philosophy. A Reassessment after 50 Years*, Kirchberg am Wechsel: Austrian Ludwig Wittgenstein Society, 162-166.

Da Penha, João (1995), *Wittgenstein*, São Paulo: Editora Ática.

Dall'Agnoll, Darley (1993), "'Crítica à linguagem' e ética: a demarcação dos limites do dizível no 'Tractatus' e seu sentido ético" (M.A. Dissertation), Universidade Federal do Rio Grande do Sul.

Engelmann, Mauro L. (2000), "O que pode *mostrar* um contra-senso (como compreender a conclusão do 'Tractatus' de Wittgenstein)" (M.A. Dissertation), Universidade Federal do Rio Grande do Sul.

Faria, Paulo F. E. (1989), "Lógica e interpretação: Wittgenstein e o problema das incompatibilidades sintéticas" (M.A. Dissertation), Universidade Federal do Rio Grande do Sul.

Faria, Paulo F.E. (1994), "O mundo exterior: uma investigação gramatical" (Ph.D. Thesis), Universidade Federal do Rio Grande do Sul.

Faustino, Sílvia (1995), Wittgenstein: a gramática do eu, São Paulo, Editora Ática.

Felix, F.J.P.C. (1963), "Situação da linguagem no 'Tractatus' de Wittgenstein" (M.A. Dissertation), São Paulo, Faculdade de Filosofia, Ciências e Letras da Universidade de São Paulo.

Flusser, Vilém (1966), "Ludwig Wittgenstein: Philosophische Bemerkungen" (Resenha), *Revista Brasileira de Filosofia*, 16, 129-132.

Furlan, Reinaldo (1998), "Introdução ao pensamento de Merleau-Ponty: contrapontos com Freud e Wittgenstein" (Ph.D. Thesis), Campinas, Universidade Estadual de Campinas.

Furlan, Reinaldo (1999), "Inconsciente e linguagem comum na teoria freudiana", *Psicologia: Teoria e Pesquisa*, 15(2), 167-175.

Giannotti, José A. (1968), "Introdução", in: *Ludwig Wittgenstein, Tractatus lógico-filosófico*, São Paulo: Nacional/Editora da USP.

Giannotti, José A. (1972), "Apresentação", in: *Ludwig Wittgenstein, Estética, Psicologia e Religião*, São Paulo: Cultrix.

Giannotti, José A. (1987), "Breves considerações sobre o método de Wittgenstein", *Manuscrito*, X(2), 77-90.

Giannotti, José A. (1990), "A sociedade travada", *Novos Estudos*, 28, 50-66.

Giannotti, José A. (1995), *Apresentação do Mundo: considerações sobre o pensamento de Ludwig Wittgenstein*, São Paulo: Companhia das Letras.

Gomes, Nelson G. (1994), "Schlick's early criticism of Russell and Russell's answer to it", in: Jaakko Hintikka/Klaus Puhl (eds.), *The British Tradition in 20th Century Philosophy*, Kirchberg am Wechsel: Austrian Ludwig Wittgenstein Society, 171-179.

Gomes, Nelson G. (1995), "Neurath, crítico de Popper, in: Maria Cecília M. de Carvalho (Org.), *A Filosofia Analítica no Brasil*, Campinas, São Paulo: Papirus, 129-142.

Gomes, Nelson G./Haller, Rudolf (2000), 'Neopositivismus' (Review), *Disputatio* 9.

Guimarães, Lívia M. (1989), "Linguagem e filosofia nas 'Investigações Filosóficas' de Wittgenstein" (M.A. Dissertation), Universidade Federal de Minas Gerais.

Hallet, G. (1975) "A oposição de Wittgenstein à filosofia científica", *Presença Filosófica* (São Paulo), 4-5, 36-47.

Hegenberg, Leonidas (1958), "La revolución en filosofia, de A. J. Ayer" (Resenha), *Revista Brasileira de Filosofia*, 9.

Hegenberg, Leonidas (1962), "Ludwig Wittgenstein: Philosophical Investigations", *Revista Brasileira de Filosofia*, 12, 134.

Hegenberg, Leonidas (1963), "A realidade para Moritz Schlik", *Revista Brasileira de Filosofia*, 13, 71-88.

Hegenberg, Leonidas (1974), "Wittgenstein, linguagem e filosofia, de Warren Shibles" (Resenha), *Convivium*, 13, 470-472.

Hegenberg, Leonidas (1990), "Wittgenstein e a ética", *Revista Psicologia* USP, I(2), 191-193.

Junqueira Smith, Plínio (1993), "Wittgenstein e o Pirronismo: sobre a natureza da filosofia", *Analytica*, 1 (1), 153-186.

Junqueira Smith, Plínio (1995), "Como distinguir entre estados subjetivos?", *Manuscrito*, 18(2), 339-366.

Junqueira Smith, Plínio (1997), "Sobre a tranquilidade da alma e a moderação das afecções", *Kriterion*, 35 (93), 22-56.

Landim Filho, Raul (1982), "Sentido e verdade no Tractatus de L. Wittgenstein", *Cadernos de História e Filosofia da Ciência*, 2, 18-37.

Landim Filho, Raul (1982), "Jogos de linguagem e análise lingüística", *Revista Filosofia Brasileira*, I(1), 25-33.

Landim Filho, Raul (1984), "Notas sobre a questão da verdade", *Aquiles* I(1), 46-50.

Landim Filho, Raul (1983), "A interpretação realista da definição nominal de verdade", *Manuscrito*, 6 (2), 7-14.

Landim Filho, Raul (1984), "Significado e verdade", *Síntese*, 32, 33-47.

Leitão-Condé, Mauro L. (1998), *Wittgenstein: linguagem e mundo*.

Lopes dos Santos, Luiz H. (1994), "A essência da proposição e a essência do mundo", in: *Ludwig Wittgenstein, Tractatus Logico-Philosophicus*, São Paulo: Editora da Universidade de São Paulo.

Lourenço, M. S. (1993), *A Cultura da Subtileza: Aspectos da Filosofia Analítica*, Lisboa: Gradiva Publicações.

Machado, Renato (1989), "Relevância espistemológica da doutrina do significado no Tracatus Logico-Philosophicus" (M.A. Dissertation), Universidade Federal de Minas Gerais.

Marcondes, Danilo (1977), "Language and Action: A reassessment of Speech Act Theory" (Ph.D. Thesis), St. Andrews University, England.

Marcondes, Danilo (1987), "Wittgenstein, Habermas, and the idea of a critical philosophy" (Abstract), *Philosophy of Law, Politics and Society*, Kirchberg am Wechsel: Austrian Ludwig Wittgenstein Society, 66.

Marcondes, Danilo (1989), "Duas concepções de análise do desenvolvimento da filosofia analítica", in: Maria Cecília M. de Carvalho (Org.), *Paradigmas Filosóficos da Atualidade*, Campinas, São Paulo: Papirus, 11-38.

Marcondes. Danilo (1995), "Ceticismo e filosofia analítica: por um novo rumo", in: Maria Cecília M. de Carvalho (Org.), *A Filosofia Analítica no Brasil*, Campinas, São Paulo: Papirus, 9-38.

Marcondes, Danilo (1996), "A intersubjetividade no discurso e a construção da realidade", in: M.I.S. Magalhães (Org.), *As Múltiplas Faces da Linguagem*, Brasília: Editora da UnB.

Marcondes, Danilo (1995), "Juizo, suspensão do juízo e filosofia cética", *Kriterion*, 35(93), 9-21.

Margutti Pinto, Paulo R. (1980), "Aspectos lógicos da implicação articulada pelas frases condicionais" (M.A. Dissertation), Universidade Federal de Minas Gerais.

Margutti Pinto, Paulo, R. (1996), "Sobre a natureza da filosofia: Wittgenstein e o pirronismo", *Kriterion*, 35(93), 164-183.

Margutti Pinto, Paulo R. (1997), "Aspectos da influência de Weininger sobre Wittgenstein", *Síntese*, 24(77), 199-225.

Margutti Pinto, Paulo R. (1998), *Iniciação ao Silêncio: análise do Tractatus de Wittgenstein*, Belo Horizonte: Loyola, 1998.

Margutti Pinto, Paulo, R. (1999), "Frege's referencial dualism concerning proper names", *Manuscrito*, 22(1), 117-142.

Marques, Edgar D.R. (1990), "Sobre a distinção entre Tatsache e Sachverhalte no Tractatus Logico-Philosophicus de Ludwig Wittgenstein", O Que Nos Faz Pensar. Cadernos do Departamento de Filosofia da PUC-RJ, 2, 54-61.

Martinez, Horácio (1996), "Voluntad y Subjectividad en el pensamiento del 'Primer' Wittgenstein: acerca de una posibilidad de una lectura ética del 'Tractatus'" (M.A. Dissertation), Universidade Estadual de Campinas, São Paulo.

Mendonça, Wilson (1991), "Wittgenstein e os números", O Que Nos Faz Pensar. Cadernos do Departamento de Filosofia da PUC-RJ, 4, 5-36.

Michielon Jr., Claudio F. (1998), "The role of reasons in living a good life", in: Peter Kampits/Karoly Kokai/Anja Weiberg (eds.), *Applied Ethics* (2 Vols.), Kirchberg am Wechsel: Austrian Ludwig Wittgenstein Society, 78-83.

Miranda, Fábio J. (1998), "Conversations on Freud: To undo a bewitchment", in: Peter Kampits/Karoly Kokai/Anja Weiberg (eds.), *Applied Ethics* (2 Vols.), Kirchberg am Wechsel: Austrian Ludwig Wittgenstein Society, 84-89.

Mojola, Norberto (1960), "O positivismo lógico", *Revista Brasileira de Filosofia*, 10, 543-554.

Moreno, Arley R. (1971), "O problema da significação em Wittgenstein: uma introdução ao estudo do Tractatus" (M.A. Dissertation), Faculdade de Filosofia, Ciências Humanas e Letras da Universidade de São Paulo.

Moreno, Arley R. (1974), "Conhecimento científico do individual e comentários filosóficos: uma análise do Tractatus", *Transform-ação*, 1, 71-77.

Moreno, Arley R. (1975), « Recherches sur le Tractatus logico-philosophicus de Wittgenstein (Ph.D. Thesis), Faculté des Lettres, Université de Provence, Aix-en-Provence.

Moreno, Arley R. (1978), "Le système de numérotation du Tractatus", in: *CNRS, Systèmes symboliques: science et philosophie*, Paris.

Moreno, Arley R. (1985), "A propósito da noção de 'estética' em Wittgenstein", *Manuscrito*, 8(2), 113-146.

Moreno, Arley R. (1986), *Wittgenstein: ensaio introdutório*, Rio de Janeiro: Taurus.

Moreno, Arley R. (1986), "Descrição gramatical como terapia filosófica", *Rev. Latinoamericana de Filosofia*, 12, 323-334.

Moreno, Arley R. (1987), "Marcas de um estilo?", *Manuscrito*, 10(2), 99-110.

Moreno, Arley R. (1989), "Duas observações sobre a gramática filosófica", *Manuscrito*, 12, 83-115.

Moreno, Arley R. (1993), *Wittgenstein: através das imagens*, Campinas: Editora da Unicamp.

Moreno, Arley R. (1995), "Fenomenologia e problemas fenomenológicos", *Manuscrito*, 18(2), 199-226.

Moreno, Arley R. (2000), *Wittgenstein: labirintos da linguagem*, São Paulo: Moderna.

Nunes, Benedito (1991), "O pensamento de Wittgenstein", in: Benedito Nunes, *A Filosofia Contemporânea: trajetos iniciais*, São Paulo: Ática, 131-135.

Palavecino, Sérgio R. (1996), "La certeza fuera de la verdad", *Kriterion*, 93, 184-194.

Palma, Jorge L. P. (2001), *Gramática filosófica e proposições necessárias* (M.A. Dissertation), University of Brasília.

Perini-Santos, Ernesto (1997), "Occasion Sentences: Disagreements we Cannot Afford", in: Paul Weingartner/Gerhard Schurz/Georg Dorn (eds.), *The Role of Pragmatics in Contemporary Philosophy* (2 Vols), Kirchberg am Wechsel: Austrian Ludwig Wittgenstein Society, 758-762.

Pires da Silva, João C. S. (1999), "Considerações sobre a edição das 'Bemerkungen über die Farben'", *Manuscrito*, 22(1), 291-308.

Pires da Silva, João C. S. (2001), "On Remarks on Colour", in: Rudolf Haller/ Klaus Puhl (eds), *Wittgenstein and the Future of Philosophy. A Reassessment after 50 Years*, Kirchberg am Wechsel: Austrian Ludwig Wittgenstein Society, 173-177.

Romano, Roberto (1991), "Wittgenstein por Rudolf Haller" (Resenha), *Revista da Universidade de São Paulo*, 9, 199-202.

Ruffino, Marco A. (1990), "O princípio do contexto em Frege e Wittgenstein" (M.A. Dissertation), Universidade Estadual de Campinas.

Ruffino, Marco A. (1994), "Wittgenstein on Russell's Use of Real Variables", in: Jaakko Hintikka/Klaus Puhl (eds.), *The British Tradition in 20th Century Philosophy*, Kirchberg am Wechsel: Austrian Ludwig Wittgenstein Society, 401-406.

Ruffino, Marco A. (1994), "The context principle and Wittgenstein's criticism of Russell's Theory of Types", *Synthese*, 98 (3), 401-414.

Saes, Sílvia, F.A. (1992), "Wittgenstein – Solipsismo e Linguagem" (M.A. Dissertation), Departamento de Filosofia da Faculdade de Filosofia, Ciências Humanas e Letras da Universidade de São Paulo.

Spaniol, Werner (1975), „Ein Kampf gegen die 'Verhexung des Verstandes'; Philosophie und Methode bei Wittgenstein" (Ph.D. Thesis), Universidade Gregoriana, Roma.

Spaniol, Werner (1989), *Filosofia e método no segundo Wittgenstein: uma luta contra o enfeitiçamento de nosso entendimento*, São Paulo: Loyola.

Spaniol, Werner (1990), "Formas de vida: significado e função no pensamento de Wittgenstein", *Síntese Nova Fase*, 51, 11-31.

Wrigley, Michael (1977), "Wittgenstein's Philosophy of Mathematics", *Philosophical Quarterly*, 27, H. 106, 50-59.

Wrigley, Michael (1980), "Wittgenstein on Inconsistency", *Philosophy*, 55, H. 214, 471-484.

Wrigley, Michael (1986), "Remarks on the origin of Wittgenstein's Verificationism", in W. Leinfellner/F. Wuketits (Hrsg.), *Die Aufgaben der Philosophie in der Gegenwart. Akten des 10. Int. Wittgenstein-Symposiums*, Vienna: Hölder-Pichler-Tempsky, 448-450.

Wrigley, Michael (1986), "Wittgenstein's Philosophy of Mathematics" (Reprint), in: S.G. Shanker (ed.), *Ludwig Wittgenstein: Critical Assessments*, Vol III, Londres: Croom Helm, 183-192.

Wrigley, Michael (1986), "Wittgenstein on Inconsistency" (Reprint), in: S.G. Shanker (ed.), *Ludwig Wittgenstein: Critical Assessments*, Vol. III, Londres: Croom Helm, 347-359.

Wrigley, Michael (1986), "Wittgenstein on Inconsistency" (Reprint), in: J.V. Canfield (ed.), *The Philosophy of Wittgenstein. Vol. 11: Philosophy of Mathematics*, New York: Garland, 1986.

Wrigley, Michael (1987), "Wittgenstein's early philosophy of Mathematics" (Ph.D. thesis), Berkeley, University of California.

Wrigley, Michael (1989), "The Origin of Wittgenstein's Verificationism", *Synthese*, 78, 265-290.

Wrigley, Michael (1993), "The Continuity of Wittgenstein's Philosophy of Mathematics", in: Klaus Puhl (ed.), *Wittgenstein's Philosophy of Mathematics*, Vienna: Hölder-Pichler-Tempsky.

Wrigley, Michael (1995), "Wittgenstein, Ramsey and the Infinite", in: Jaakko Hintikka/Klaus Puhl (eds.), *The British Tradition in 20th. Century Philosophy*, Vienna, Hölder-Pichler-Tempsky.

Wrigley, Michael (Ed.) (1995), "Wittgenstein", *Manuscrito*, 18(2), 470 pages.

Wrigley, Michael (1995), "Wittgenstein e a Filosofia Austríaca: questões, de Rudolf Haller" (Resenha), *Manuscrito*, 18, 465-468.

Wrigley, Michael (1996), "Review of *Wittgenstein's Philosophy of Mathematics* by Pasquale Frascolla (London/New York: Routledge 1994)", *Manuscrito*, XIX (2), 237-252.

Wrigley, Michael (1998), "Review of *Frege: Importance and Legacy* (ed. by Matthias Schirn) & *The Philosophy of Mathematics Today* (ed. by Matthias Schirn)", *Manuscrito*, XXI (1), 269-274.

Wrigley, Michael (1999), "A Note on Wittgenstein, Real Numbers & Metaphilosophy", *Manuscrito*, XXII (2), 561-566.

Zilhão, António (1993), *Linguagem da Filosofia e filosofia da Linguagem: estudos sobre Wittgenstein*, Lisboa: Edições Colibri.

Zilhão, António (1995), "Acção, Explicação e Explicação da Acção", *Manuscrito*, 18(2), 367-405.

Translations of Secondary Literature

Assoun, Paul-Laurent (1990), *Freud e Wittgenstein*, Rio de Janeiro: Ed. Campus.

Brockman, J. (1982), *Einstein, Gertrud Stein, Wittgenstein e Frankenstein*, São Paulo: Companhia das Letras.

Brown, Norman (1972), *Vida Contra Morte*, Petrópolis: Vozes.

Carnap, Rudolf (1988), *Coletânea de Textos*, São Paulo: Nova Cultural (Col. Os Pensadores).

Cavell, Stanley (1997), *Esta América Nova, Ainda Inabordável – Palestras a partir de Emerson e Wittgenstein*, São Paulo: Editora 34.

Chauviré, Christine (1991), *Wittgenstein*, Rio de Janeiro: Zahar.

Chisholm, Roderick M. (1974), *Teoria do Conhecimento*, Rio de Janeiro: Zahar.

Ferrater-Mora, José (1982), *A Filosofia Analítica: mudança de sentido em filosofia*, Porto: Rés.

Gargani, Aldo G. (1988), *Wittgenstein*, Lisboa: Edições 70.

Glock, Hans-J. (1998), *Dicionário de Wittgenstein*, Rio de Janeiro: Zahar.

Granger, Giles G. (1948), "O Verdadeiro, o Falso e o Absurdo", *Boletins da Faculdade de Filosofia da Universidade de São Paulo*, LXXXVIII, Filosofia 3, 32p.

Granger, Giles G. (1955), *Lógica e Filosofia das Ciências*, São Paulo: Melhoramentos.

Granger, Giles G. (1958), "A arte e a interpretação do mundo atual", *Boletim de Psicologia* (USP), X, n. 35/36.

Granger, Giles G. (1962), "Introdução", in: *Descartes – Obra Escolhida* (Coleção Clássicos Garnier), São Paulo: DIFEL, 9-36.

Granger, Giles G. (1962), "Acontecimentos e estruturas nas ciências do homem", *Kriterion* (Belo Horizonte), 59-60, 40-80.

Granger, Giles, G. (1974), *Filosofia do Estilo*, São Paulo: Perspectiva.

Granger, Giles G. (1975-1976), *Pensamento Formal e Ciências do Homem*, São Paulo: Martins Fontes.

Granger, Giles G. (1981), "Was in Königsberg zu sagen wäre", *Manuscrito*, 5(1), 66-90.

Granger, Giles G. (1982), "Sobre a unidade da ciência", *Ciência e Filosofia* (São Paulo), 2.

Granger, Files G. (1987), "Contenus formels et dualité", *Manuscrito*, 10(2), 195-210.

Granger, Giles G. (1987), "Bibliografia de Giles Gaston Granger (até 1985)/ Publications of Giles Gaston Granger (up to 1985)", *Manuscrito*, 10(2), 211-215.

Granger, Giles G. (1990), "Arley Ramos Moreno, Wittgenstein através das imagens" (Review), *Manuscrito*, 18(2), 439-443.

Hacker, P.M.S. (2000), *Wittgenstein: sobre a natureza humana*, São Paulo: Editora UNESP.

Haller, Rudolf (1990), *Wittgenstein e a Filosofia Austríaca: questões*, São Paulo: Editora da Universidade de São Paulo.

Haller, Rudolf (1991), "A ética no pensamento de Wittgenstein", *Estudos Avançados* (USP), 5(11), 71-88.

Haller, Rudolf (1995), "Wittgenstein no período intermediário – um fragmento", *Manuscrito*, 18(2), 141-158.

Hintikka, Jaakko/Hintikka, Merril (1994), *Uma Investigação sobre Wittgenstein*, Campinas: Papirus.

Janik, A./Toulmin, S. (1991), *A Viena de Wittgenstein*, Rio de Janeiro: Campus.

Langer, Susanne K. (1971), *Filosofia em Nova Chave*, São Paulo: Perspectiva.

Marcuse, Herbert (1967), *A Ideologia da Sociedade Industrial*, Rio de Janeiro: Zahar.

Monk, Ray (1995), *Wittgenstein – O dever do gênio*, São Paulo: Companhia das Letras.

Pears, David (1982), *As idéias de Wittgenstein*, São Paulo: Cultrix.

Resweler, J.-P. (1982), *Filosofia da Linguagem*, São Paulo: Cultrix.

Rorty, Richard (1988), *A Filosofia e o Espelho da Natureza*, Lisboa: Publicações Dom Quixote.

Rossi-Landi, Ferruccio (1985), *A Linguagem como Trabalho e como Mercado: uma teoria da produção e da alienação lingüísticas*, São Paulo: DIFEL.

Scruton, R. (1982), *Introdução à Filosofia Moderna: de Descartes a Wittgenstein*, Rio de Janeiro: Zahar.

Shibles, Warren (1974), *Wittgenstein, linguagem e filosofia*, São Paulo: EDUSP/Cultrix.

Stegmüller, Wolfgang (1977), *A Filosofia Contemporânea*, São Paulo: Editora da USP.

Strathern, Paulo (1997), *Wittgenstein em 90 Minutos*, Rio de Janeiro: Zahar.

Tugendhat, Ernst (1992), "'Wittgenstein I: a impossibilidade de uma linguagem privada' e 'Wittgenstein II: a saída da campânula'", in: *Novos Estudos*, 32 and 33, São Paulo: Cebrap.

Tugendhat, Ernst/Wolf, Ursula (1996), *Propedêutica Lógico-Semântica*, Petrópolis: Vozes.

Wallner, Friedrich (1997), *A Obra Filosófica de Wittgenstein como Unidade*, Rio de Janeiro: Tempo Brasileiro.

AXEL ARTURO BARCELÓ ASPEITIA

Grammatical Necessity in Wittgenstein's Middle Period

I. Introduction

This article recapitulates several arguments to defend Wittgenstein's view during the middle period of his philosophical career[1] that mathematical statements ultimately belong to grammar. In particular, it aims at debunking those arguments based on the mistaken premise that statements of grammar describe the usage of words and, as such, cannot express necessary propositions. Thus, the overall strategy of this work is to demonstrate, first, that statements of grammar, at least under Wittgenstein's notion, do not *describe* the usage of words, and second, that Wittgenstein's grammatical account of mathematics can accurately account for mathematical necessity.

The first part of this article deals with the Quine/Carnap debate on so-called 'truth by convention' and its relevance to Wittgenstein's grammatical account of mathematics. Since Carnap asserted that he developed his view of mathematics as syntax inspired on Wittgenstein's views on the same subject, taking a stance regarding the Quine/Carnap debate on this issue is crucial for the purposes of this article. It is also indispensable to clarify whether or not Wittgenstein held a view like the one Carnap championed, as is defending him against Quine's criticisms.

The second part assembles a defense of Wittgenstein's grammatical account of mathematical necessity out of arguments from Morris Lazerowitz's "Necessity and Language", Zeno Vendler's "Linguistics and the *a-priori*" W. E. Kennick's

---

[1] Wittgenstein's middle period ranges from his return to Cambridge, early in 1929, to 1933. In this point, I side with Dale Jacquette, who wrote, in the introduction to his *Wittgenstein's Thought in Transition*, "I designate [the middle period] from 1929 to 1933. [...] The dates are significant and by no means arbitrary. [...] In 1930, Wittgenstein began lecturing at Cambridge University. The end of the transition period can be dated approximately to 1933, because Wittgenstein's lectures from this term recorded in the Blue Book, together with the *Brown Book* of 1934, already contain his new methodology and nearly all of the central ideas of his later philosophy as they were to appear in the *Philosophical Investigations*." (West Lafayette: Purdue University Press 1998, 9)

"Philosophy as Grammar"[2], and J. Michael Young's "Kant on the Construction of Arithmetical Concepts."[3] These arguments show that the objections raised against Wittgenstein equivocate on the meaning of the adjectival phrase 'of grammar'.

II. Wittgenstein's Grammatical Account of Mathematical Necessity and 'Analyticity'

A. Brief Historical Background

According to the middle Wittgenstein, internal descriptions ascribe essential properties to objects, while external descriptions ascribe accidental properties.[4] A description is internal if the concept in the subject includes or implies the concept in the predicate. This characterization of internal descriptions is very close to one of Kant's definitions of analytic judgements. Since Wittgenstein also includes mathematical statements among internal descriptions, this commits him to believe that mathematical statements are somehow analytic.

Before Kant's classical account of analyticity, Locke had already distinguished two kinds of analytic propositions. In *An Essay concerning Human Understanding* (pp. 306, 308), he distinguished between 'trifling' and 'predicative' propositions. Trifling propositions have the form '$a = a$', in which "we affirm the said term of itself." In predicative propositions, "a part of the complex idea is predicated of the name of the whole." For Locke, mathematical propositions are not analytic in either of these senses. After Locke, Kant added a new account of analyticity to Locke's notion of trifling proposition. For Kant, an analytic judgement is (*i*) one whose subject contains its predicate, or (*ii*) one whose negation is a logical contradiction. By offering these two different accounts, Kant laid the foundations for what became the two main doctrines of analyticity in modern

---

[2] W. E. Kennick, "Philosophy as Grammar", in: G. E. Anscombe/M. Lazerowitz: *Ludwig Wittgenstein, Philosophy and Language*, Bristol: Thoemmes Press 1996.

[3] J. Michael Young, "Kant on the Construction of Mathematical Concepts", *Kant-Studien* 73, 1982, 17-46. Michael Young's article differs from those of Vendler, Lazerowitz and Kennick's in that it focuses on questions in the philosophy of mathematics. Michael Young uses an argument similar to the present one to "show that Kant is right in thinking that to ground *a priori* judgements, at least in arithmetic, upon ostensive constructions" is possible (p. 17). Kant's and Wttgenstein's position regarding the construction of arithmetical concepts differ primarily because the rules of calculation that Kant refers to as 'the universal conditions of construction', are distinct from the concepts whose constructions they govern. *Cf. Ibidem*, 28, 29.

[4] *Philosophical Remarks*, §94.

western philosophy.[5] For Kant, a judgement is analytic if the subject contains the predicate. However, he allows for two possible interpretations of this 'containment': what Jerrold J. Katz in *The New Intentsionalism* calls 'logical-containment' and 'concept-containment'.[6] Kant's notion of analyticity fused these two notions, and they remained so until the seminal work of Frege. For Frege, Kant's account of analyticity in terms of conceptual containment was a psychologistic error. In *The Foundations of Arithmetic* §3, Frege defines analyticity as 'being a consequence of logical laws plus definitions without scientific assumptions.' Wittgenstein's account of logical necessity in the *Tractatus* follows Frege away from the conceptual path and into logicism. This path leads from Wittgenstein directly into the Quine/Carnap controversy.

It is also worth mentioning that at the end of his 1944 article on 'Russell's Mathematical Logic' Kurt Gödel distinguished two senses of 'analyticity'.

> As to this problem [if (and in which sense) mathematical axioms can be considered analytic], it is to be remarked that analyticity may be understood in two senses. First, it may have the purely formal sense that the terms occurring can be defined (wither explicitly or by rules for eliminating them from sentences containing them) in such a way that the axioms and theorems become special cases of the law of identity and disprovable propositions become negations of this law. [...]

> In a second sense a proposition is called analytic if it holds "owing to the meaning of the concept occurring in it", where this meaning may perhaps be undefinable (i.e., irreducible to anything more fundamental). [Note 47. The two significations of the term 'analytic' might perhaps be distinguished as tautological an analytic.][7]

According to Carnap, Wittgenstein's *Tractatus* endorsed the view of mathematical propositions as analytic in the tautologous sense. However, by the beginning of the thirties, Wittgenstein's view on the analyticity of mathematics had evolved from a purely formal notion into Gödel's second sense.

After the *Tractatus*, considerations about color and the nature of space changed Wittgenstein's mind about the logicist's path. In the *Tractatus*, he had maintained that "there is only *logical* necessity" (6.375). However, by the late twenties, he could hardly see how the *Tractatus*' logical necessity could account for the necessity of such propositions as 'The blue spot is not red at the same time'. In the early thirties, the notion of grammatical necessity had become a substitute for the *Tractatus*' 'logical necessity'.

---

[5] They have also been called the 'logicist' and the 'idealist' doctrines.
[6] Jerrold J. Katz, *Mind*, New Series, CI, 404, 1992, 691.
[7] Kurt Gödel, *Works. English & German Collected Works*, edited by Solomon Feferman et al., New York: Oxford University Press, 1986, 139.

B. Carnap

Despite their alleged mutual personal dislike, Carnap always recognized Wittgenstein's influence on this and other philosophical matters. In his "Intellectual Autobiography," Carnap states that "Wittgenstein was perhaps the philosopher who, besides Russell and Frege, had the greatest influence on my thinking."[8] From Carnap's own appraisal, the sources of this influence were triple: (*i*) careful and intense reading of the *Tractatus* by the Vienna Circle, (*ii*) personal contact between Carnap and Wittgenstein from the Summer of 1927 to the beginning of 1929, and (*iii*) "Waismann's systematic expositions of certain conceptions of Wittgenstein's on basis of his talks with him."[9]

According to Carnap,

> The most important insight I gained from his [Wittgenstein's] work was the conception that the truth of logical statements is based only on their logical structure and the meaning of terms. Logical statements are true under all conceivable circumstances; thus their truth is independent of the contingent facts of the world. On the other hand, it follows that these statements do not say anything about the world and thus have no factual content.[10]

From Wittgenstein, Carnap received the idea that logical truths are tautologies. In the *Tractatus*, Wittgenstein unsuccessfully argued for the tautologous nature of logical truth for the first time in the history of logicism.

However, the issue of logical truth is both the source of the main agreement and most important divergence between Carnap and Wittgenstein. Michael Friedman has already pointed this out in his "Carnap and Wittgenstein's *Tractatus*", where he writes:

> This conception of the tautologous character of logical and mathematical truth represents Carnap, the most important point of agreement between his philosophy and that of the *Tractatus*. But there is also an equally important point of fundamental disagreement. Whereas the *Tractatus* associates its distinctive conception of logical truth with a radical division between what can be said and what can only be shown but not said a division according to which logic itself is not properly an object of theoretical science at all – Carnap associates his conception of logical truth with the idea that logical analysis, what he calls "logical syntax," is a theoretical science in the strictest possible sense.[11]

---

[8] Rudolf Carnap, "Intellectual Autobiography", in: Paul Arthur Schillp (ed.), *The Philosophy of Rudolf Carnap*, La Salle, Illinois: Open Court Pub. Co., 1963, 46.
[9] *Ibidem*, 28.
[10] *Ibidem*, 25.
[11] Michael Friedman, "Carnap and Wittgenstein's *Tractatus*", in: William W. Tait (ed.), *Early Analytic Philosophy. Frege, Russell, Wittgenstein. Essays in Honor of Leonard Linsky*, Chicago: Open Court, 1997, 20.

In terms of the middle Wittgenstein, the main point of divergence between Carnap and Wittgenstein was the autonomous character of mathematics and grammar. Under the influence of Frege and Russell, Carnap was convinced of "the philosophical relevance of constructed language systems."[12] During his years in the Vienna Circle, Otto Neurath nurtured Carnap's idea that a descriptive science of the structure of language – what would become the "Logical Syntax of Language" – was possible. Finally, Carnap's study of Hilbert and his continuous talks with Tarski and Gödel convinced him of the philosophical power of metamathematics. By the time he had developed his theory of logical syntax, virtually all connection with Wittgenstein's notion of tautology and analyticity seemed lost.[13] Most strikingly, Carnap's logical syntax of language, unlike Wittgenstein's grammar, had lost its autonomy.

Carnap conceived philosophy as a descriptive, scientific enterprise geared towards formulating the logic of science in a precise meta-language.[14] Instead of an indescribable, but displayable grammar, Carnap expresses his logical syntax in its own object language. Carnap uses Gödel's arithmetization method to embed the syntactic meta-language in the object language (provided that the object language includes elementary arithmetic), allowing it to express its own syntax. However, it immediately follows from Gödel's work that, for a language containing classical arithmetic, 'truth' is a non-arithmetical predicate and thus, not definable in the language itself. Carnap understood this and, consequently, qualified his remarks on this method in *Logical Syntax*. Commenting on the Wittgenstein-Carnap connection, Michael Friedman interprets this as a point in favor of Wittgenstein's autonomous grammar over Carnap's logical syntax.[15]

The failure of Carnap's attempt to syntactically define analyticity is a point in favor of the autonomy of mathematics. Carnap followed Wittgenstein in his

---

[12] Carnap 1963, 28.
[13] Friedman 1997, 23.
[14] Rudolf Carnap, *The Logical Syntax of Language*, New York: Harcourt, 1937, §73.
[15] "Carnap, characteristically, has transformed an originally philosophical point into a purely technical question – in this case, the technical question of what formal theories can or cannot be embedded in a given object language. Considered purely as a technical question, however, the situation turns out to be far more complicated than it initially appears. [...] For it turns out, again as a consequence of Gödel's researches, that it is as a matter of fact not possible in most cases of interest to express the logical syntax of a language in Carnap's sense in the language itself. [...] Thus, the logical syntax in Carnap's sense for a language for classical mathematics can only be expressed in a distinct and essentially richer metalanguage; the logical syntax for this metalanguage can itself only be expressed in a distinct and essentially richer meta-metalanguage; and so on. [...] Does this same situation does not represent the kernel of truth – from Carnap's point of view, of course – in Wittgenstein's doctrine of the inexpressibility of logical syntax?" (Friedman 1997, 35-36)

search for mathematics among the grammatical rules of language. However, while natural language grammar contains embedded mathematical calculi, Carnap was wrong in believing that mathematics' job is to describe this application in a formal meta-language. For Wittgenstein, in contrast, mathematics is autonomous. Every calculus is its own internal application. As such, it does not require an external description or a meta-mathematical formulation.

It is possible to describe a calculus' external application in a meta-language. However, this description is *not* the calculus itself. Describing a syntax is substantially different from calculating. Unlike calculation, description is not autonomous. The truth of a descriptive proposition point outside the description itself. Calculation determines the correctness of its own propositions. The mere description of a calculus' external application cannot fully determine the correctness or incorrectness of its propositions. Gödel showed that Carnap's attempt failed technically, while Wittgenstein showed that the project was also philosophically inadequate.

C. Quine

1. Two Dogmas and the Analytic Nature of Grammar

> The linguistic doctrine of logical truth is sometimes expressed by saying that logical truths are true by linguistic convention. (Quine 1963, 391)

The analytic/synthetic distinction has a long history in modern philosophy. According to Quine's "Two Dogmas of Empiricism", the writings of Leibniz, Hume and Kant foreshadow the contemporary distinction. However, both Hume's "relations of ideas" and Leibniz's "truths of reason" are quasi-psychological notions. It was Kant who first inserted language at the core of the philosophical characterization of analyticity. The idea of 'truths independent of fact' precedes Kant. Nonetheless, starting with him, these truths became also 'true by virtue of meaning'. Thus, it could be said that the current notion of 'analyticity' originates in Kant. After the seminal work of Frege, analyticity secured a central place in contemporary philosophy of logic and mathematics. The discussion of analyticity in this century has grown largely from his conception. Nevertheless, Quine offered the principal arguments against the analytic/synthetic distinction, not in response to Frege, but in response to Carnap's *The Logical Syntax of Language*. Those arguments are so convincing that even today a large number of philosophers and mathematicians consider some of the points made in these seminal writings settled matters. For example, Paul A. Boghossian, starts his 1996 article 'Analyticity Reconsidered' with the following remarks:

> This is what many philosophers believe today about the analytic/synthetic distinction: In his classic early writings on analyticity – in particular, in "Truth by Convention," "Two Dogmas of Empiricism," and "Carnap and Logical Truth" – Quine showed that there can be no distinction between sentences that are true purely by virtue of their meaning and those that are not. In so doing, Quine devastated the philosophical programs that depend on he notion of analyticity – specifically, the linguistic theory of necessary truth. [...] Now, I do not know precisely how many philosophers believe all of the above, but I think it would be fair to say that it is the prevailing view.[16]

Quine's strategy against the analytic/synthetic distinction is stunningly novel and elegant. It targets its putative linguistic dimension through the syntax/semantics distinction. For Quine, if some propositions are true in virtue of linguistic conventions, then either their syntax or their semantics determines their truth. In "Two Dogmas," he distinguishes between '*logically true*' (syntactic) and others (semantic) analytic statements.[17] According to Quine, both the proof theoretical and model theoretical approaches to necessity can only account for analytic statements of the first kind. For the rest of the article, Quine attacks different attempts – mostly Carnap's – at reducing analytic sentences of the second class to those of the first class. According to Quine, Carnap's account of analyticity is unsuitable, because it tries to reduce semantics to syntax. For Quine, 'analytic' is an irreducible semantic notion. He finds no non-circular, suitable, syntactic account of analyticity. Semantics is simply irreducible to syntax.

Wittgenstein's account of analyticity is not semantic, but syntactic. However, it does not correspond fully to Quine's notion of logical truth. Quine's definition of logical truths reformulates Yehoshua Bar-Hillel's reconstruction of Bolzano's definition of analytic proposition.[18]

> First, we suppose indicated, by enumeration if not otherwise, what words are to be called logical words; typical ones are 'or', 'not', 'if', 'then', 'and', 'all', 'every', 'only', 'some'. The logical truths, then, are those true sentences which involve only logical words *essentially*. What this means is that any other words, though they may also occur in a logical truth (as witness 'Brutus', 'kill', and 'Caesar' in 'Brutus killed or did not kill Ceasar'), can be varied at will without engendering falsity.[19]

---

[16] *Nous* XXX, 3 (August 1996).

[17] W. V. O. Quine, "Two Dogmas of Empiricism", *The Philosophical Review* LX, 1 (January 1951a), 23.

[18] "If we suppose a prior invertory of *logical* particles, comrpising 'no', 'un-', 'not', 'if', 'then', 'and', etc., then in general a logical truth is a statement which is true and remains true under all reinterpretations of its components other than the logical particles." *Ibidem* 23

[19] W. V. O. Quine, *From a logical point of view*, 2nd edition, New York: Harper books, 1963, 387.

As a matter of fact, Wittgenstein's grammatical method is indeed very similar to one of the attempts at defining analyticity syntactically discussed in "Two Dogmas". In section III, Quine discusses the account of analyticity, according to which (*i*) "any analytic statement could be turned into a logical truth by putting synonyms for synonyms"[20] and (*ii*), (cognitive) synonymy[21] is "interchangeability *salva veritate* everywhere except within words."[22] According to him, the main flaw of this latter account is that interchangeability *salva veritate* fails to capture cognitive synonymy. It only captures co-extensionality. In consequence, not only analytic truths, but also synthetic truths may be transformed into logical truths through *salva veritate* substitution. For example, since the current president of Mexico in August 2002 is Vicente Fox, the singular terms 'current president of Mexico in August 2002' and 'Vicente Fox' are interchangeable *salva veritate*. In consequence, substituting 'current president of Mexico in August 2002' for 'Vicente Fox" in the logical truth 'The current president of Mexico in August 2002 is the current president of Mexico in August 2002' results in the synthetic truth 'The current president of Mexico in August 2002 is Vicente Fox'. An endorser of this account may object that distinguishing between 'current president of Mexico in August 2002' and 'Vicente Fox' remains possible. The terms cannot substitute for each other in a sentence like 'Necessarily the current president of Mexico in August 2002 is the current president of Mexico in August 2002', because 'Necessarily Vicente Fox is the current president of Mexico in August 2002' is false. However, Quine retorts, this objection begs the question.

> The above argument supposes we are working with a language rich enough to contain the adverb "necessarily', this adverb being so construed as to yield truth when and only when applied to an analytic statement. But, can we condone a language which contains such an adverb? Does the adverb really make sense? To suppose that it does is to suppose that we have already made satisfactory sense of 'analytic'. Then what are we so hard at work on right now?[23]

It is clear that Wittgenstein's grammatical method is very similar to that of Section III in "Two Dogmas". However, they are also significantly different, and these differences are strong enough to elude Quine's criticisms. First of all, Wittgenstein's interchangeability criterion is not *salva veritate*, but *salva grammaticality*. Second, it is not an attempt at defining general synonymy, but grammatical synonymy. In other words, it applies only to terms of grammar, not to all terms in general. Hence, it does not attempt to reduce genuine semantics to

---

[20] Quine 1951a, 28.
[21] Quine distinguishes cognitive analyticity from "synonymy in the sense of complete identity in psychological associations or poetic quality." *Ibidem*, 28.
[22] *Ibidem*, 28.
[23] *Ibidem*, 29.

syntax – certainly a doomed enterprise. It attempts to give a synonymy criteria for those words whose grammar entirely determines their meaning.

Wittgenstein's distinction between genuine propositions and those of grammar is similar to that between analytic and synthetic statements. However, Wittgenstein's distinction presumes nothing about its empirical nature, while Quine's primary concern is with the empirical dimension of the analytic/synthetic distinction. Wittgenstein's distinction between genuine propositions and those of grammar is closer to the current logical distinction between syntax and semantics. Wittgenstein bases his distinction at the level of propositions on a distinction at the level of concepts and objects. For Wittgenstein, terms of grammar are those whose grammar entirely determines their meaning. Since grammatical concepts lack intensionality, co-extensionality offers suitable synonymity criteria for them.

Indeed, Wittgenstein never maintained that grammar fully determined the meaning of every expression in a language. However, he argued that it did for those he called 'of grammar'. In Wittgenstein's grammar, two terms are grammatically equivalent if they are interchangeable *salva grammaticality* in all contexts. If the terms belong to grammar, they are also synonymous.

At the level of statements, a statement belongs to grammar if its concepts belong to grammar's vocabulary. In consequence, its grammar completely determines its 'meaning' and 'truth'. Nevertheless, grammar cannot fully determine the truth of other statements, especially those expressing genuine propositions, i.e. possible states of affairs. It can only determine its grammaticality, that is, whether they are well or ill formed. However, since grammaticality is a necessary condition for the expression of possible states of affairs, modality is built into the language's grammar. In consequence, Wittgenstein's grammatical account does not require a previous understanding of analyticity to explain necessity and, hence, is not circular in Quine's sense.

2. Convention and Justification

> But still there was no truth by convention, because there was no truth. (Quine 1963, 392)

The breadth of Quine's arguments in "Truth by Convention" focuses on the foundational role of linguistic conventions. In consequence, it is mostly irrelevant for Wittgenstein's grammatical project, for Wittgenstein clearly found such a foundational enterprise absurd. Hence, his philosophy of mathematics during the middle period is not a conventionalism in that sense.

The target of Quine's anti-conventionalist arguments is linguistic conventions' inability to found mathematics or calculus. In "Truth by Convention," Quine questions linguistic conventions' capacity to justify mathematical or logical truths. However, Wittgenstein's grammatical account of mathematics is not a foundational enterprise. In Wittgenstein's account, rules of grammar certainly have no justificatory power. Wittgenstein most likely would sympathize with Quine's efforts to demonstrate the impossibility of justifying logical and mathematical truths by inferring them from syntactic conventions.

> [...] the difficulty is that if logic is to proceed *mediately* from conventions, logic is needed for inferring logic from the conventions.[24]

Dummett reiterates this point when he says, in his "Wittgenstein on Necessity":

> The moderate conventionalist view was never a solution to the problem of logical necessity at all, because, by invoking the notion of consequence, it appealed to what it ought to have been explaining: that is why it appears to call for a meta-necessity beyond the necessity it purported to account for. The conventionalists were led astray by the example of the founders of modern logic into concentrating on the notion of logical or analytic *truth*, whereas precisely what they needed to fasten on was that of deductive *consequence*. [...][25]

Wittgenstein would agree with Quine and Dummett that logical truths and linguistic conventions do not logically entail each other. If conventions logically entailed logical truths, justifying this relation would itself require logic. 'Logical entailment' and 'justification' are concepts that do not apply to propositions of grammar, at least not in the same sense as they apply to genuine propositions.

If 'to justify p' means to demonstrate the truth of p, then justification applies only to genuine propositions. Correct calculations are also called mathematical truths, but mathematical truth is not a sub-species of 'truth' in general. For Quine, "We may mark out the intended scope of the term 'logical truth', within that of the broader term 'truth'."[26] However for Wittgenstein, and at least since the *Tractatus*, the scopes of 'truth' and 'logical truth' do not overlap. In Ramsey's words, "It is important to see that tautologies are not simply true propositions, though for many purposes they can be treated as true propositions."[27] Ramsey presented Wittgenstein's position very clearly in his 'Foundations of Mathematics' where he wrote:

---

[24] W. V. O. Quine, *Mathematical Logic*, Cambridge: Harvard University Press, 1951b, 97.
[25] Michael Dummett, *The Seas of Language*, Oxford: Clarendon Press, 1993, 460.
[26] Quine 1963, 386.
[27] Frank P. Ramsey, "The Foundations of Mathematics (1925)", in: *Philosophical Papers*, Cambridge: Cambridge University Press, 1990, 173.

The assimilation of tautologies and contradictions with true and false propositions respectively results from the fact that tautologies and contradictions can be taken as arguments to truth-functions just like ordinary propositions, and for determining the truth or falsity of the truth-function, tautologies and contradictions among its arguments must be counted as true and false respectively. Thus, if '*t*' be a tautology, '*c*' a contradiction, '*t* and *p*', 'If *t*, then *p*', '*c* or *p*' are the same as '*p*', and '*t* or *p*', 'if *c*, then *p*' are tautologies.[28]

For Wittgenstein, the 'being true' predicate has only an evaluative function when applied to tautologies. Hence, it means something different when applied to genuine propositions. In the logical calculus of propositions, being true is nothing more than having 'truth' as its truth-value. In the truly semantic case, being true means that the proposition is the case. "For what does a proposition's *'being true'* mean? *'p' is true = p*. (That is the answer.)"[29] In the case of tautologies and contradictions, nothing could or could not be the case. In consequence, saying that they are true (or false for that matter) in the same sense as true genuine propositions makes no sense. The 'being true' predicate defined for genuine propositions does not apply to tautologies or contradictions.

Mathematics is pure calculus, and every calculus is a rule-governed practice. In this respect, calculi are more like chess than like natural science. Asking for the justification of a mathematical truth is like asking for the justification of the truth of chess rules. Both are nonsense. It makes sense to justify 'that *p*', but not to justify 'to *p*'. Unless justification means something different when applied to rules and practices than to genuine propositions. For Carnap, a calculus is as 'justified' as its application. In this sense, Carnap's conventionalism is also a pragmatism. Application justifies calculation. Wittgenstein offers a different interpretation. For him, following a rule justifies it. A rule is justified if it is possible to follow it. This sense of justification does not require metamathematics. Performing the calculation is sufficient. It demonstrates that following the rule is constructively possible. Wittgenstein's grammatical necessity is the necessity of calculations, not of propositions.[30]

Finally, Wittgenstein is not a conventionalist in Dummett's sense either. According to Dummett, Wittgenstein is a *radical* conventionalist, because he grounds mathematical necessity on the *decision* of not questioning mathematical truth. However, for the middle Wittgenstein, mathematical statements have no genuine propositional content. Therefore, deciding whether or not to question mathematical truth is absurd. Questioning the truth of statements of grammar

---

[28] *Ibidem*, 174.
[29] *Remarks on the Foundations of Mathematics*, Pt. I, Appendix I, §6.
[30] His interest is precisely what Dummett calls necessary consequence: what necessarily *follows* according to a rule.

does not make any sense at all. Accordingly, the mere notion of such a decision is nonsensical. Mathematical truths are not the kind of things it makes sense to question. Hence, mathematics contains no decisions and, in consequence, no radical conventions, either.[31]

D. Wittgenstein

Wittgenstein's grammatical account of the grammatical necessity of internal descriptions in general, and mathematical propositions in particular, differs from Carnap and most recent accounts of analyticity, because it is not metaphysical or epistemological, but logical. In his 1996 article 'Analyticity Reconsidered', Paul Boghossian distinguishes between two different notions of analyticity: a metaphysical and an epistemological one.

> Here, it would seem, is one way: *If mere grasp of S's meaning by T sufficed for T's being justified in holding S true.* [...] On this understanding, then, 'analyticity' is an overtly *epistemological* notion: a statement is 'true by virtue of its meaning' provided that grasp of its meaning alone suffices for justified belief in its truth.

> Another, far more *metaphysical* reading of the phrase 'true by virtue of its meaning' is also available, however, according to which a statement is analytic provided that, in some appropriate sense, it *owes its truth value completely to its meaning*, and not at all to 'the facts'.

Wittgenstein's analyticity is neither metaphysical nor epistemological, but grammatical. Wittgenstein agrees with Kant that separating analyticity from aprioricity is important. 'Analyticity' is a logical notion, while 'apriori' is epistemological. However, Wittgenstein understands analyticity not as 'true by virtue of meaning', but 'true by virtue of grammar.'[32] Grammatical analyticity is not a

---

[31] Do not confuse convention with stipulation. Rules of grammar may be conventions, but they are certainly not stipulations.

[32] However, some scholars consider Wittgenstein's analyticity epistemological. Alberto Coffa ["Carnap, Tarski and the Search for Truth," *Nous* 21, no. 4 (December 1987), 547-572] interprets Wittgenstein's account of analyticity – from the *Tractatus* to the middle and late periods of his philosophy – as epistemological. Wittgenstein characterizes logical sentences in the *Tractatus* as those "one can recognize [*erkennen*] from the symbol alone that they are true" (6.113) Coffa also recognizes "that this determination is embodied in constructive procedures that allow someone who understands the given langauge to 'recognize' the truth-values in question." (pp. 547, 548) Nevertheless, he does not interpret this procedure as a syntactic/grammatical one, but as an epistemic one. Michael Hymers ["Internal Relations and Analyticity: Wittgenstein and Quine" *Canadian Journal of Philosophy* 26, no. 4 (December 1996), 591-612] also sustains that Wittgenstein's criteria for recognizing analytic propositions [internal descriptions] remained epistemological from the *Tractatus* to *Philosophical Grammar*. (p. 594) He writes, "Also implicit here [in the

semantic notion, but a logical one. Wittgenstein's account says that a statement S is analytic if and only if the mere inclusion of S in the language suffices for its truth. The term 'inclusion' in this characterization is deeply misleading, since the 'included' statement does not actually make sense outside S. Accordingly, the mere meaningfulness or grammaticality of S guarantees its truth. A statement of grammar S cannot make sense and be false.

The truth of a mathematical calculus is not contingent on the existence of genuine objects, but only those mathematical ones it constructs for itself. No calculus requires the existence of any spatio-temporal objects or events. For example, arithmetical addition is not contingent on any particular numerals, or additions. A mathematical statement like '3 + 4 = 7' says that the correct result of adding three to four is seven. However it does not refer to any particular numerals or additions. The equation refers to numbers as *roles* in the calculus and to additions as calculations: entities fully defined by the calculus' rules.

Mathematics is part of the syntax of language. However, mathematics does not describe this syntax in a formal meta-language. Describing syntax is a substantially different task than calculating. A meta-linguistic description of logical syntax, like Carnap's, is external to the calculus, while calculation occurs only within the calculus it belongs to. This is what Wittgenstein means when he says that mathematics is autonomous. The correctness of the calculations in a calculus is fully determined by the calculus' rules. In contrast, the mere description of a calculus' rules cannot fully determine the truth of its propositions.

Mathematics is pure calculus, and mathematical propositions are calculation rules. 'Justification' and 'truth' apply to genuine propositions only. They do not apply to rules. Grammatical necessity is the necessity of calculations, not of propositions. It requires no further justification. Performing the calculation is enough 'justification', because it demonstrates that the rule can be followed, and there is nothing more to it. Calculations may be right or wrong, depending on whether they are performed in accordance to the calculus' rules or not. However, there cannot be *false* calculations.

Philosophical Grammar], is a further revision of the epistemic criterion for internal relations: two concepts, or instruments of language, are internally related if in order to understand one I must also understand the other. [...] However, concepts have no existence here, independently of norms and practices. Understanding a concept is, paradigmatically, to be able to use a word correctly, where correctness ammounts to accord with the rules of a calculus." (pp. 596-597)

III. On the Grammatical Nature of Mathematics

A. Arguments against the Grammatical Nature of Mathematics

In general, four major arguments are raised against the claim that mathematical propositions belong to grammar:

1. Linguistic practice is an empirical fact. Hence, propositions of grammar about verbal usage are empirical generalizations and, consequently, not necessary. In contrast, mathematical propositions are necessary.

2. Understanding propositions of grammar as those that describe the usage of words implies that propositions of grammar are not necessary. This is so because negating a true proposition about verbal usage is not a contradiction, but a false proposition.[33] Morris Lazerowitz, presents this objection as follows:

> The negation of a true verbal proposition is a false verbal proposition, but not a proposition which could not, in principle, be true. [...] To use an expression of Wittgenstein's, we know what it would be like for a verbal *proposition,* which happens to be true, to be false. By contrast we do not know what it would be like for a false arithmetical proposition to be true, for example, for 4 + 3 to be less than 7.[34]

3. If propositions of grammar record the usage of words, they must describe particular words in a particular language. Mathematical propositions do not, in general, say anything about vocabulary. Furthermore, if statements of grammar are about words, morphemes, etc. and their uses, then their truth depends on the existence of these linguistic entities. If, as Wittgenstein contended, '3 + 4 = 7' does not deal with abstract entities called numbers 3, 4 and 7, but with numeral types '3', '4' and '7', then it features a commitment to the existence of these numerals.

4. Finally, mathematical truths do not depend on the language expressing them. Hence, mathematical propositions cannot belong to grammar. The peculiarities of one language are not sufficient to solve genuine mathematical problems.
The objection that propositions of grammar, unlike mathematical ones, are language-specific is at least as old as Moore's notes on Wittgenstein's lectures of Lent and May terms of 1930. He reports that Wittgenstein stated, "[...] the proposition 'red is a primary color' was a proposition about the word 'red'.[35]

---

[33] Morris Lazerowitz, Introduction to M. Lazerowitz and Alice Ambrose (eds) *Essays in the Unknown Wittgenstein*, Buffalo: Prometheus Books, 1984, 6.
[34] Morris Lazerowitz: "Necessity and Language", in: Lazerowitz 1984, 235.
[35] *Philosophical Papers*, 275, quoted in: Lazerowitz 1984, 16-17.

Immediately after, Moore observed that,

> [...] if he had seriously held this, he might have held similarly that the proposition or rule '3 + 3 = 6' was merely a proposition or rule about the particular expressions '3 + 3' and '6'.[36]

Moore himself recognized the absurdities that his interpretation of Wittgenstein implied, when he commented,

> [...] he cannot have held seriously either of these views, because the *same* proposition which is expressed by the words 'red is a primary color' can be expressed in French or German by words which say nothing about the English word 'red'; and similarly the *same* proposition or rule which is expressed by '3 + 3 = 6' was undoubtedly expressed in Attic Greek and in Latin by words which say nothing about the numerals '3' and '6'. And this was in fact what he seemed to be admitting in the passage at the end of (I).[37]

Mathematical propositions do not say anything about vocabulary. Furthermore, their truth does not depend on the language expressing them. For Moore, this meant that they cannot belong to grammar.

What these arguments have in common is the mistaken premise that propositions of grammar are descriptions of the grammatical rules underlying language use. From this, they infer their putative empirical, contingent and language-dependent nature. However, this picture does not apply to all propositions that may accurately be characterized as belonging to grammar. In Wittgenstein's conception, mathematical propositions of grammar express language rules without describing them or even mentioning any explicitly linguistic entity like morphemes, words, etc. These propositions do not describe grammatical rules, but display them in their application. As such, they make no mention of grammatical rules or categories. They display them in their use.

B. Statements of Grammar

In order to understand the grammatical nature of mathematical propositions, it might be helpful to make an informal comparison between mathematical and

---

[36] *Ibidem*, 275.

[37] *Philosophical Papers*, 41, quoted in: Lazerowitz 1984, 17. Leaving aside for a moment the possibility that Wittgenstein might have actually said that 'red is a primary color' is *about* the word 'red', Moore's assumption that, if a statement of grammar is about words, it must be about the words that occur in it is surprising. In many cases, statement of grammar address the correct use of terms not in them. 'Number words can function as adjectives' is a statement of grammar about the correct use of number words. Still, no number words occur in it. On the other hand, "'Spanish' is spelled with capital 'S'" is about the spelling of the word 'Spanish' in it.

more obvious propositions of grammar. The following section develops this comparison in two parts. The first part sets out the different senses in which statements are said to 'belong to grammar'. The second part develops an analogy between these statements of grammar and properly mathematical ones. This analogy's goal is to clarify the sense in which mathematical statements can be correctly characterized as belonging to grammar.

Consider an obviously grammatical transition of ordinary English language: the transition from passive to active forms. This transition may easily be formulated as a purely syntactic rule:

(1) The passive form of an active sentence a_B_c_d (where a is the sentence's subject, B its verb, c the verb's direct compliment, and d is the string of indirect compliments of B) is the string c_BE(c/B)_PP(B)_'by'_a_d, where BE(c/B) is the conjugation of the verb 'to be' in the number of c and the time of B, and PP(B) is the past participle form of verb B.

This rule allows us to transform active sentence (2) into passive sentence (3):

(2) Many persons have attended the dance marathon since its inception.

(3) The dance marathon has been attended by many persons since its inception.

This transformation may also be expressed in a single sentence (just like the conditionalization of a *modus ponens*):

(4) If many persons have attended the dance marathon since its inception, then the dance marathon has been attended by many persons since its inception.

This illustrates the double nature of grammatical application. The same grammatical rules may be applied both in the formation (as in 4) and transformation (as from 2 to 3) of acceptable strings.[38]

Finally, the following statement also expresses the same application of the rule expressed in (1):

(5) The passive form of "Many persons have attended the dance marathon since its inception" is "The dance marathon has been attended by many persons since its inception."

---

[38] Hence, he does not make a distinction between formation and transformation rules, as most traditional grammarians do.

Since the rule for the transformation from active to passive belongs to grammar, statements (1), (4) and (5), and the transition between statements (2) and (3) may correctly be said to belong to grammar. However, they belong to grammar in different ways. Their relation to the rules of grammar is different. Both (4) and the transition from (2) to (3) are applications of a grammatical rule. Statements (1) and (5), on the contrary, are expressions of that same rule. As such, they are *about* the grammatical rule. In consequence, they are *heteronomous* statements of grammar. Statement (4), in contrast, is a necessary *autonomous* statement of grammar. When Wittgenstein talks about statements of grammar, he mostly means statements like (4), that is autonomous statements of grammar which do not express or are about any grammatical rule, but merely display it in its application.

This difference becomes essential once questions of truth and necessity come into play. It is clear that the question of truth can only be brought about genuine propositions and not about transitions like that between (2) and (3). In those cases, the question of grammatical necessity is not that of necessary truth, but necessary transition. This difference played an essential role when dealing with Quine's criticisms above. For the moment, let us center on statements (1), (4) and (5).

Most objections to grammatical necessity focus on statements like (1), also called *external*[39] or *explicitly*[40] grammatical statements. These statements, as descriptions of rules of grammar, are language-dependent and contain ontological commitments that render them not necessary. Wittgenstein considers statements like (1) to be contingent. Thus, he had no problem with this sort of

---

[39] This nomenclature originates in the work of Zeno Vendler's *Linguistics in Philosophy*, Ithaca: Cornell University Press, 1967, 147-171. According to Vendler, a statement of grammar is *external* if it mentions a word, morpheme or any other linguistic entity, and says something about its use. Otherwise, it is *internal*. Consider the statement "'Spanish' is spelled with a capital 'S'." This statement of grammar is external, because it mentions the word 'Spanish' and it says something about its use: that it is spelled with a capital 'S'. Now look at an internal statement of grammar: 'Names of languages are capitalized'. This statement does not mention any words, but still expresses a rule of grammar in grammatical vocabulary. Other examples of external statements of grammar are: "'Dog' is a noun" and 'the gerund of 'walk' is 'walking''. Examples of internal statements of grammar are: 'Number words function as adjectives' and 'Noun and adjective must agree in gender'. In Chomskian grammars, this distinction corresponds to terminal (external) rules, and non-terminal (internal) rules.

[40] This convention is present in Kennick (1996) and Morris Lazerowitz (1984). However, it does not completely match with Vendler's notion of 'external grammatical' statement. For Kennick and Lazerowitz, a statement is explicitly grammatical if its vocabulary belongs to grammar, and implicitly grammatical if it does not include terms of grammar, "but still expresses a rule, convention, or decision about verbal usage." (Lazerowitz 1984, 142)

like (1) to be contingent. Thus, he had no problem with this sort of objections. For him, a statement like (1) does not belong to grammar. Instead, it is *about* grammar. It is not completely clear from Wittgenstein's writings whether statements like (5) belong to grammar as well. However, this is a minor issue. There is a unique grammatical rule expressed in (1) and (5), which is also displayed in (4) and the transition from (2) to (3). This rule is the real proposition of grammar.

Consider, now a mathematical calculation, for example, the addition of two naturals lower than 100. The rule that governs the performance of such calculation on decimal notation numerals can be expressed the following way:

(6) The addition of two numerals a_b and c_d is the string R(((R(b + d) + a) + c)_ (((R(b + d) + a) + c)_(b + d), where R(n) = '1' if n ≥ 10 and R(n) is the empty string otherwise.

This rule applies to the addition of 27 to 34. This calculation may be represented in the following way:

(7)   1
       27
      +34
       61

This calculation is also expressed in the form of an equation as:

(8) 27 + 34 = 61

Mathematics also features the double nature of grammatical application presented above for natural language grammar. For Wittgenstein, calculation rules may be applied both in the formation (as in 8) and transformation (as in 7) of expressions.

The following statement also expresses the same application of this rule:

(9) The result of adding 27 to 34 is 71.

Since the rules governing calculation are grammatical, (6), (8) (9), and (7) all belong to grammar as well. However, just like in the case of (1) to (5), they all belong to grammar in radically different senses, since their relation to the aforementioned mathematical rule is different.

(7), (8) and (9) all express the same calculation. Yet, when people think about mathematical statements, expressions like (8) most typically come to mind. For Wittgenstein, however, this same calculation is displayed in (7) as well as in (8). A mayor difference is that strings like (8) have the further disadvantage of looking too similar to natural language statements. It is customary to call (8) a mathematical *statement*. However, it is important not to think that, as a statement, it must be about something. Furthermore, it is also important not to infer that it is about the addition, either as a calculation or as a mathematical operation. The relation between calculation and mathematical statement is not one of aboutness, but of trace. Statement (8), just like display (7), is the trace left by the calculation. Statement (9), in contrast, expresses this same calculation externally. Unlike (7) and (8), (9) is not a trace of the calculation. It expresses a genuine proposition. This proposition is not the calculation itself. It is *about* the calculation. Even if it does not include explicit mention of numerals, it still lacks the autonomy of belonging to the calculus that (7) and (8) do. In that sense, it is similar to (6). Both (6) and (9) are external mathematical statements. They describe the calculation from outside the calculus it belongs to.

The common criticisms to the grammatical nature of mathematics are dissolved by paying closer attention to the analogy between statements (1) to (5), and (6) to (9). In mathematics, as in ordinary natural language grammar, it is very important to distinguish between statements of grammar and statements *about* grammar. Mathematical statements like (8) and (7) belong to grammar, yet they are not about grammar. In strict sense, they are not about anything.

From (7) to (9), there is a unique calculation and, in consequence, a unique mathematical proposition. It is displayed in (7) and (8), but described in (9). Questions about the truth or necessity of mathematical propositions commonly stem from misguided analogies between mathematical statements and descriptive ones. These analogies conceal important differences between the descriptive and mathematical propositions behind the statements. Most of all, they hide the important difference between displaying a rule by following it and describing it.

Summarizing, mathematical statements belong to grammar because they display grammatical rules in their application. As such, they have no descriptive content. They do not describe any grammatical phenomenon or fact about language usage. Their relation to grammar is not that of description. They do not mention or describe any grammatical entities like words or formulae. Instead, they display them in their use. As such, they are not dependant on them or on the language they belong to. Mathematical statements belong to grammar only in this sense. They are autonomous grammatical displays.

JESÚS PADILLA-GÁLVEZ

"Metamathematics Does Not Exist"
Wittgenstein's Criticism of Metamathematics[1]

Introduction

In the year 1933 L. Wittgenstein wrote an article with the provocative headline: "Metamathematics does not exist" [„Es gibt keine Metamathematik"].[2] This occurs in Paragraph 109 of his *Philosophical Grammar* and is also mentioned in the *Big Typescript*. However, this article was never really noticed among his colleagues and didn't generate any discussion in the secondary literature. The aim of this paper is to find out why his article didn't elicit any response within the scientific community.

In 1931 Wittgenstein was working on various topics of philosophy and logic. He wrote down his thoughts in several pocket notebooks. In one of his notebooks holding the bookmark 153a[3] (Trinity College) he deals with the problems of meaning, color and the "Gesichtsfeld", to name but a few.[4] In notebook 154 he talks about some questions of logic from B. Russell and in his other notebooks there are remarks about rules. He also mentions which people he was intellectually influenced by.[5] Apart from that, his overall interest always remained the question of logical proof and general induction as well as demonstrative definitions.[6] Between 1932 and 1934 he was preoccupied with the problem of meaning.[7]

---

[1] I would like to thank Prof. Dr. von Wright for giving me permission to read the Wittgenstein Manuscripts in the Trinity College at the University of Cambridge.
[2] Wittgenstein PG, Teil II. Über Logik und Mathematik, 12 and Wittgenstein TS213, § 109, 539-541.
[3] Wittgenstein Pocket notebook *Anmerkungen* (339 pp.), 1931, Trinity College, 153a.
[4] Wittgenstein Pocket notebook *Continuation of 153a* (122 pp.), 1931, Trinity College, 153b.
[5] Wittgenstein Pocket notebook (190 pp.), 1931, Trinity College, 154.
[6] Wittgenstein Pocket notebook (189 pp.), 1931, Trinity College, 155.
[7] Wittgenstein, Pocket notebook (121 pp.), 1932-4, Trinity College, 156a and Wittgenstein, Pocket notebook (121 pp.), 1932-4, Trinity College, 156b.

Many of the comments in his notebooks were summarized in 1932 in the form of a typescript which became an important work of reference.[8] This was a big collection of type-written material containing all his thoughts and ideas which were prepared for publication. These were to be published later in his *Philosophical Investigations*.

Wittgenstein seemed to handle his scripts in a rather unusual way by taking his typescript, cutting it into pieces according to topics of interest and having these topics retyped. These were to form *The Big Typescript*.[9] In the course of this procedure he took his topics of interests, put them in several folders which he indexed by titles. One of these folders was labeled "Metamathematics does not exist". Both, the original typescript and *The Big Typescript* contain parts of texts which were taken out of their context.[10] This leads us to asking, which concept of metamathematics did Wittgenstein have and which areas did he consider relevant? In this paper we will look for answers to these questions.

1. Historical Questions

During the 1930s the discussion on metamathematics didn't lead to any constructive results. However, R. Carnap[11], A. Tarski[12], K. Gödel[13] and others appreciated the importance of Wittgenstein's point of view and considered it a basic element for the syntax, metalogic and metamathematics, as is expressed in the following statement:

> My syntax has two historic roots: 1. Wittgenstein, 2. Metamathematics (Tarski, Gödel)
>
> Meine „Syntax" hat historisch zwei Wurzeln: 1. Wittgenstein, 2. Metamathematik (Tarski, Gödel).[14]

---

[8] Wittgenstein, Typescript based on 109-113 and the beginning of 114 (771 pp.), c 1932, Trinity College, 211.
[9] Wittgenstein, Typescript consisting of cut part from 208, 210 and 211 (3 boxes), c 1932-3, Trinity College, 212.
[10] Wittgenstein, *The "Big Typescript"* (776 pp), c 1933, Trinity College, 213.
[11] Carnap, Letter to Neurath of 23. 12. 1933. Hilman-Library, RC 29-03-06 A. Padilla-Gálvez 1999, 169, footnote 8.
[12] Tarski 1936, 11.
[13] Gödel 1995, 171.
[14] Letter from R. Carnap to O. Neurath from 23 December 1933 in: *Archives of Scientific Philosophy*, Hilman-Library, RC, Nr: 029-03-06, S1. Padilla-Gálvez, 1998, 26.

In 1953 Gödel wrote a paper about mathematics in which he summarized Wittgenstein's position as follows:

> Around 1930 R. Carnap, H. Hahn, and M. Schlick, [...] largely under the influence of L. Wittgenstein, developed a conception of the nature of mathematics[...] which can be characterized as being a combination of nominalism and conventionalism.[15]

Inspite of Tarski's and Gödel's appreciation of his point of view, Wittgenstein did not accept his colleagues' views. For many years, he was fixated with the problem of metamathematics:

> I have long been tempted to believe that "understand" is a metalogical expression.
>
> Ich war lange versucht zu glauben, „verstehen" sei ein metalogisches Wort.[16]

As we can see from the above statement, Wittgenstein had a very strong opposition towards metamathematics. During this period metamathematics was a highly contentious issue, this was at a time when Gödel had presented some interesting arguments. This leads us to the following questions: Which arguments led Wittgenstein to such an opposing view? Is there a connection between the logic rejection of any metatheory (mainly by G. Frege and B. Russell)? These questions have not been touched upon in the secondary literature so far and we will therefore bring them to light in this paper.

2. The Question of Metamathematics

The study of Wittgenstein's scripts suggests that he didn't seem to be interested in resolving the issue in metamathematics. On several occasions he mentions that the solutions made so far are worthless. In the secondary literature one can find critical remarks attributed to his view of metamathematics. These are characterized by the so-called "praxeologic fundamentalism"[17]. This was nothing less than a tendency towards ordinary language. However, this reference is not in accordance with Wittgenstein's text, because he first mentions his opposed attitude after the proposition of Hilbert's term of "rule". He says,

---

[15] Gödel 1986 [1995], III, 334 and Gödel 1995, 171.
[16] Trinity College Library, Item 116, Bd. XII *Philosophische Bemerkungen*, 16. The argument is often repeated: "Es gibt keine Metalogik. Auch das Wort "verstehen" und der Ausdruck "einen Satz verstehen", sind nicht metalogisch." Trinity College Library, Item 114, Bd. X *Philosophische Grammatik*, 2. Or: "<Eine> Versuchung [÷],] zu glauben "meinen", das Wort "[V|v]erstehen", seien metalogische Worte." Trinity College Library, Item 116, Bd. XII *Philosophische Bemerkungen*, 2.
[17] Haller 1981, 57 ff. and Sedmak 1997.

Hilbert proposes rules of a certain calculus as rule of / the / a / metamathematic.

Hilbert stellt Regeln eines bestimmten Kalküls als Regel / der / einer / Metamathematik auf.[18]

It is not quite clear, which concept Wittgenstein had in mind when he was talking about metamathematics. The actual term goes back to Hilbert who saw a certain resemblance to metaphysics. It was supposed to deal with the whole field of mathematics and should be a mathematical, rather than a philosophical theory. Hilbert writes:

> A new mathematics adds to the original formalist mathematics, a metamathematics, which is necessary to protect the one, in which – contrary to the purely formalistic reasoning of conventional mathematics – the reasoning within a context is applied in order to prove the logic order of the axioms.
>
> Zu der eigentlichen so formalisierten Mathematik kommt eine gewissermaßen neue Mathematik, eine Metamathematik, die zur Sicherung jener notwendig ist, in der – im Gegensatz zu den rein formalen Schlußweisen der eigentlichen Mathematik – das inhaltliche Schließen zur Anwendung kommt, aber lediglich zum Nachweis der Widerspruchsfreiheit der Axiome. In dieser Metamathematik wird mit den Beweisen der eigentlichen Mathematik operiert, und diese letzteren bilden selbst den Gegenstand der inhaltlichen Untersuchung.[19]

Some years later he adds to this and says:

> If mathematics is described in a formalist way, the suitable metalanguage will be the metamathematics.
>
> Wird speziell die Mathematik in formalisierter Gestalt, so heißt die zugehörige Metasprache die *Metamathematik*.[20]

Metalanguage can be defined as the language for terms, sentences, etc. and calculi, but it is different from the language of calculus. The attempt to define the language for calculi led to fundamental difficulties which was to put the whole endeavor into question. If metamathematics was supposed to be a theory it was by the same token an object which consequently led to a vicious circle. This problem could only be solved by considering the mathematical theory as axiomatic. This seems relatively easy nowadays but involved some important fundamental work then. Wittgenstein defined his motives in Volume 10 of the *Philosophical Grammar* in which he says:

---

[18] Wittgenstein 153a, 136 links.
[19] Hilbert 1923, 153.
[20] Hilbert/Ackermann 1972, 162.

> We don't interfere with the mathematician's work unless he states to do metamathematics, then we will control him.
>
> Wir mischen uns nicht in das, was der Mathematiker tut, erst wenn er behauptet Metamathematik zu treiben, dann kontrollieren wir ihn.[21]

Mathematics was in the middle of a fundamental crisis and the confrontation between axiomatic logic[22], formalism[23] and intuitionism[24] remained unresolved. Wittgenstein was interested in the mathematics of metamathematics which he based on certain arguments. The first proposition for the argument dealt with the question, would the term calculus in the metalevel be the same as that in logics? The intention of the second proposition was to try out whether what had been defined as rule could be used for metamathematics. The answer and conclusion to this problem forms the title of the paragraph: "Metamathematics does not exist." Wittgenstein intends to show that the ideas proposed do not provide any answer for metamathematics. His argument is intended to show the inconsistency of the concept of metamathematics. We will follow the line of this argument.

3. The Purpose of Calculus

If we want to find a definition for the term calculus, one might think that it is similar to answering questions like: "What is meant by water, air, fire, etc.?" Thus we have the following definition: Calculus is a way of operating with numbers on the basis of rules. The meaning of symbols will be introduced intuitively including only the formal structure of the symbols. Calculi not only contain the formal language but also the method of calculation. The investigation of the properties of structure of calculus needs the concept of metamathematics.

Wittgenstein sees the problem from a completely different angle: being able to calculate is the presupposition for supplying a definition for calculus. In 1932 calculus was defined as, "[...] to operate on the basis of fixed rules //, e. g. the process of fixed rules. //" „[...] operieren nach festgelegten Regeln // d.h. als Vorgang nach festgesetzten Regeln //".][25] Does the expression "rule" have several meanings? The question in this respect is whether "rule" can have several meanings. He draws the attention to a restriction, when he asks:

---

[21] Wittgenstein 114, 30 v.
[22] Hilbert 1923, 151-165.
[23] Carnap 1935.
[24] Heyting 1930, 42-56.
[25] Wittgenstein 211, 40.

> And shouldn't we therefore talk about rules in general, as well as of languages in general? Or only about rules in specific cases.
>
> Und sollen wir also nicht von Regeln im Allgemeinen reden, wie auch nicht von Sprachen im Allgemeinen? Sondern nur von Regeln in besonderen Fällen.[26]

Thus he stands against the Platonism of general description of theory of knowledge. He reaches the following conclusion:

> One can't step behind the rule, because there is no such behind.
>
> Hinter die Regeln kann man nicht dringen, weil es kein Dahinter gibt.[27]

He thinks that a certain assumption can be made and that is another calculus than the one we already use. Therefore, the question as to whether there is a need for another calculus, cannot be answered. Thus he is completely opposed to Plato's view of the common.[28] He says,

> It is clear that the question "what is a calculus" is of the same kind as the question "what is a game" or as "what is a rule".
>
> Das ist klar, daß die Frage „was ist ein Kalkül" von genau der gleichen Art ist wie die: „was ist ein Spiel" oder wie die: „was ist eine Regel."[29]

When we play, we can describe what we have done. On dealing with calculi we can therefore describe what we do when we calculate. We can therefore make an attempt at finding a definition of what is a calculus.[30] In the same line of argument he points out the impossibility of finding a solution to philosophical problems when he says,

> I mentioned above that "calculus is no mathematical term", which means that the term 'calculus' is no *chess-figure* of mathematics.
>
> Ich sagte oben „Kalkül ist kein mathematischer Begriff"; dass heisst, das Wort, 'Kalkül' ist kein *Schachstein* der Mathematik.[31]

There is quite clearly a distinction between what Wittgenstein calls a quotation and quasi-quotation. We can see this from the following statement, "'calculus' is no *chess-figure* of mathematics", meaning calculus doesn't belong to the basic mathematical terminology. The quasi-quotation in this instance refers to nebu-

---

[26] Wittgenstein 211, 41.
[27] Wittgenstein 211, 42.
[28] Wittgenstein 211, 44.
[29] WA 4, 37 and 211, 44.
[30] Wittgenstein TS213, 539.
[31] WA 4, 39; TS213, 539 and 211, 45.

lous terms. This brings to light the issue of a proper mathematical definition for the term, which has so far not been defined. The paradox lies in the act of marrying the definition with the practical application. Once we have a proper definition of calculi we can address the issue of an application to the description of metacalculi. If this can be done, all the following calculi would then simply be inference of a metacalculus. He says the following:

> This need not happen in mathematics. – And if it would still be used in a calculus, then this is not a metacalculus. *This word* is then no more than a chess-figure as all the others.
>
> Es brauchte in der Mathematik nicht vorzukommen. – Und wenn es doch in einem Kalkül gebraucht wird, so ist dieser nun kein Metakalkül. Vielmehr ist dann *dieses Wort* wieder nur ein Schachstein wie alle andern.[32]

4. What are Rules?

In contrast to Wittgenstein's point of view, we are familiar with David Hilbert's way of defining a class of accepted rules to every calculus. Thus metarules are then considered as rules about rules. The property of the metarules can be described as follows: applied to the rules of a calculus it creates another new rule. Wittgenstein states the following:

> (Hilbert sets up the rules of a specific calculus as rule of a / the / metamathematics.
>
> (Hilbert stellt Regeln eines bestimmten Kalküls als Regeln einer / der / Metamathematik auf.)[33]

Thus on the distinction between *a* and *the* hangs the existence of metamathematics. For the first case Hilbert sets up the rules of a specific calculus to serve as a model for metamathematics. The case of metamathematics is quite different. The use of indefinite and definite articles, *a* and *the*, does not seem like a relevant argument to prove the existence of metamathematics. After the introduction of Hilbert's rules of a specific calculus as a base for metamathematics nobody has doubted the existence of metamathematics. But Wittgenstein has done so.

These calculi as rules of metamathematics are called metacalculi. Metacalculi are different from traditional calculi in the sense that the former establish rules. Starting from metacalculi and in relation to metarules, we have to repeat the

---

[32] WA 4, 39; TS213, 539 and 211, 45.
[33] PG 297 and TS213, 539.

procedure. This repetition can be carried out variously and it becomes obvious that we will be receiving the same sentences about a calculus on every level. At that point we are confronted with a fundamental problem: how can logical arguments be solved? Let's assume that we have the following implication:

(1) $\neg \forall x Px \rightarrow \exists x \neg Px$.

Obviously, implication (1) can be inferred within the first-order predicate calculus. If we want to examine the reliability of the implication by finding out about the truth-values, the whole thing becomes more complicated. In this instance Wittgenstein would refer to a natural feeling for language and describe statement (1) as follows:

(2) If Px is not valid for all x, then some x are valid not Px.

This is only valid in the case of assuming (2) to be true. Hilbert is not convinced about going back to the ordinary language. The aim of metamathematics is to justify the predicate calculus with mathematics as its basis rather than the ordinary language. Wittgenstein is surprised by the proposition of a rule. He thinks that the rule must not be used as an explanation.[34] But what does he mean by "rule" and how did he use it in 1932? The answer to these questions is uncertain.[35] Every index of rules is usually incomplete and uncertain towards borderline cases ("Grenzfälle"). Therefore we need definition, especially a definition of what is supposed to be a rule. These definitions should not contain presuppositions. It is interesting to point out that there are usually references needed to list all single cases that give an explanation of general cases.

Contrary to Hilbert's position, Wittgenstein sees the mistake within mathematics in the following assumption:

> Logic and mathematics don't rest on axioms, as well as a group is not defined by the elements that makes up its whole. This mistake can be seen in the acceptance of: a) enlightenment, b) evidence and c) axioms, being seen as a criteria for logical correctness.
> A fundament, that doesn't stand on anything, is a rather bad fundament.
>
> Die Logik und die Mathematik *ruht* nicht auf Axiomen; so wenig eine Gruppe auf den sie definierenden Elementen und Operationen ruht. Hierin liegt der Fehler, das Einleuchten, die Evidenz, der Grundgesetze als Kriterium der Richtigkeit in der Logik zu betrachten.
> Ein Fundament, das auf nichts steht, ist ein schlechtes Fundament.[36]

---

[34] Wittgenstein 211, 46.
[35] Wittgenstein 211, 60.
[36] PG, 297 and TS213, 540 f.

Or even more precisely expressed, the mistake in mathematics lies in the following assumption: A calculus could be the metamathematical fundament for metamathematics. There is a crucial question of metamathematics, whether a calculus can be set up for mathematically true sentences, which can reduce the proof of such a statement to the form of an inference of the calculus. This question was earlier negated by K. Gödel on the ground of his results about the incompleteness theorem ("Unvollständigkeitssatz"). Wittgenstein approaches these results by examining them closely and says:

> Gödel <u>indirectly</u> says that it cannot be proved" – what does then the opposite of i.e. the negation of Gödel's sentence mean? Gödel's negated sentence
> Does „δp" imply that „δp" can be proved? In other words: given that "p" has an inner property of proof, does that imply that it is true? The proof for proof can be seen as proof for „δp, but at the same time that does not lead to inferring from the unproved sentence „δp can be proved".
>
> „Gödel<s> sagt in <u>indirekter</u> Weise aus, daß er nicht beweisbar ist." – was sagt also das Gegenteil von „d.h. die Verneinung" von Gödels aus Satz aus? der verneinte Satz Gödel<sche> Satz aus
> Folgt aus „δp ist beweisb. „δp"? D.H.: folgt daraus, daß „p" die (interne) Eigenschaft der Beweisbarkeit hat, daß es wahr ist? – Der Beweis für die Beweisbarkeit gilt allerdings als Beweis von „δp", aber das heißt nicht, daß man aus dem unbewiesenen Satz „δp ist beweisbar" folgern darf.[37]

It must be said that Gödel's controversal results put into doubt the method that he used.

> I am inclined to say: which ever decision you take, don't decide for Gödel's reason, because that's a rather stupid reason.
>
> Ich möchte beinahe sagen: wofür immer Du Dich entscheidest, entscheide Dich nicht aus dem Gödelschen Grund, denn das ist ein dummer Grund.[38]

5. Completeness and Internal Consistency

We have outlined earlier that one of the most important aims of metamathematics is to provide a justification for the predicate calculus, having as its basis mathematics and logic rather than the ordinary language. Consequently its task is to find a proof for the internal consistency. It has to be proved that any theory of calculus should avoid contradiction. A theory of a formula A can't therefore prove A and non-A at the same time. The internal consistency of logic corresponds to that of mathematics. D. Hilbert expressed this thought as follows:

---

[37] Trinity College Library, Item 121, Bd. XVII *Philosophische Bemerkungen*, 82v.
[38] Trinity College Library, Item 121, Bd. XVII *Philosophische Bemerkungen*, 82r.

> The absolute truths are those insights that were given by my theory of proof and the internal consistency of those formula-systems.
>
> Als die absoluten Wahrheiten sind vielmehr die Einsichten einzusehen, die durch meine Beweistheorie hinsichtlich der Beweisbarkeit und der Widerspruchsfreiheit jener Formelsysteme geliefert werden.[39]

Wittgenstein summarized his discussions of 28 December 1930 as follows:

> The problem of internal consistency of mathematics stems from two different sources: 1. From the ideas of non-Euklidean geometry, which was dealing with the problem of proving the parallel axiom after the principle of reductio ad absurdum. 2. From the antinoms of Burali-Forti and from Russell.
>
> Das Problem der Widerspruchsfreiheit der Mathematik stammt aus zwei Quellen: 1. Aus der Ideen der nicht-euklidischen Geometrie, wo es sich darum gehandelt hat, nach dem gegebenen Vorbild einer reductio ad absurdum das Parallelaxiom zu beweisen. 2. Aus den Antinomien von Burali-Forti und von Russell.[40]

The arguments can be outlined as follows: The problem of internal consistency is derived from the antinoms. But Wittgenstein thinks that these two elements don't have anything in common, because the antinom never occurs in the calculus but it appears in the ordinary language. The reason is that words are often used in an ambiguous way. This problem can be solved by using words precisely and distinctly, which would lead to the disappearance of antinomy, "but by analysis rather than by proof."[41] Then the types of different proofs applied in mathematics were listed:

> 1. The proof, that gives evidence for a certain formula. This formula occurs in the proof as its last element. [1]
> 2. The inference proof. What is striking is that the sentence that is supposed to be proved doesn't appear in the proof. This means, that the inference is not a method that leads to a sentence, but it shows us infinite possibilities which is a relevant characteristic of the inference proof."
>
> 1. Ein Beweis, der eine bestimmte Formel beweist. Diese Formel kommt im Beweis selbst, als ihr letztes Glied vor. [1]
> 2. Der Induktionsbeweis. Hier fällt zunächst auf, daß im Beweis selbst der zu beweisende Satz gar nicht vorkommt. Der Beweis beweist also auch gar nicht den Satz. Das heißt, die Induktion ist nicht ein Verfahren, das zu einem Satz führt. Sondern die Induktion läßt uns eine unendliche Möglichkeit sehen, und darin allein besteht das Wesen des Induktionsbeweis.[42]

---

[39] Hilbert 1923, 153.
[40] Wittgenstein WWK, 121.
[41] Wittgenstein WWK, 122.
[42] Wittgenstein WWK, 135.

L. Wittgenstein believes that the antinomy has encouraged him to deal with the problem of internal consistency. His line of argument seems to be wrong in this aspect because the antinomy doesn't relate to the internal consistency of mathematics. The antinomy normally appears in the ordinary language rather than in the calculus, because words are often used in an ambiguous way. The solution to this problem would be to replace ambiguous meanings with precise ones. The antinomy disappears through analysis rather than by proof. Thus, if ambiguity leads to contradictions in mathematics, it can never be solved by a proof. And as a result of this, he states, that there can never be a proof for internal consistency (comparing the contradictions in mathematics to those in predicate calculus). On the basis of the discussion with Hilbert's 'New Foundation of Mathematics', Wittgenstein points out, that a proof for internal consistency must evolve to understand the rules. These rules are usually described by the inference proof. The inference suggests infinite possibilities. A contradiction cannot be considered as rule because the grammar of the word "rule" is of a kind, that a contradiction is not a rule.[43]

References

Carnap, R. (1935), *Logische Syntax der Sprache*, Wien/New York.
Carnap, R. (1995), "Metalógica – Metalogik" (ed. J. Padilla-Gálvez), *Mathesis*, 11, 137-192.
Gödel, K. (1930), "Einige metamathematische Resultate über Entscheidungsdefinitheit und Widerspruchsfreiheit", *Anzeiger der Akademie der Wissenschaften in Wien, mathematisch-naturwissenschaftliche Klasse*, 67, 214-215.
Gödel, K. (1931), Über formal unentscheidbare Sätze der *Principia Mathematica* und verwandter Systeme I", *Monatshefte für Mathematik und Physik*, 38, 173-198.
Gödel, K. (1986 ff.), *Kurt Gödel. Collected Works*, Vol. I/II/III. Oxford.
Gödel, K (1995), *Unpublished Philosophical Essays*, Basel/Boston/Berlin.
Haller, R. (1981), "Die gemeinsame menschliche Handlungsweise", in: R. Haller (ed.), *Sprache und Erkenntnis als soziale Tatsache*, Wien, 57-68.
Heyting, A. (1930), "Die formalen Regeln der intuitionistischen Logik", *Sitzungsberichte der Preussischen Akademie der Wissenschaften. Physikalisch-Mathematische Klasse II*, 42-56.
Hilbert, D. (1923), "Die logischen Grundlagen der Mathematik", *Mathematische Annalen*, 88, 151-165.
Hilbert, D. (1935), *Gesammelte Abhandlungen*, Berlin.
Hilbert D./Ackermann, W. (1972), *Grundzüge der theoretischen Logik*, Berlin/Heidelberg/New York, [6]1972.
Hilmy, S. (1987), *The Later Wittgenstein*, Oxford.
Kleene, St. C. (1971), *Introduction to Metamathematics*, Amsterdam/New-York/North-Holland.
Padilla-Gálvez, J. (1994), "Gödels Vorschlag innerhalb der selbstbezüglichen Sätze", *Grazer Philosophische Studien*, 47, 43-57.

---

[43] Wittgenstein WWK, 194.

Padilla-Gálvez, J. (1998), "Was trägt Wittgenstein zu der Carnapschen Metalogik bei?", in: J. Padilla-Gálvez/R. Drudis Baldrich (eds.), *ittgenstein und der Wiener Kreis*, ed. UCLM, Cuenca, 25-36.

Padilla-Gálvez, J. (1999), "Metamathematik versus deskriptive Metalogik", *Grazer Philososphische Studien*, 57, 167-182.

Sedmak, C. (1997), "Metaphysik, Metamathematik, Metasprache. Zu Wittgensteins deskriptivem Programm in den Umbruchsjahren", *Wittgenstein Studies* 1/97, Datei: 09-1-97.TXT.

Siitonen, A. (1989), "On the operational interpretation of logic and mathematics in the Tractatus", *Akten des Wittgenstein Symposiums*, Wien, 411-413.

Tarski, A. (1930a), "Über einige fundamentale Begriffe der Metamathematik", *C. R. des Séances de la Société des Sciences et des Lettres de Varsovie*, Cl. III, 23, 22-29.

Tarski, A. (1930b), "Fundamentale Begriffe der Methodologie der deduktiven Wissenschaften", I, *Monatsh. Math. Und Phys.*, 37, 361-404.

Tarski, A. (1935), "Der Wahrheitsbegriff in den formalisierten Sprachen, *Studia Philosophica*, 1, 261-405.

Tarski, A. (1936), "Über den Begriff der logischen Folgerung", *Actes du Congrès International de Philosophie Scientifique*, Paris 1935, Vol. VII, *ASI*, 394, Paris, 1-11.

Tarski, A. (1986), *Collected Papers* (eds. Steven R. Givant and Ralph N. McKenzie), Basel/Boston/Stuttgart: Birkhäuser.

Tarski, A. (1987), "A philosophical letter", *The Journal of Philosophy*, 84, 28-32.

Tarski, A. (1992), "Alfred Tarski: Drei Briefe an Otto Neurath" (ed. By Rudolf Haller, translated into English by Jan Tarski), *Grazer Philosophische Studien*, 43, 1-31.

Tarski, A. (1995), "Some Current Problems in Metamathematics" (ed. By Jan Tarski and Jan Wolenski), *History and Philosophy of Logic*, 16, 159-168.

FRANCISCO RODRÍGUEZ-CONSUEGRA

Wittgenstein and Russell on Propositions and Forms

Russell's logical atomism can be regarded, to some extent, as the stage where Russell's philosophy had to pay the price for the continuous delay of a true and deep facing with "fundamental principles", as Bradley liked to say. This price was really expensive, for it involved the abandonment of a major project in philosophy of logic and epistemology (the manuscript *Theory of knowledge*), and the subsequent devoting to only particular problems, but already without the hope to find an acceptable global philosophy out. The inconsistencies which made the project impossible were already present in former stages, and the main problems which made it necessary the abandonment of the global construction had been already pointed out by Bradley, in spite of the fact that Wittgenstein's criticisms were the sole apparent main cause of Russell's disappointment with his own philosophy.[1]

In the following, I will describe the main traits of the interaction between Russell and Wittgenstein from 1912 to 1914, and will provide with an attempt of a global explanation of the main causes why Russell's theory of proposition and judgement was abandoned, as well as of the role that Wittgenstein's criticisms played on that abandonment. Then the lines of development of both philosophers, from 1914 onwards, will be explained as a partial compromise with the important difficulties which were raised as a result of that interaction, which have mostly to do with the notion of form and Bradley's paradox against relations.[2]

---

[1] Griffin *1986* contains a good survey of Wittgenstein's criticisms. As it can easily be seen with only having a look at Pears 1967 and Stock 1972, resorting to unpublished material is indispensable to explain Russell's evolution. Pears 1989 has offered a further study by taking into consideration Russell's unfinished 1913, but, as I have pointed out in my review 1991c, with doubtful results.

[2] This paper contains partial English translations of some of the materials which already appeared in my 1992, together with new material, especially on the notion of form in the manuscript "What is logic?" (section 1), as well as on Russell's and Wittgenstein's ways out (sections 4 and 5). This new material includes unpublished notes and correspondence in the Russell Archives, McMaster University, Hamilton, On., Canada, where the copyright is held.

1. What is logic?

Wittgenstein's influence on Russell started probably in 1912, in a way that some the features of Russell's main philosophical project were already a partial response to some of Wittgenstein's criticisms. Yet there is a very important, although short, manuscript from 1912 which allows us to verify that the fundamental apparent novelty of *Theory of knowledge* (written in 1913), i.e., the introduction of forms as explicit constituents of complexes, was a possibility rejected before as being contradictory, in the same way than similar attempts were also rejected in former stages. The unfinished manuscript was entitled "What is logic?" (1912).

The manuscript shows that Russell did not yet solved the problem of characterizing the notion of the form of a complex, exactly in the same way than 1903, where form (or rather constancy of form) was regarded as a primitive idea. Also, the manuscript shows that Russell still needed this notion as the only way of characterizing logic, which was indispensable to make sense of the logicist thesis. Thus, the starting-point is the definition of logic: "Logic is the study of the forms of complexes", where the first thing to do is deciding the status of forms and complexes.

As for the notion of complex, Russell starts by accepting it as a primitive idea. But, according to his already old project, it is necessary to provide with some explanation for every primitive idea, in order to show that we are actually "acquainted" with the "object" involved. This explanation should provide some link with propositions, as they are apparently so fundamental for logic. So it was also necessary to explain the status of true and false propositions, supposedly through the multiple relation theory of judgment. Concerning propositions Russell says that they may be judgments, forms of words, or Meinong's objectives, although as they can be false they must be judgments (which are psychological) or mere forms of words. Thus, he finishes by deciding that logic is not concerned with propositions at all.

Concerning complexes, the only characterization offered is that they have a correspondence with true propositions, but not with false ones. Accordingly, they cannot be true or false in themselves. Russell tried so to locate truth and falsehood outside logic, which is admittedly done "in order not to have to give being to non-entities". Yet this device is just the old Russellian recourse of adding a theory of correspondence to his multiple relation theory of judgment, for obviously the most natural way to define a proposition as true is by means of some correspondence with a complex. Thus, we are told: "Don't say a complex *true;* say a judgment or proposition *true* when *corresponds* (in definable sense) to a complex". As we already know, this should be followed by a full explanation of the status of this correspondence, on pain of falling down into Bradley's (and Moore's) paradox of truth, yet we find no sign of such an explanation.

Regarding forms, the situation is hardly more satisfactory. Russell starts by returning to the way he explained them in 1903: "The *form* of a complex is what it has in common with a complex obtained by replacing each constituent of the complex by something different".[3] He immediately adds that to speak about "what such complexes have in common is of course a problem —a problem for logic". However, he says nothing concerning the notion of "constituent", probably to avoid the formidable problems involved in any attempt to explain the relations among them into a complex, and the relations between them and the complex itself. Of course the admission of forms was a device to avoid, honestly, this problem, but then we face a similar problem when trying to know whether or not forms are constituents of complexes, given that we have to avoid Bradley's paradox (1912, 2):

> In a complex, there must be something, which we may call the *form*, which is *not* a constituent, but the way the constituents are put together. If we make this a constituent, it would have to be somehow related to the other constituents, and the way in which it was related would really be the form; hence an endless regress. Thus the form is not a constituent.

This shows Russell as maintaining the old scheme of forms and constituents intact: when he thought of constituents he regarded them as mere simple and "external" objects, whose nature is not affected by the fact of their combination. This is exactly the view which leads directly to the unsolved problem of giving a philosophical account of relations. Also, it shows that Russell was completely convinced, as he was in former stages, that forms can by no means be regarded as constituents, precisely because he included the notion of form to avoid the problem of the relation between relations and the related terms, which is supposed to be solved through undefined "forms". Yet it seems to me that calling "forms" to ghostly second order relations is only an *ad hoc* way to leap over the philosophical problem involved.

As for the technical problem, it seems easily solved by making the form to be a primitive idea. Russell considered, to finish the manuscript, several ways to do that, but with no definite result. I think this was so precisely because of the philosophical problems involved, which had be faced in trying to introduce this primitive idea into the several complexes. Thus, he rejected making the predicate "to have the same form" to be a primitive idea, for it would give rise to non-existent complexes, given that "it is possible for a form to be *impossible,*

---

[3] The examples which Russell mentions are propositional functions, dyadic and multiple relations, and the two standard forms of quantification.

e.g. x ≠ x" (1912, 3).[4] Finally, Russell abandoned any attempt to characterize forms when trying to make the several needs involved compatible. This is particularly clear in considering the need for admitting atomic and simple forms, for "what is 'part' of a form? Are there simple and complex forms?" (1912, 4).

As a whole, we can then conclude that this manuscript was a failure, precisely because Russell was trying to be consequent with the impossibility to make forms to be constituents of complexes. Bradley's paradox was respected, and for the same reason any possible violation of the theory of types was apparently avoided, for any attempt to consider forms at the same ontological level than constituents would be such a violation. On the other hand, the multiple relation theory already entailed, even without forms, some kind of problem concerning types, as it allowed "relating relations" to be constituents of complexes, at the same level that individuals.

2. *Theory of knowledge* and Wittgenstein's criticisms

That is why it is so strange that in *Theory of knowledge* (1913) Russell's main recourse was the open admission of forms as constituents of complexes. Yet this was also an attempt to overcome Stout's and Bradley's criticisms, which forced him to introduce some changes to avoid the idealist consequences of regarding complexes, then propositions, as a mere product of our minds. However, by then Russell was also trying to reply to Wittgenstein's first criticisms, which took place before he began to write *Theory of knowledge*.

I think that those first criticisms were relevant mainly because they forced Russell to face a very unpleasant dilemma: either maintaining the old theory of types by abandoning the multiple relation theory of judgment, and by renouncing to characterize complexes, then logic, or abandoning some philosophical consequences of the theory of types by complementing the multiple relation theory with some explicit device making the admission of forms, as some sort of constituents, possible.

We can consider Wittgenstein's letter from January 1913 the source of this dilemma. In that letter, Wittgenstein clearly wrote that as there cannot be different types of things, the correct analysis of propositions must point out, just through an appropriate symbolism, that types are unnecessary.[5] The suggested analysis is

---

[4] And this apart from the problem of definitions by abstraction, which Russell seems not to remember.

[5] Wittgenstein's attack against Russell's theory of types is here underlying the later famous objection that the very formulation of the theory sins against itself. However, the authors

well known. Wittgenstein proposes to analyze "Socrates is mortal", not into "Socrates", "Mortality" and the quantificational form involved, for this would make erroneous substitutions possible (e.g. "Mortality is Socrates"), but into "Socrates" and "there is at least an x, and x is mortal" (1974, R.9). These kind of analysis is likely to have led Russell to the attempt to openly include forms in complexes, as Wittgenstein clearly said that the second constituent of his former analysis is not complex, in spite of the fact that he did not provide with any explicit treatment of forms.

Russell's solution in 1913 was clearly a compromise between the two horns of the dilemma, although the final details seems to involve rather the second alternative, despite the fact that it is quite obvious that it involved at least some violation of Bradley's prohibitions. Russell starts by rejecting that the form can be a mere constituent of complexes, with the usual Bradleyan argument. Thus, in "Socrates is human", "is" represents the form, and then cannot be a constituent: "for if it were, there would have to be a new way in which it and the two other constituents are put together, and if we take this way as again a constituent, we find ourselves embarked on an endless regress" (1913, 16). But when he tries to explain the nature of forms, according to his usual method of analyzing the notions involved, in order to "prove" that we are acquainted with them, he rejects not only regarding them as equivalence relations (which was already rejected in 1912), but also as primitive ideas, which would lead to the usual paradox. Therefore, the only solution, already within the Wittgensteinian framework, was regarding forms as the indefinable objects which correspond to certain general expressions (which are "shown" by those expressions, we can add, to recall Wittgenstein's language).

Thus, the form of subject-predicate complexes will be "some has some predicate", and the form of dyadic complexes will be "something has some relation to something". Russell tried to avoid the obvious objection of circularity in this

---

who explicitly have proposed this objection (Weiss 1928, Black 1944) unfortunately did not state the necessary connection. On the other hand, it is clear that the objection itself has much to do with Bradley's in virtue of his self-referential character, which is rather clear on reading Russell's own objections against logical form in 1912 (see above in the main text). In his reply to Black's criticism, Russell himself recognized the force of the objection and confessed: "This is a point which formerly troubled me a good deal; the very word 'type' sinned against the letter of the theory", although unfortunately he does not state any link with his celebrated idea, in the introduction to the *Tractatus,* according to which it is possible to establish different levels of language. Rather, he says that some escape from the difficulty should be possible by regarding differences in type as syntactical differences (1944, 692). It seems then clear that Russell was thereby reacting along the Carnapian syntactical lines at that time. But if my arguments here are correct, syntax —through "forms" and similar notions— offers as much reasons of relational ineffability as semantics from Russell's viewpoint.

passage, which is the kernel of the book from our viewpoint, in this way (1913, 114):

> The logical nature of this fact is very peculiar. If we take some particular dual complex xRy, this has three constituents, x, R, and y. If we now consider "something has the relation R to y", we get a fact which no longer contains x, and has not substituted any other entity for x, since "something" is nothing. Thus our new fact contains only R and y. For similar reasons, "something has the relation R to something" contains no constituent except R; and "something has some relation to something" contains no constituent at all. It is, therefore, suitable to serve as the "form" of dual complexes. In a sense, it is simple, since it cannot be analyzed. At first sight, it seems to have a structure, and therefore to be not simple; but it is more correct to say that it *is* a structure. Language is not well adapted for speaking of such objects. But in spite of the difficulties of language, it seems not paradoxical to say that, in order to understand a proposition which states that x has the relation R to y, we must understand what is meant by "something having some relation to something". I shall therefore assume that his may be defined as the "form" of dual complexes, and that similar definitions may be adopted for other forms.

However, the compromise gives rise to many unsolved problems, especially by taking into consideration that the only change in the general scheme of the multiple relation theory of judgment consists precisely in incorporating a symbol for the form (γ) to the general complex constituting the judgment: "U (S, x, R, y, γ)" (see below for more details).

Thus, it is difficult to deny that the form is being regarding as a new constituent. And this is not only an attempt to leap over Bradley's paradox, but also an attempt to give an objective status to the form. For this means that we have to be acquainted with forms in the same way that we are acquainted with the rest of the constituents of a complex. So we have to face here the same problem than the one we already had with R as being both a relating relation and a term. The only change is now regarding γ as the general form of dual complexes, and so trying this form to absorb the "relating" part of R. Yet in so doing we still need to explain the status of γ into the complex, so that the main problem remains unsolved.

Therefore: (i) the theory of types is incompatible with the general scheme of the judgment complex, for individuals, properties, relations, and forms or structures are located at the same ontological level, and nothing is said as to whether the theory is proposed to dispense with types or not; (ii) the nonsense continues to be possible, for there is no additional device avoiding wrong replacements by just altering the order; (iii) the new theory falls again into Bradley's paradox, for the "relating" part of the relation is obviously a constituent of the complex; (iv) the problem concerning idealism remains, for we have to interpret that the form, as an object of our acquaintance, is that which imposes the true order to the "secondary" complex, given that no other theory is provided. Although it seems that the form is supposed to be something objective, we cannot forget that judgment (judging) is psychological in itself, and if it imposes the order (or sense) to the secondary complex, the result is that there is no independent source of objectivity to maintain any theory of correspondence (which, once again, also sins against Bradley's prohibitions). Let us try to develop these problems in considering Wittgenstein's more definite criticisms to the new theory.

In the present stage Russell, in order to obtain a non psychological notion of judgment, needed a scheme presenting the symbol for proposition as an incomplete symbol, and at the same time as something objective and mind-independent. Then, it is not strange that he arrives at the same problem which had arisen with forms: to give the pre-eminence both to the structural and to the atomistic viewpoints. The compromise consists, simply, of incorporating the very form to the scheme, by representing the multiple relation existing between the mind and the several constituents of the complex which is judged. Thus, calling S to the subject, U to the "relating" multiple relation, x and y to the terms which are joined by the relation R, and γ to the form itself (in this case the one corresponding to dyadic relations), the whole complex would be given by the formula: "$U(S, x, R, y, \gamma)$". This formula, in being the same for every subject and for every propositional relation which are affected by the same proposition, can be used, according to Russell, to give to this proposition all the treats of a genuine entity (1913, 115), although the price which have to pay seems to be converting the form into an object.

With this manoeuvre Russell expected to overcome the troubles with his notion of sense, in order to "put order" among the objects of the judgment, without requiring that order to be was directly referred to in the analysis. However, the old argument against false propositions continues to be defended, as the "false multiple relation" is attributed to our erroneous "idea" (1913, 116), and this is, once again, the seed of similar problems: if the form is something objective and we are only mistaken in "combining" it with certain other objects (the ones constituting the judgment), then the role which in fact the form is playing is that of one more constituent, no matter how much we may dislike this last conclusion.

Russell himself insisted in saying, through his principle of acquaintance, that we cannot understand a proposition without being acquainted with every of its constituents. Thus, the complex that *we* construct by ourselves includes the form as being one more "object", no matter that we can be mistaken in interpreting it in a way which is different from the one which is actually taking place. So, in replacing the particular form by the abstract one we would again obtain a combination which erroneously presents *every* one of its constituent objects as being located at the same ontological level.

For example, in the case of the form of dyadic relations applied to "A and B are similar", we would have (1913, 117):

$$U \{S, A, B, \text{similarity}, R(x, y)\}.$$

We come thus to the exact point in which the theory of types is violated, as we are putting at the same level individuals, relations and properties. At the same time, nonsense is again possible, by only changing the order actually exhibited. Finally, we fall into Bradley's paradox, as we have to explicitly refer to the relation between a relation and its terms.

Russell realizes this last problem when he writes the following (1913, 117):

> It is obvious, in the first place, that S is related to the four other terms in a way different from that in which any of the four other terms are related to each other. It is obvious, in the second place, that $R(x, y)$ enters in a different way from the other three objects, and that "similarity" has a different relation to $R(x, y)$ from that which A and B have, while A and B have each the same relation to $R(x, y)$.

However, the fact that he offers a graphic scheme —which looks like being tridimensional— to represent the "structure" of the whole thing, leads him just to regard so important a problem as being already —provisorily— solved. Yet he does not mention the theory of types, neither here nor in any other place in 1913, with which he is probably showing his doubts after Wittgenstein's criticisms in the January letter.

Only in the final summary of part II (first section) a doubtful reference can be found, when Russell writes that understanding a proposition is a relation between a subject and certain objects, which are (i) the form of certain atomic complexes; (ii) entities of the same logical species than the constituents of such complexes (1913, 176-7). However, this shows only that Russell was aware of the problem, but not that he had some solution available. Once again we have to point out the unsatisfactory compromise consisting in admitting the form as an entity and, at the same time, in rejecting it as such, on pain of facing the three problems pointed out above.

3. The final criticism

We come now at Wittgenstein's definitive criticism, that is, the celebrated letter he wrote to Russell in June 1913, after he knew Russell's *1913*, which remained unfinished. In that letter he made his criticisms to Russell's theory of judgment more precise (*1974*, R.12):

> I can now express my objection to your theory of judgment exactly: I believe it is obvious that, from the proposition "A judges that (say) a is in the Relation R to b", if correctly analysed, the proposition "aRb . v . ~aRb", must follow directly *without the use of any other premiss.* This condition is not fulfilled by your theory.

For a long time this criticism, which is very obscure, was seen as something isolated, which required some specific explanation, and the same took place as for other criticisms contained in Wittgenstein 1913 or the *Tractatus,* which are usually pointed out mainly because they clearly allude to Russell.[6] I am thinking about the following criticisms:

(i) the one referred to the need for a theory which makes it impossible to judge *nonsense (1913, 97):*

> Just as one arrow behaves to another arrow by being in the same sense or the opposite, so a fact behaves to a proposition; it is thus bi-polarity and sense come in. In this theory p has the same meaning as not-p but opposite sense. The meaning is the fact. A proper theory of judgment must make is impossible to judge nonsense.

This can be illustrated by the famous example: "every right theory of judgment must make it impossible for me to judge that 'this table penholders the book' (Russell's theory does not satisfy this requirement)" (1913, 96);

(ii) the one requiring the object of judgment to be a proposition, and not simply several constituents and a form (1913, 96):

> When we say A judges that, etc., then we have to mention a whole proposition which a judges. It will not do either to mention only its constituents, of its constituents and form but not in the proper order. This shows that a proposition itself must occur in the statement to the effect that is is judged;

(iii) the one directly attacking the notion of form (1913, 99):

> There is no *thing* which is the form of a proposition, and no name which is the name of a form. Accordingly we can also not say that a relation which in certain cases holds between things holds sometimes between forms and things. This goes against Russell's theory of judgment.

This criticism, by the way, is nothing but a form of Bradley's paradox against relations, which, as we have seen above, was already used by Russell himself against the notion of form in 1912, and is also included in the *Tractatus.*[7]

---

[6] This can be seen in a whole series of publications, at least from Anscombe 1959, p. 46, to Blackwell 1981, p. 22.

[7] Which is usually unnoticed, except for the first one, which appears also in 4.0621 and 5.5422, but the second is closely related to the strange theory that "A believes p" is of the form "'p' says p" (5.542), which already appears in 1914, p. 206, while the third (Brad-

However, I think that no explanation of such criticisms can be satisfactory without being global, that is, without providing with a a general conception from which they can be inferred, together with other central theses from 1913:

(i) the protest about Russell's regarding "complexes" as "simples", which also embraces the impossibility of distinguishing certain logical types of the rest of them (1913, 99);

(ii) the rejection of "logical objects", which arise in regarding propositions as names (1913, 100-1; see also 1916, 37 and *Tractatus* 4.0312, 4.441);

(iii) the attack against relations, predicates and real variables (1913, 99, 103), already appearing in Wittgenstein's correspondence with Russell from 1912.[8]

This global explanation is the one I will attempt in the following, by trying, at the same time, of taking into consideration a few arguments on the secondary literature which seems to me particularly close to truth.

Wittgenstein's criticism contained in the letter of June 1913, as we have seen, is rather cryptic. One of the consequences of this has been that most of the treatments of the question have been very unsatisfactory.[9] An important exception was Sommerville 1981, which, by starting from a doctoral thesis from 1979, offered, for the first time, an acceptable beginning of explanation.[10] This explanation was specific, that is, not global, but it had however the merit of paving the way for the global explanation I referred to in the previous paragraph. The kernel of Sommerville's explanation consists, precisely, of the thesis that Wittgenstein's criticism to the possibility of judging nonsense, and the one requiring "A judges that aRb" to be inferred directly from "aRb . v . ~aRb", are *one and the same* criticism, under different forms. Actually, Sommerville continues, Russell had already offered the following proposition (*Principia*, *13.3):

---

ley's paradox in the bottom line) appears again in 4.12 in close connection to Moore's paradox of truth. See below in the main text for more details on some of those passages.

[8] Curiously enough, all this appeared together with other theses which are apparently contradictory. I think this can be interpreted, like in Russell himself, as proceeding from the defence of an atomistic view, which ultimately gave rise to important tensions in the *Tractatus,* and finally to the "second" Wittgenstein. With that I am thinking, for example, of the admission of indefinables and their classification into names and forms (1913, 98), or of the theory according to which a proposition is understood when every of its indefinables has been understood (*ibid.*).

[9] As for instance Pears (1977, 190-1), Iglesias (1984, 298-9) and Griffin (1985, 240-1). The recent Landini 1990 is clever and original, but I think it has a basic flaw: it has almost anything to do with the actual, historical Russell.

[10] Which was later efficiently discussed by Griffin 1980, 1985, 1986, and Blackwell 1981.

$$\emptyset a \lor \sim\emptyset a . \supset \therefore \emptyset x \lor \sim\emptyset x . \equiv : x = a . \lor . x \neq a$$

According to it, "if a is any argument for which 'ϕa' is significant, *i.e.* for which we have $\emptyset a \lor \sim\emptyset a$, then '$\emptyset x$' is significant when, and only when, x is either identical with a or not identical with a" (1910, 171-2). This can be immediately applied to relational propositions (like in Wittgenstein's case) and is equivalent to say that the *sense* of a proposition depends upon its possibility of being true or false (like Russell himself had already said in 1913). In Sommerville's words (1981, 187):

> That "aRb .v. –aRb" follow without further premisses is, then, the requirement that, if "aRb" is genuinely an elementary judgment (at the base-level of the hierarchy of orders), its analysis alone must reveal the items so related to belong to the appropriate type. Otherwise, that "aRb" is elementary would depend upon the truth of a further judgment —that a and b are individuals (of type-0); when it is the *account* of elementary judgment itself which is intended to provide independent support for classifying the ranges of significance of functions into types. so the type of significant argument to xRy depends upon the kind of judgment made in asserting xRy of a, b and so on; whilst the kind of judgment made depends, in part, upon the type of argument related by R in the complex.

Which is, obviously, circular in showing that the theory of judgment of 1913 tries to justify a classification into types and, at the same time, to do it by taking advantage of a theory of types already constituted. As I said above, the main merit of Sommerville is to have taken a first step towards a global explanation, but it is a real pity that this author did not notice that to obtain a more global conception, it is enough to retake Wittgenstein's attack to the notion of form (already advanced in Russell 1912, as we have seen), under the argument of Bradley's paradox.

A sign of that can be also found in Kenny (1973, 100-1), who extended the former viewpoint in inserting it into the framework of the general criticism of belief propositions. Thus, Kenny writes, when Wittgenstein wrote that we cannot judge (or believe) nonsense, he was saying, at the same time, that, from A's belief in aRb, "aRb or no aRb" can be directly inferred: "anyone who knows what 'Grass is green' means, and thus has the appropriate mental elements, knows *eo ipso* that either grass is green or grass is not green".[11] And this is the same as saying, we can add, that to believe in a proposition we have first to understand it, and this can only take place if it shows a sense, that is, if it can be true or false.

---

[11] Kenny points out to Wittgenstein 1916, p. 94. There we can read: "I understand the proposition 'aRb' when I know that either the fact that aRb or the fact that not aRb corresponds to it; but this is not to be confused with the false opinion that I understand 'aRb' when I know that 'aRb or not aRb' is the case".

However, and this the important thing that Kenny adds to the former analysis, to *say* that "A believes *p*"is always a pseudo-proposition, because it not only asserts that in A's mind certain elements are related in certain form, but also that the form in which these elements are related says that "*p*". And this is precisely what we cannot say, because, in general, *we* cannot say what is shown in a proposition: its sense, e.g. its possibility of being true or false: "A proposition *shows* how things stand *if* it is true. And it *says that* they do so stand" (*Tractatus*, 4. 022). That is why Wittgenstein wrote, already in 1914: "The relation of 'I believe p' to 'p' can be compared to the relation of '"p" says p' to p: it is just as impossible that *I* should be a simple as that 'p' should be" (1914, 118); which is repeated in the *Tractatus*; "'*A* believes that *p*', '*A* has the thought *p*', and '*A* says *p*' are of the form '"*p*" says *p*': and this does not involve a correlation of a fact with an object, but rather the correlation of facts by means of the correlation of their objects" (5.542). Summing up: we cannot refer with sense to the relation of correspondence between propositions and facts.

However, it seems to me that Kenny does not state the decisive connection with the notion of form either, which we need to reach our global explanation. In fact, Russell himself came a little closer to the real problem in realizing that the kernel of Wittgenstein's criticism to his theory of judgment already appeared in the proposition 5.542 of the *Tractatus*. Thus, Russell wrote that the really fundamental in propositional attitudes "is the relation of a proposition, *considered as a fact,* to the fact which makes it true or false, and that this relation of two facts is reducible to a relation of their constituents" (Russell 1922, 20). I said that this came a little closer to the real problem because to reach it we need only to add the following: and we cannot refer with sense to this relation because, in trying to do so, we unavoidably introduce another proposition, then we would be force to refer to the relation of this last proposition to that to which it is pointing out, and so on, in a clear Bradleyan (and Moorean) endless regress.

Consequently, the global viewpoint I have been referring to consists of realizing: (i) not only, with Sommerville (and Griffin 1985, who follows him), that the criticism to the possibility of judging nonsense is the same than the one according to which the disjunction corresponding to each proposition has to be directly inferred from it (from "p" to "p or no p") without any other premise; and that this gives immediately rise to difficulties for the theory of types; (ii) not only, with Kenny (and Russell), that it is the general scheme of propositional attitudes the one which introduces an apparent breaking with truth functions, which can be overcome only in realizing that it is based mainly upon the unacceptable presupposition that we can refer to the correspondence between a proposition and the facts which make it true or false.

The global viewpoint can be reached only by realizing, in addition, that (i) the criticism to the possibility of judging nonsense; the thesis that the disjunction has to be immediately inferred from any proposition; the rejection of propositional attitudes; the attack against the theory of types; and, in general, Wittgenstein's conviction that it is impossible to conceptually grasp certain formal notions, proceed once and for all from a common root: Wittgenstein's criticism to the notion of form as being able to be one more constituent of propositions;[12] (ii) this criticism came from Russell's difficulties to construct forms both as relations and as terms, that is, ultimately, from Bradley's and Moore's paradoxes.[13]

---

[12] Stout's criticism (1915, 343) to the multiple relation theory of judgment shows that to obtain genuine acquaintance the complex which is the object of the judgment has to exist previously to the fact that the relation to our mind is stated. Yet Russell's theory could hardly agree with that, as it was created precisely to locate on the subject the whole responsibility of mistakes (then of false propositions).

[13] Therefore, it is not enough, as it takes place in Hylton 1984, to mention Moore's theory of judgment as a precedent to these problems. It is necessary to show, as I try here, not only that this is so, but also that Wittgenstein's rejection of atomism led him to a somewhat holistic position; and that this was caused for similar reasons than the ones which led Bradley to his general position. In his 1990 Hylton has devoted a long section to Russell's multiple relation theory of judgment (pp. 333-361), but I am afraid that he offers only a set of comments on some of the relevant passages which can be found in Russell's writings, with no attempt to provide any global, let alone original interpretation. I find substantial problems in his account. First, although Hylton admits that Russell considered a first formulation of the theory in a previous manuscript (p. 355), he provides us with no exegesis of the manuscript, nor does he seems to be aware that there are other manuscripts of the same period in which Russell actually *endorses* the theory, as I have pointed put in my 1989. Second, Hylton regards *Theory of knowledge* as the next step to the official statement of the theory in the publications of 1910, as can clearly be seen in his writing that the notion of *form* was first introduced in the manuscript of the finally unfinished book (p. 343). With that we can see that he is obviously unaware of the fact that, as we have seen, Russell introduced and discussed the nature of that notion very keenly in a previous manuscript: "What is logic?", written in 1912 in the context of Wittgenstein's first influence (see Russell 1992, 54). And this is important, because the kernel of the question involved, which is a form of Bradley's paradox, is clearly exposed in that manuscript, although it is explicitly avoided in *Theory of knowledge*. Furthermore, this leads Hylton to ignore (p. 358) the fact that Wittgenstein's first criticism to Russell's theory (from January 1913) was *previous* to Russell's writing of *Theory of knowledge,* which means that in that unfinished book he may have been reacting against that criticism. Finally, Hylton offers no explanation at all of Wittgenstein's criticisms against the theory as exposed in *Theory of knowledge,* so he is unable to see the fundamental problem involved in the globality of Wittgenstein's position which I have tried to offer in my account. (In fact Hylton does not even seem to know the relevant secondary literature, as he only mentions Pears 1989 and Sommerville 1981 —p. 357, footnote 37— but not the important papers by Griffin and others which I have mentioned.)

I have already quoted Wittgenstein's passage from 1913 where he repeats Russell's idea, which was also quoted above. Here I would like to add the corresponding text from the *Tractatus*, which is particularly interesting because it includes Moore's paradox of truth. This paradox constitutes a rejection of the possibility of explicitly *stating the* correspondence between a proposition (which is already a fact) and facts: "Propositions can represent the whole of reality, but they cannot represent what they must have in common with reality in order to be able to represent it —logical form" (4.12). It is then clearer why this text paves the way in the *Tractatus* to a whole series of passages in which a Bradleyan point of view is frankly adopted, which is characterized by the defense of the ineffability of "internal relations" and "formal properties" and, ultimately, by the doctrine of showing.[14]

4. Russell's way out: the chaotic forms

Probably, the failure of a general philosophical justification of the logical notions employed in *Principia* led Russell, as a sort of way-out, to particular epistemological problems, as the one dealing with the logical construction of external world. But in that change the influence of Whitehead's methods supposed an additional element in favour of an increasing importance of abstract structures over their terms. This, together with the monism involved in those methods, must have been the beginning of the holistic alternative that Russell chose from 1919 onwards. Thus, although it is unnecessary to consider here the details of Russell's logical constructions of physical objects, points and instants, in which he followed Whitehead's ideas, yet it would be important to try to discover the philosophical implications of those ideas for our main problem.

Whitehead's method of extensive abstraction was explicitly designed to construct what is supposedly simple out of what is complex, i.e. points and instants out of a framework of relations.[15] Apart from the obvious influence of Veblen and his device of triadic relations, which had already been employed by Whitehead in his works of the first decade of the century, this was the result of several

---

[14] The impossibility to refer to internal relations appears also in the *Prototractatus:* "[...] the definitions can be left tacit and the word does not then lose its meaning, since it still stands in the same relation to the objects which are depicted by means of the definitions —only we do not specifically depict that relation" (3, 202111); "So the logical structure of a situation is mirrors in a proposition -we cannot express it by means of language- the proposition *show* it" (4, 10221); "A common form is not a common constituent" (p. 237).

[15] The unpublished correspondence with Russell contains several letters where Whitehead clearly says he completely rejected the existence of simples. In chapter 14 of my 1987 I tried to explain in detail how Whitehead's methods led Russell to the before rejected "relationism".

deep philosophical tendencies that we can summarize into one main notion: monism. Whitehead's monism involved several inter-related consequences. On the one hand, it supposed the open rejection of any possible "dualism" between subject and object, and this implied the rejection of any causal theory of perception; hence the attempt to present the supposedly physical reality in terms of just one sort of stuff, common to mental realities. Thus, certain idealistic tendency can by no means by denied here. On the other hand, Whitehead's monism, as a theory trying to dispense with the philosophical "subject", has a strong link with what we can call "holism", i.e. the tendency to concede pre-eminence to relations (structures, forms, etc.) over terms (fields, logical atoms, etc.), and therefore it supposed a rejection of any theory admitting "absolute", atomistic realities like points, instants, and so on.

Russell was in 1913-14 hardly prepared to assume so strong consequences of the method he decided to accept from Whitehead, although doubtless the first seed of the sort of holism involved here was already present in the theory of descriptions. As his efforts to present forms as constituents point out, Russell maintained, to some extent, the remains of the old atomistic theory inherited from Moore, despite the rejection of propositions as genuine complexes. And this theory was the ultimate source for the pre-eminence of terms over relations, whose main metaphysical consequence was the absolutist theory of position, order, space and time, together with a strong rejection of any alternative relationistic theory as contradictory, and too close to idealism, as can bee seen in ch. 51 of *Principles*.

On the other hand, Russell's old realism, resting upon the strong distinction between act and object, could hardly allow him to accept Whitehead's monism, which rejected such a distinction. That is why Russell, although admitting some partial return to relationism, at least in some loose places of his writings at this stage, he continued to believe that monism involved idealism. Yet in the last analysis he also said that all his constructions were compatible with monism (as for instance with "neutral" monism), and that there must be a way to make a causal theory of perception to be compatible with phenomenalism. Finally, the theory of logical constructions, by explicitly accepting that inferences can be replaced by any construction which fulfil certain conditions, can serve to recognize the fact that there can be many acceptable different logical constructions for the same inference to be constructed. But this was hardly compatible with the old theory of analysis, according to which there is only one true analysis for every complex to be analyzed. And this obviously involved another strong element of relativity.

At least in theory, the relationism involved in Russell's new devices must have led him to some acceptance of the pre-eminence of relations and forms over terms and logical atoms, and then to some form of monism. However, the open acceptance of these implicit consequences took place only in 1919, once a new theory of judgment, more compatible with the new implicit holism, was available. In the meantime, Russell apparently continued to maintain most of his old views about relations and terms, and even his previous theory of judgment, which, although it was rejected in the personal correspondence, continued to appear in the publications up to 1918, with only some more or less implicit recognition of its defects. We come so to Russell's explicit treatment of the problem of forms and complexes between 1914 and 1918 (including 1919a, which, although published in 1919, it was written in 1918).

Our knowledge of the external world (1914) included a whole chapter devoted to "Logic as the essence of philosophy", and we can find there the Russellian alternative to the Hegelian and Bradleyan logic, which, as usual, is again wrongly characterized as the one maintaining that every proposition ascribes a predicate to a subject. That Russell continued to regard a fuller treatment of Bradley as necessary is shown by the two pages he devotes to Bradley's argument against relations and predicates in the first chapter. Unfortunately, we cannot find there any reply to that argument.

Russell starts by declaring forms to be the proper object of "philosophical logic" (1914, 52). However, by resorting to the "replacing" device, he says only that "form is not another constituent, but is the way the constituents are put together", i.e. something "abstract and remote". Thus, with no word about his previous failure in constructing an acceptable epistemology on logic (in 1913), he adds the expected claim that we have knowledge of forms, which allows us to understand sentences (1914, 53):

> In order to understand a sentence, it is necessary to have knowledge both of the constituents and of the particular instance of the form... Thus some kind of knowledge of logical forms, though with most people it is not explicit, is involved in all understanding of discourse. It is the business of philosophical logic to extract this knowledge from its concrete integuments, and to render it explicit and pure.

We have thus the two traditional arguments: (i) form cannot be a constituent of propositions (Bradley's paradox is then clearly involved);
(ii) there is some knowledge of forms, and this knowledge should be made explicit and serve to construct the relevant inventory of those entities (just what Wittgenstein claimed to be impossible). Yet we know nothing about the status of forms in the judging complex, with which Russell seems to give an old argument only for the sake of propaganda.

On the other hand, it is certainly difficult to accept that this supposed a knowledge of forms, because forms are abstract objects (then universals), and

Russell's favourite model for knowledge was knowledge by acquaintance, which seemed to be reserved only to particulars. In a letter from Broad of February 6, 1914, we find the problem explicitly posed, with the additional interest of the claim that Russell's rejection of propositions in favour of propositional functions may involve an endless regress. Broad's arguments concerns, in his own words, "a difficulty in reconciling your theory of judgment with your theory of knowledge by description", and reads this way:

> When I make a judgment about something that I only know by description —e.g. Charles I— I am really making a judgment about a certain propositional function and asserting [?] that it is not always false. If then the judgment is really about this propositional function I must surely be acquainted with it; and if I can be acquainted with propositional functions why not with propositions? If on the other hand I am not acquainted with it I must know it in turn [?] by another description, which will introduce another function and so start a vicious ∞ regress.

Here is Russell's reply of Feb. 10, 1914:

> The difficulty you raise is a very real one. The fact is that "acquaintance" cannot be applied straight off except to particulars, i.e. the only two-term cognitive relation of the form s.—$\xrightarrow{K}$.o has its converse domain confined to particulars. Knowledge by description is knowledge of a general proposition of the form $(\exists x) . \phi x$. In such cases, we cannot properly speak of *acquaintance* with $\hat{\phi x}$; "$\hat{\phi x}$" must be never put in a *subject*- place, i.e. it must only occur in positions where it is doing the proper work of a function. Universals, propositions, functions, facts cannot be *named,* and cannot occur in subject-places; they are not "things". The symbols which are concerned with them are never simple, and do not name them. E.g. *redness* is introduced by "the meaning of 'x is red' whatever x may be". This is Wittgenstein's theory and I am sure it is right.

Therefore, Russell's whole theory about our knowledge of forms cannot be inserted in his traditional epistemological way of explaining our immediate knowledge of the "genuine" indefinables, as for instances he told us in 1903. Thus, this knowledge cannot no longer be "acquaintance", as he recognized later in the same letter. However, Russell did not provide us with any alternative, apart of insisting that this knowledge has nevertheless to be immediate.[16]

---

[16] In the last lecture of *1914* Russell openly recognizes that logical constants, being ultimately forms (or at least being "formal"), are not objects, which I think is other way to admit that Wittgenstein was right, as he also explicitly says:

"If the theory that classes are merely symbolic is accepted, it follows that numbers are not actual entities, but that propositions in which numbers verbally occur have not really any constituents corresponding to numbers, but only a certain logical form which is not a part of propositions having this form. This is in fact the case with all the apparent objects of logic and mathematics. Such words as *or, not, if, there is, identity, greater, plus, nothing, everything, function,* and so on, are not names of definite objects, like 'John' or 'Jones,' but are words which require a context in order to have meaning. All of them are *formal,*

Russell continued his arguments in 1914 with his usual attacks against the subject predicate form of propositions. Yet propositional functions, the basis of *Principia,* are essentially based on them, and can only be described by properties, which are expressed by predicates. Russell also said that the subject-predicate view is infected by mysticism and idealism, but, as we have seem, his own treatment of forms as almost ineffable realities which are more or less a product of our minds was the one admitted in 1913.

A rather popular treatment of relations and the usual arguments in favour of asymmetrical relations follow. However, the claim that "the existing world consists of many things with many qualities and relations" (1914, 60) is not followed by any explanation as to how is it possible that relations, claimed to be mere incomplete symbols in *Principia,* can be real constituents of the world. The possible response that relations in *Principia* were only relations in extension is not acceptable, for we had the same with classes (or propositions) in that work, then why not to regard classes "in intension" as further constituents of the world? The truth is that Russell was forgetting that all formal concepts are fictions expressed by incomplete symbols, including of course properties.

I think that is why Russell's introduction of qualities and relations as "facts" explains nothing, while their epistemological status as to the possible correspondence between propositions and facts is not clarified either. This is really understandable, as any attempt to state that correspondence was abandoned as impossible in 1913 thanks to Bradley's and Wittgenstein's criticisms. And I think that is why the description of propositions as "forms of words", which can be true or false, is not followed by any attempt to relate propositions and facts through assertions, although the traditional theory that facts are "objective" is also added, with no further treatment of the obvious difficulties.

Also, we find even the explicit claim that looking for *forms* is the purpose of philosophy (1914, 189-90):

> But in philosophy we follow the inverse direction: from the complex and relatively concrete we proceed towards the simple and abstract by means of analysis, seeking, in the process, to eliminate the particularity of the original subject-matter, and to confine our attention entirely to the logical *form* of the facts concerned. [...]

---

that is to say, their occurrence indicates a certain form of proposition, not a certain constituent. 'Logical constants,' in short, are not entities; the words expressing them are not names, and cannot significantly be made into logical subjects except when it is the words themselves, as opposed to their meanings, that are being discussed." ([Footnote:] See *Tractatus Logico-Philosophicus,* by Ludwig Wittgenstein (Kegan Paul, 1922).) This fact has a very important bearing on all logic and philosophy, since it shows how they differ from the special sciences. But questions raised are so large and so difficult that it is impossible to pursue them further on this occasion."

> While mathematics, starting from comparatively simple propositions, seeks to build up more and more complex results by deductive synthesis, philosophy, starting from data which are common knowledge, seeks to purify and generalize them into the simplest statements of abstract form that can be obtained from them by logical analysis.

Which, by the way, is very similar to the theory maintained in "On scientific method in philosophy" (in 1918a, 84-5), where Russell called his philosophy "logical atomism or absolute pluralism".

Finally, we have clear signs that the multiple theory of judgment is more or less maintained, or at least not completely rejected, mainly because Russell does explain the nature of judgment precisely as an instance of a problem which was solved thanks to the discovery of a new form: that of the multiple relation (1914, 66 ff):

> The case of judgment demands the admission of more complicated forms. If all judgments were true, we might suppose that a judgment consisted in apprehension of a *fact,* and that the apprehension was a relation of a mind to the fact. From poverty in the logical inventory, this view has often been hold. But it leads to absolutely insoluble difficulties in the case of error. Suppose I believe that Charles I died in his bed. There is no objective fact "Charles I's death in his bed" to which I can have a relation of apprehension. Charles I and death and his bed are objective, but they are not, except in my thought, put together as my false belief supposes. It is therefore necessary, in analysing a belief, to look for some other logical form than a two-term relation.

Before that, I am unable to see any weight in the usual claim that Russell "abandoned" the multiple theory in 1913 because of Wittgenstein's criticisms.[17] As a

---

[17] Russell seems to have maintained some sort of multiple relation theory in his lectures in America. The following are some notes from V. Lenzen's "Notes on Russell lectures", which were taken in March 1914 (and are based chiefly on *1913* and *1914*), that is to say, once Russell had abandoned *1913* and, supposedly, the theory of judgment it contained. In Lenzen's notes we can read, for example, about propositional attitudes as involving not a dual but a multiple relation:
"Judgment: all objects must be things with which you are acquainted.... Acquaintance with universal —logical form of occurrence— not same as acq. with particulars. Possibility of error in any cognitive occurrence shows that occurrence is not dual relation.... I believe Jones hates Smith -single fact- contains 2 verbs. Constitutes oddity of propositional thought [...] logical form of occurrence is different from that of presentation."
Lenzen's term paper dealt precisely with Russell's theory of judgment, and it contained two main criticisms: judgment cannot be a relation, for (i) truth *is* a relation; that is why we say there are true judgments; (ii) relations are universals, while judgment is a process in time. Russell's reply, under the form of notes added to the paper, says: "*Judgment* is a relation, *a judgment* is not a relation. Thus *man* is a universal, but *a man* is not. Your argument (...) on this point sins against philosophical grammar". Also: "'A judgment' will

whole I have then to conclude that Russell made no progress in trying to solve the real problems underlying all his rather loose talk of relations.

"The philosophy of logical atomism" (1918b) was Russell's last attempt to maintain a consistent theory before officially abandoning the multiple theory of judgment; yet we find again exactly the same unsolved problems in those lectures. The constructive doctrine is as usual, with only the systematic language of "facts", which are supposed to be the objective counterpart of propositions as linguistic realities. As for the old convictions that complexes are composed of terms and concepts, and that predicates are mainly monadic relations, they are repeated again. This is done by saying that atomic facts have two kinds of components. A first one is expressed by a verb representing a quality or predicate (or by an adjective in case of monadic relations), or a relation (a dyadic relation, a triadic one, and further). A second kind of component consists of the terms of the former relations, which are to regarded as "particulars", and are supposed to be expressed by names (1918b, 199). Likewise, predicates and relations, as occurring in facts, can only take place as such predicates and relations, and not as subjects, in spite of some misleading verbal usages. However, although this is claimed on the basis of the theory of types (1918b, 205-6), we already know that there is hardly any compatibility between this theory and the admission of forms, which takes place in the following.

Regarding forms, the same idea of constituting an inventory (which appeared in 1914) is introduced, by only replacing "forms of propositions" by "forms of facts" (1918b, 216). This is presented as a "realistic bias", despite the need for providing an account of false "facts" in terms of some kind of multiple relation theory, which, as we have seen, can hardly avoid to be committed to some form of idealism. And this multiple relation theory is *still maintained here* (1918b, 224):

> It is not accurate to say "I believe the proposition p" and regard the occurrence as a twofold relation between me and p. The logical form is just the same whether you believe a false or a true proposition. Therefore in all cases you are not to regard belief as a two-term relation between yourself and a proposition, and you have to analyse up the proposition and treat your belief differently. Therefore the belief does not really contain a proposition as a constituent but only contains the constituents of the proposition as constituents.[18]

---

be a positive fact in which the principal relation is *judging;* but a judgment is not itself a relation. What is related to an objective is a judgment, not a judgment". Thus, Russell does not confess his strong doubts concerning the multiple relation theory after Wittgenstein's Bradleyan criticisms, but he seems to continue to maintain the theory rather *explicitly.*

[18] For, as stated before, "Every fact that occurs in the world must be composed entirely of constituents that there are, and not of constituents that there are not" (1918b, 220).

This presupposes that "propositions are nothing" (*ibid.*), and therefore that once again we have only a change in the terminology. Where we had before the judging complex and the secondary complex, we have now a belief apparently containing a unity as one of its components (the proposition), and a fact, which can or cannot be expressed by the proposition.

This does not mean, however, that Russell once again did accept that the judging complex (here the belief) can be reconstructed through some sort of map, as the one presupposed in the usual scheme of the multiple relation theory. Now Russell says, according to Wittgenstein, that the subject of the belief cannot be related to the relation taking place between the terms constituting the object of the belief. Such a map would be mistaken, and the wrong thing "is that in the symbol you have this relationship relating these two things and in the fact id doesn't really relate them" (1918b, 225).

However, Russell is here presupposing the impossibility to speak about the correspondence between belief and fact, while only an incidental reference to that problem can be found, under the claim about "the impossibility of putting the subordinate verb on a level with its terms as an object term in the belief" (1918b, 226). The ultimate reason of this impossibility was Bradley's paradox, which, as I pointed out above, was underlying Wittgenstein's criticisms. That is why a few pages later Russell admits that the reason why we cannot put the verb (the secondary relation) on the same level than its correspondent terms is because it is an instance of form, which, again, can by no means be a further constituent (1918b, 239):

> If you assert that "Socrates loves Plato", the form of that proposition is the form of the dual relation, but this is not a constituent of the proposition. If it were you would have to have that constituent related to the other constituents. Your will make the form much too substantial of you think of it as really one of the things that have that form, so that the form of a proposition is certainly not a constituent of the proposition itself.

The conclusion is certainly surprising, for Russell is trying to maintain, at the same time, that some sort of multiple relation theory of judgement has to be accepted to explain false propositions, and that the form involved in it cannot be regarded as a constituent of the complex in question. This was already maintained in the past, but the present novelty is that Russell explicitly regards Bradley's paradox as the one making the representation of the form as a constituent impossible. Yet this representation is somehow needed in the multiple relation theory, so I think he was implicitly admitting that Wittgenstein's prohibition and Bradley's paradox are one and the same.

A further link with the previous problems concerning the rejection of propositions involved in the solution of semantic paradoxes is here very important. It shows us that Russell was moving himself within the same conceptual world all the time, in spite of the different influences he was receiving. Thus, he says that at any rate the form "may possibly be a constituent of general statements about propositions that have that form, so I think it is *possible that* logical propositions might be interpreted as being about forms" (*ibid.*). Therefore, Russell seems to be thinking exactly of the same problem which led him in 1906 to dispense with propositions, but keeping general statements to state logical laws.[19] At the same time, he seems to be thinking of the same problem which, from 1903 onwards, he was somehow forced again and again to maintain that relations can and cannot be regarded as terms. The fact that Russell forgot about these rather obvious facts by immediately concluding that the question of the constituents of logical propositions constitutes "a problem rather new", is only a sign that he was thinking mainly in Wittgensteinian terms. Yet these terms, as we have seen, were still referred to Bradley's old objections against relations, predicates, or any other formal concept.

The extraordinary persistence of these ideas can even be shown once again through the arguments appearing in *Introduction to mathematical philosophy* (1919a, 198 ff), which can be regarded as the final attempt to philosophically founding logical complexes. We can read there that "the 'form' of a proposition is that, in it, that remains unchanged when every constituent of the proposition is replaced by another", although Russell clearly recognizes that he did not know "What are the constituents of a proposition". Thus, to explain forms in terms of replacing constituents without explaining how can we find them seems to be useless. Besides, Russell was perfectly aware that when a proposition contains variables and functions, the constituents approach is a failure, for we need also to consider "positions" in the proposition, which can by no means be occupied by any constituent.

In a book explicitly devoted to explain the logicist foundations of mathematics Russell obviously needed some definition of logic,[20] so he resorts to the usual "solution": "we may accept, as a first approximation, the view that *forms* are what enter into logical propositions as their constituents"; thus, "logic is con-

---

[19] See my 1989 for all the details about what is asserted here.

[20] In a letter of 1918 —to Frank Russell— Russell says that the most important things still to be reached at that stage were: (i) a theory of judgment; (ii) a definition of logic. The new orientation, as to the *solutions,* is now openly psychological, but the *problem* is still the same: the unity of complexes. I think is worth quoting the letter (Russell 1986, 249):

"'Facts, Judgments, and Propositions' opens out —it was for its sake that I wanted to study behaviourism, because the first problem is to have a tenable theory of judgment. I see my way to a really big piece of work, and incidentally to a definition of "logic", hitherto lacking. All the psychology that I have been reading and meaning to read was for the sake of logic; but I have reached a point in logic where I need theories of (a) judgment (b) symbolism, both of which are psychological problems."

cerned only with *forms,* and is concerned with them only in the way of stating that they are always or sometimes true". Therefore, Russell says, not only that forms are constituents, but also that we can have second order propositions in which we can refer to these forms and the rest of the constituents, so he is obviously ignoring again the two forms of Bradley's paradox (the relations-form and the truth-form). However, some lines before he himself had already stated that Bradley's paradox made the attempt impossible:

> Given a proposition, such as "Socrates is before Aristotle", we have certain constituents and also a certain form. But the form is not itself a new constituent; if it were, we should need a new form to embrace both it and the other constituents.

There are, however, some progress in these pages, mostly when Russell openly identifies the notion of form with that of logical constant, and also when, along the same lines, he says that it is possible to avoid explicit words for forms by trying to represent them only in a syntactical way. However, the syntactical approach, which was already implicit in Wittgenstein, led Russell to an explicit abandonment of any form of realism, and even to declare, in the 50's, that logic and mathematics are merely linguistic.

If I have to include here some conclusion, I can only add that this chaotic philosophy, usually called "logical atomism", can be hardly regarded as "logical" or as atomistic. It was mainly non logical, but rather the compromise between two purely *metaphysical* and incompatible traditions: that from Moore, and that from Bradley (ultimately through Wittgenstein). And it can hardly be regarded as atomistic, as it was mainly devoted to try to include forms in the ultimate inventory of the world, which was impossible as it was attempted by making forms (ultimately relations) to have a twofold nature, that of terms and that of non-terms.

Furthermore, we can even deny that that philosophy was ultimately realistic, for the unavoidable idealistic implications of the multiple relation theory of judgment, together with the monism implicit in the logical constructions of the external world, made it impossible to continue to maintain that complexes are to be ultimately regarded as genuine, objective realities. Under those problems complexes are, at most, the result of our direct intuition of forms, and of the further application of these forms to the terms we perceive in the world. But these terms, even when they are the simplest possible, can be further constructed out of relational structures, which ultimately are nothing but "incomplete symbols" (as they are made out of relations, and they are exactly like classes in their ontological status). Thus, the old realistic and atomistic world is replaced by an unavoidable idealistic and holistic one, where terms can no longer be opposed to relations, where relations can no longer be regarded as true terms (i.e. as logical subjects), and where the seed of the later abandonment of the distinction between subject and object was already present. The next, and last, stage was only the drawing of the consequences here already involved.[21]

5. Wittgenstein's way out: the formal concepts

On Wittgenstein's way out the first to say is that it is not enough to point out that the doctrine of showing is a reaction to the theory of types, as it has been correctly said by J. Griffin (1964, 19 ff) and Hacker (1972, 20). It is also necessary to add that the whole picture theory of propositions, which was mainly a result of the doctrine of showing, is properly the only possible way out to the problem of the nature of forms. That is way we can also say that the main result of the picture theory consists of "absorbing" forms until eliminating them (Pears *1977,* 189). And this, again, can be regarded as the first example, perhaps the supreme one, of the method of dissolving —rather than solving— apparent philosophical problems.

I think we can locate here the origin of the need for eliminating logical objects in general, and also the deep significance of Wittgenstein's idea that the theory of types has to replaced by a correct theory of symbolism. The "formal concepts" of the *Tractatus* would met this need, by breaking with any possibility of stating different ontological levels among facts. In the same way, Moore's first philosophy, which was partially inherited from Bradley, contained the thesis that judgment is nothing more that a *single* concept (no matter how complex it could be). It also contained the interpretation that the rest of "special" simple concepts (i.e., existence and truth), have to be located at the same ontological level than the rest of concepts, so that they can fulfil their main function merely by mere "presence", that is, without introducing new relations.[22]

---

[21] As I pointed out in my 1987b (and my 1991a, ch. 5), the inconsequences as to the evolution of the principle of abstraction were another element doubtless contributing to this general evolution towards holism and monism. Thus, this principle was reinterpreted, precisely at this stage (from 1914 onwards), as no longer capable of replacing properties by relations, but rather as only replacing properties by membership to certain classes. However, another surprising feature of Russell's evolution was his rejection (at least in practice) of Wiener's simplification of the logic of relations, which was presented as capable of being reduced to the logic of classes, through his ingenious definition of the ordered pair in set-theoretical terms. This can be seen as a further sign that Russell continued to think, despite all the inconsistencies we are pointing out, of relations in an intensional way, i.e. as objective realities capable of being regarded as independent from their terms.

[22] That is why it is not strange that Hope 1969 was already able to construct a whole list of similarities between the picture theory and Moore's early theory of judgment. As we have seen, it was Russell's own theory that which made this historical transition possible.

In the end, Russell's very paradox of classes must have arisen because of Russell's incapacity of overcoming the inconsistency existing between the class as one (the class-concept or property) and the class as many. Yet this paradox could not take place in Moore's philosophy, although this was certainly due to his difficult theory according to which the proposition is a *complex* concept but *one* concept, then necessarily simple in some sense. Besides, Wittgenstein's rejection of the —perhaps natural— supposition that formal concepts can also give rise to genuine differences of ontological levels would make the paradox impossible. Russell had tried to free himself of forms by transforming them insidiously into constituents of the propositions, no matter how different they can be as regard the rest of the other constituents. However, Wittgenstein was forced to absolutely dispense with forms, so he was also forced to dispense with any attempt of stating a correspondence theory, even after having tried to maintain himself within the general framework of some form of correspondence theory.

I think this idea is clearly expressed already in 1914: "I always said that truth is a relation between the proposition and the situation, but could never pick out such a relation" (1916, 20e), and this idea, which I think is underlying the picture theory of proposition, as well as the doctrine of showing, must have been the one which made the first rejection of any theory of types possible, which, in the end, made any linguistic hierarchy impossible too. That is why Wittgenstein denied that we can *say* anything about types: we are all inside the framework of symbols, and we cannot go outside them (1914, 190); and that is why "internal relations" (the only alternative to Russell's hierarchical atomism) appear so early in Wittgenstein as being relations between types, which cannot be expressed in propositions, but only shown in the corresponding symbols (1914, 202). Again, the link with Moore and Bradley seems to me to be clear, although it does not seem to fit very well with the supposed influence from Hertz's proto-picture theory.[23]

If, then, formal concepts were Wittgenstein's main recourse to escape from Russell's unsolvable problems, we must devote some space to its development in the *Tractatus,* as well as to their relationships to our main problem: the different forms of Bradley's endless regresses.

Wittgenstein introduced formal concepts in the *Tractatus* through the notions of formal property and formal relation (i.e., internal property and internal relation) of objects, states of affairs and structures, which are the opposite to genuine (external) properties and relations. Their basic characteristic is that they cannot be asserted by means of propositions, but propositions *show* them in representing objects and states of affairs (4.122). Thus, an internal property of a possible state

---

[23] McGuinness (1981, 61 ff) has insisted that Hertz's influence on Wittgenstein was not an empiricist one.

of affairs can be expressed only through an internal property of the proposition which represents it, and to this proposition we cannot refer directly (4.124). As for the internal relation between states of affairs, it can be expressed only by means of an internal relation between the propositions which represent them (4.125).

It is then when formal concepts do appear, as being the opposite to proper concepts, and as being characterized by formal properties:

> When something falls under a formal concept as one of its objects, this cannot be expressed by means of a proposition. Instead it is shown in the very sign for this object. (a name shows that it signifies an object, a sign for a number that it signifies a number, etc.)
> Formal concepts cannot, in fact, be represented by means of a function, as concepts proper can.
> For their characteristics, formal properties, are not expressed my means of functions.
> The expression for a formal property is a feature of certain symbols. (...)
> So the expression for a formal concept is a propositional variable in which this distinctive feature alone is constant. (4.126).

> The propositional variable signifies the formal concept, and its values signify the objects that fall under the concept (4.127).

> Every variable is the sign for a formal concept. For every variable represents a constant form that all its values possess, and this can be regarded as a formal property of those values (4.1271).

> A formal concept is given immediately any object falling under it is given. It is not possible, therefore, to introduce as primitive ideas objects belonging to a formal concept *and* the formal concept itself (4.12721).

Wittgenstein's final list of formal concepts is rather short: object, complex, fact, function, number, and a somewhat mysterious "etc.", but I think we can add, without further ado, other formal concepts like: name, predicate, proposition, relation, and perhaps even other like: truth, representation, logical form and similars.

At first glance this would mean, among other things, that formal concepts are some sort of second order concepts. This would explain that, contrary to proper concepts, they cannot be represented by mere functions, in which we can see that Wittgenstein seemed to follow Frege's view of concepts as functions.[24] And this, again, would mean, exactly like in Frege's paradox of concepts, that although we can say "x is a horse", by replacing x by the name of a horse, we cannot say "x is a function", by replacing x by the name —the symbol— of a function, because a function cannot be the logical subject of a proposition.

---

[24] For Frege a function-name is a sign whose essence is that of predicativeness or unsaturation.

Thus, the fact that Wittgenstein used a rather obscure notion of propositional variable seems to me to be something secondary, since he understood it simply as a variable whose values are the propositions which contain a particular expression (3.313). Thus, although a given expression determines a form (that which is common to a series of propositions), this presupposes the very notion of form, which is that which leads to the very problem which we are trying to handle. Therefore, we need to delve deep into the notion of form and, consequently, into that of relation (which underlies it), and this lead us directly to the old problems of the ontological status of terms, relations and relational notions (as for instance that which is presupposed in every theory of truth as correspondence).

Most of the authors dealing with the *Tractatus* seem to me to elude an explicit treatment of formal concepts (an important instance is Stenius), or they limit themselves to paraphrase the relevant passages. I would like to answer the question why formal concepts lack sense when they are misused. My answer is that formal concepts are inexpressible because, when one tries to use them as proper concepts, then paradoxes, vicious circles and endless regresses arise. Thus, although it is true that Wittgenstein follows Frege in the functional approach to concepts, in the end he tries to solve Frege's paradox precisely by ignoring his distinction between saturate and unsaturate expressions (entities), so rejecting Frege's "relation" of subsumption between objects as being ineffable.[25] Let us have a look at a few passages where Wittgenstein refers directly to those problems.

Such passages are a sign that it is precisely when we try to explicitly speak of logical form (and similar notions) that we can find in Wittgenstein what I have been calling Bradley's paradox of relations and Moore's paradox of truth. To recall them: Bradley's paradox of relations consists in denying that relations can be regarded as new terms which we can add to the terms already connected by them, on pain of having to accept new relations between those relations and the rest of terms, which lead us to and endless regress. Moore's paradox of truth consists in denying that truth can be defined through some sort of correspondence between a proposition and something more, on pain of having to show how is it possible that the proposition through which we state that correspondence can be true, which seems to require another correspondence with something else, so leading to and endless regress.[26]

---

[25] The relations between Wittgenstein's *Tractatus* and Frege's paradox of concepts has been usefully studied by Copi 1976, who was the first in pointing out Wittgenstein's ideas as being a "solution" to Frege's paradox.

[26] For Bradley and Frege this last paradox can be generalized to *any* definition of truth; see my 1999.

Both paradoxes are clearly related to one another: the second is a particular form of the first. Thus, when we try to *relate* a supposedly true proposition with something external to it, the need appears for transforming the stating of this *relation* into something true as well, which obviously would need the stating of a new *relation,* and so on, in an endless regress. Wittgenstein's solution is also common to both problems: there is no connection (relation, glue, etc.) between propositions and reality,[27] nor is there any connection between objects and concepts. The first version leads to the doctrine of showing, the second to the doctrine of formal concepts.

To my knowledge, the most important passages in Wittgenstein which can be taken as clear examples of the actual occurrence of both paradoxes are the following:

> The method of portrayal must be completely determinate before we can compare reality with the proposition at all in order to see whether it is true or false. ... Whether a proposition is true or false is something that has to appear (1916, 23e);

> The reality that corresponds to the sense of the proposition can surely be nothing but its components parts, since we are surely *ignorant* of *everything* else. If the reality consists in anything else as well, this can at any rate nether be denoted nor expressed; for in the first case it would be a further component, in the second the expression would be a proposition, for which the same problem would exist in turn as for the original one (1916, 31e);

> Propositions can represent the whole of reality, but they cannot represent what they must have in common with reality in order to be able to represent it —logical form. In order to be able to represent logical form, we should have to be able to station ourselves with propositions somewhere outside logic, that is to say outside of the world (*Tractatus,* 4.12);

> What connects the elements of a state of affairs? But have we any right to ask this question? the elements are not connected with one another *by anything.* They simply are connected, and that concatenation just is the state of affairs in question. After all, does the other conception explain anything? If cement is needed to hold the elements together —what is it that connects the cement and the elements? (Waismann 1967, 252).

The obvious conclusion is precisely the doctrine of showing: "Propositions cannot represent logical form: it is mirrored in them. [...] Propositions *show* the logical form of reality" (4.121). Under my interpretation, this simply means that if we try to represent logical form, we only obtain a new logical form, and so on, in an endless regress. To see this more clearly, it seems to me that we do not need any form of mysticism or ineffability, although is rather clear that Bradley,

---

[27] Or between names and things, in whose case Wittgenstein said: "that connection is not a relation but only the holding of a relation" (1916, 26e).

Frege, Moore and Russell were also involved in some form of semantic —and even syntactic— ineffability.

Much later, Wittgenstein would eventually reject even the atomistic philosophy which was the basis of the *Tractatus,* which seems to me to be hardly compatible with the pre-eminence of logical forms in that work, because that pre-eminence should lead to the pre-eminence of relations (then concepts and functions) over terms.[28] With that, we can notice the existing parallelism between Wittgenstein's most interesting problems and Russell's and Moore's internal difficulties in developing a pluralist way out to escape from Bradley's holism. It is precisely at this point where we can see more clearly the importance of Wittgenstein's rejection of logical indefinables (or logical objects). However, that rejection was obviously incomplete, for: (i) he managed to use the Sheffer functor to state what perhaps could be called an absolutely indefinable logical object, which was needed to reconstruct the "general form of propositions"; (ii) he maintained certain arguments to show that there *must* be simples. That is why the complete pre-eminence of the estructural, holistic viewpoint can be seen to begin precisely in Wittgenstein's rejection of any form of simplicity, which is definitive in the *Investigations.* Let us then finish by briefly considering that rejection.

In that work, simplicity is always relative to a particular context: there is no absolute simplicity. With this sole idea it is enough to destroy, not only the logic of the *Tractatus,* but also his theory of language, and with it any possibility to maintain the need for explicit, constructive definitions (like the ones involved in Russell's methods). The pre-eminence of the estructural (the formal) involved, then, perhaps even the explicit renounce to the possibility to throw the ladder once we have already arrived at our point of destination.[29]

Perhaps there is no passage in the *Investigations* which is a better instance of the rejection of absolute simplicity (then of linguistic and ontological atomism) that the following one: "'Simple' means: not composite. And here the point is: in what sense 'composite'? It makes no sense at all to speak absolutely of the

---

[28] The problem is similar in Russell, who defended a extreme form of atomism in *Principles* while, at the same time, needed also to give the ultimate pre-eminence to functions. For Frege the ontological pre-eminence of functions, and also of the context principle, was however clear from the beginning (see Kluge 1980).

[29] I vaguely remember reading something about the origins of this famous comparison in Mauthner, but it can be surprisingly found, almost literally, in Sextus Empiricus:

"[...] just as it is not impossible for the man who has ascended to a high place by a ladder to overturn the ladder with his foot after his ascent, so also it is not unlikely that the Sceptic, after he haws arrived at the demonstration of this thesis by means of the argument proving the non-existence of proof, as it were by a step-ladder, should then abolish this very argument." (*Against the logicians*, II, 480-1; Loeb edition, vol. II, p. 489).

'simple parts of a chair" (1953, §47). And it makes no sense because "we use the word 'composite' (and therefore the word 'simple') in an enormous number of different and differently elated ways", which makes impossible to ask with sense for the simplicity of something outside a particular language-game (*Ibid.*).

As a consequence, the connection between simplicity, analysis and the myth that a whole is necessarily greater than its parts (and is *constituted* by them) is definitively broken: "the concept of complexity might also be so extended that a smaller area was said to be 'composed' of a greater area and another one substracted from it". It is then the particular circumstances that which makes that "we are sometimes even inclined to conceive the smaller as the result of a composition of greater parts, and the greater as the result of a division of the smaller" (*ibid.*, §48). To finish, Wittgenstein even explicitly noticed the Platonic origin of the belief in simplicity (as he quotes the celebrated passage from the *Theaetetus*) and, although he does not point out the development of this idea through Aristotle, Locke and others, this is enough to destroy the primitive, absolute, raw elements of any form of logical atomism.

Bibliography

Anscombe, G.E.M. (1959), *An introduction to Wittgenstein's Tractatus,* London: Hutchinson.

Black, M. (1944), "Russell's philosophy of language", in: Schilpp 1944, 227-55.

Blackwell, K. (1981), "The early Wittgenstein and the middle Russell", in: Block 1981, 1-30.

Block, I. (1981) (ed.), *Perspectives on the philosophy of Wittgenstein,* Cambridge, Ma.: The MIT Press.

Copi, I. (1976), "Frege and Wittgenstein's *Tractatus*". Rep. in Shanker, S. (ed.), *Ludwig Wittgenstein. Critical Assessments,* vol. I, London: Croom Helm, 1986.

Griffin, J. (1964*), Wittgenstein's logical atomism,* Oxford: University Press.

Griffin, N. (1980), "Russell on the Nature of Logic (1903-1913)", *Synthese* 42, 117-88.

Griffin, N. (1985), "Russell's Multiple Relation Theory of Judgment", *Philosophical Studies* 47, 213-247.

Griffin, N. (1986), "Wittgenstein's Criticisms of Russell's Theory of Judgment", *Russell* 5, 132-45.

Hacker, P.M.S. (1972), *Insight and illusion,* Oxford University Press.

Hope, V. (1969), "The picture theory of meaning in the *Tractatus* as a development of Moore's and Russell's theories of judgment". *Philosophy* 44, 140-8.

Hylton, P. (1984), "The nature of the proposition and the revolt against idealism", in: J.B. Schneewind/Q. Skinner (eds.), *Philosophy in history,* Cambridge (Univ. P.)

Hylton, P. (1990), *Russell, idealism, and the emergence of analytic philosophy,* Oxford: Clarendon.

Iglesias, M. T. (1984), "Russell's Theory of knowledge and Wittgenstein's earliest writings", *Synthese* 60, 285-332.

Kenny, A. (1973), *Wittgenstein,* London: Penguin, 1976.

Kluge, E.-H.W. (1980), *The metaphysics of Gottlob Frege,* The Hague: Martinus Nijhoff.

Landini, G. (1990), "A new interpretation of Russell's multiple-relation theory of judgment", *Hist. Philos. Log.* 12, 37-69.

McGuinness, B. (1981), "The so-called realism of Wittgenstein's *Tractatus*", in: Block 1981.

Pears, D. (1967), *Bertrand Russell and the British tradition in Philosophy,* London: Collins.

Pears, D. (1977), "The relation between Wittgenstein's picture theory of propositions and Russell's theories of judgment", *Phil. Rev.* 86, 177-96.

Pears, D. (1989), "Russell's 1913 *Theory of knowledge* manuscript". In Wade Savage and Anthony Anderson 1989, 169-182.

Rodríguez-Consuegra, F. (1987a), *El método en la filosofía de Bertrand Russell*, Ph. D. thesis, University of Barcelona, x + 800 pp.

Rodríguez-Consuegra, F. (1987b), "Russell's logicist definitions of numbers 1899-1913: chronology and significance", *Hist. Phil. Log.* 8, 141-69.

Rodríguez-Consuegra, F. (1989), "Russell's theory of types, 1901-1910: its complex origins in the unpublished manuscripts", *Hist. Phil. Log.* 10, 131-164.

Rodríguez-Consuegra, F. (1991a), *The mathematical philosophy of Bertrand Russell: origins and development,* Basel, Boston and Berlin: Birkhäuser.

Rodríguez-Consuegra, F. (1991b), "El logicismo russelliano: su significado filosófico", *Crítica* 67, 15-39.

Rodríguez-Consuegra, F. (1991c), "A global viewpoint on Russell's philosophy". Essay-review of C. Wade Savage and C. Anthony Anderson 1989, *Diálogos* 57, 173-86.

Rodríguez-Consuegra, F. (1992), "El impacto de Wittgenstein sobre Russell", *Theoria* VII/16-7-8, 875-911.

Rodríguez-Consuegra, F. (1999), "Bradley, Frege and relatedness", *Bradley Studies* 5, 113-125.

Russell, B. (1903), *The principles of mathematics,* Cambridge (Univ. Press). Second edition with a new preface, London: Allen & Unwin, 1937.

Russell, B. (1910) (with A.N. Whitehead), *Principia mathematica*, vol I, Cambridge: University Press. Vols. II and III respectively appeared in 1912 and 1913. Second edition with a new introduction (by Russell) in 1927.

Russell, B. (1912), "What is logic?", 5 f. Rep. In: 1992, 54-6.

Russell, B. (1913), *Theory of knowledge*. Published in 1984.

Russell, B. (1914), *Our knowledge of the external world,* London: Allen & Unwin. Second edition with a new preface and some changes in 1929.

Russell, B. (1918a), *Mysticism and logic*, London: Longmans Green.

Russell, B. (1918b), "The philosophy of logical atomism", *The Monist,* 28-29 (1918-1919). Rep. in 1956. (1986, 157-244.)

Russell, B. (1919a), *Introduction to mathematical philosophy*, London: Allen & Unwin.

Russell, B. (1919b), "On propositions: what they are and how they mean?", *Proc. Arist. Soc.,* sup. v. II, 1-43. Rep. in 1956: 285-320 (1986: 276-306).

Russell, B. (1922), "Introduction" to Wittgenstein 1922 (1988, 96-112).

Russell, B. (1944), "Reply to criticisms". In Schilpp 1944, 681-741.

Russell, B. (1956), *Logic and knowledge,* ed. R.C. Marsh, London: Allen & Unwin.

Russell, B. (1986), *The philosophy of logical atomism and other essays, 1914-19,* ed. by J.G. Slater (*Papers,* vol. 8), London: Allen & Unwin.

Russell, B. (1988), *Essays on language, mind and matter, 1919-26,* ed. by J.G. Slater (*Papers,* vol. 9) London: Unwin Hyman.

Russell, B. (1992), *Logical and philosophical papers, 1909-13,* ed. by J.G. Slater (*Papers,* vol. 6), London: Routledge.

Schilpp, P. (1944) (ed.), *The philosophy of Bertrand Russell,* La Salle, Ill.: Open Court, 1971.

Sommerville, S. (1981), "Wittgenstein to Russell (July, 1913)...", in: *Language, logic and philosophy,* Proceedings 4 th. Int. Wittgenstein Symp. Vienna: Holder Pichler), 182-7.

Stock, G. (1972), "Russell's Theory of Judgment in Logical Atomism", *Rev. Port. Fil.* 28/4, 458-89.

Stout, G. F. (1915), "Mr. Russell's Theory of Judgment", *Proc. Arist. Soc.* 15, 332-52.

Wade Savage, C./Anthony Anderson, C. (1989) (eds.), *Rereading Russell: Essays in Bertrand Russell's metaphysics and epistemology,* vol. XII of Minnesota Studies in the Philosophy of Science, Minneapolis: University of Minnesota Press.

Waismann, F. (1967), *Wittgenstein and the Vienna Circle,* Oxford: Basil Blackwell, 1979.

Weiss, P. (1928), "The Theory of Types", *Mind* 37, 338-48.

Wittgenstein, L. (1913), "Notes on logic", in: 1916.

Wittgenstein, L. (1914), "Notes dictated to G.E. Moore in Norway", in: 1916.

Wittgenstein, L. (1916), *Notebooks 1914-1916,* Oxford: Basil Blackwell.

Wittgenstein, L. (1918), *Prototractatus,* London: Routledge 1971.

Wittgenstein, L. (1922), *Tractatus logico-philosophicus,* London: Routledge.

Wittgenstein, L. (1953), *Philosophical investigations,* Oxford: Basil Blackwell.

Wittgenstein, L. (1974), *Letters to Russell, Keynes and Moore,* Oxford: Basil Blackwell.

JOSEP-MARIA TERRICABRAS

(Theology as Grammar) Wittgenstein in Brackets[1]

Ludwig Wittgenstein (1889-1951) is considered by many to be one of the greatest philosophers, or even the greatest philosopher, of the 20th century. This recognition, however, is often more academic and theoretical than real, or philosophical, in nature. In actual fact, we have at our disposition some five hundred dissertations and doctoral theses on Wittgenstein's work that have been accepted by universities all over the world. Thousands of books and articles have likewise been published offering many different comments and interpretations on his thought. Nevertheless, as often lamented by Anthony Kenny, it remains true that the real influence of Wittgenstein on the philosophy that is actually taught in universities seems to be diminishing or is, in any case, of minor importance.

The phenomenon is not strange at all and was, in fact, to be foreseen. The academic world is always more inclined to dissect, analyse, repeat and compare than to create from new stimuli and models. This is, however, precisely what is demanded of us by great philosophers, and by Wittgenstein in an exemplary fashion. He desired neither epigones nor imitators, but simply that others would succeed in thinking for themselves.

For this reason, the best and most faithful contribution to Wittgenstein's thought consists of leaving behind scholasticism, and applying his philosophical outlook to the many questions – some already alluded to by Wittgenstein himself – that fill us with perplexity when we look around us.

It is in this spirit that I wrote the present article, not in the strict sense of Wittgensteinian hermeneutics, but by drawing on the thought of Wittgenstein and applying it to a field that calls for a less conventional approach than that which is customary.

Wittgenstein showed a deep interest in ethics and religion throughout his whole life. This interest was not merely theoretical, but was, above all, a concern that pervaded and troubled his very existence. This is clear from the fact that most of his thoughts and notes on religion and ethics are to be found in his personal diaries and journals, rather than on the pages that he himself had prepared for publication.

---

[1] Girona, on the 29th April 2001, fiftieth anniversary of the death of Ludwig Wittgenstein.

However, it is neither inappropriate nor venturesome to state that the – relatively small – bulk of philosophical observations by Wittgenstein on these subjects is firmly anchored in the body of his thought. It is precisely this conviction that brings me to comment on an annotation, which on first reading could seem quite unimportant and, moreover, only appears in brackets. I refer to that which appears in paragraph 373 of the *Philosophical Investigations* (PI). With this paper, I also hope to contribute towards exemplifying the huge scope offered by Wittgenstein's thought for the understanding of other disciplines, even those that seem to defy treatment of a strictly philosophical nature.

Paragraph 373 of the PI merely consists of this very brief text: "Grammar tells what kind of object anything is. (Theology as grammar)". The sharp, often aphoristic tone that Wittgenstein adopts in both the *Tractatus* and the *Investigations* can obscure the meaning of many of his thoughts. Needless to say, the observations placed in brackets are particularly difficult to understand, among other reasons because Wittgenstein used them as connecting links to comments made elsewhere, or as reminders of subjects that required further discussion.

In fact, it is important to bear in mind that, two paragraphs above, Wittgenstein wrote, "*Essence* is expressed by grammar" (PI, 371). Therefore, the intention of the parenthesis in paragraph 373 would appear to be as follows: after saying that essence is expressed by grammar and that it is in grammar where we see what kind of object anything is, Wittgenstein wishes to offer a practical field to exemplify all that. It is at this point that he points to theology. Wittgenstein maintains that in order to know who god is and what god is like, we must examine the grammar of the language of faith. The object of which theology speaks is to be discovered within the grammar of theology itself. In this paper, I would like to explain Wittgenstein's allusion and, thus, make it plausible. Wittgenstein does not intend to speak of words but of concepts, and he certainly does not say – contrary to some interpretations – that god is just a word, but rather says that what god is, or the way we understand what god is, can only be discovered through the grammar with which we speak about god. This statement is neither daring, nor iconoclastic but, on calm reflection, is actually quite obvious. After all, Wittgenstein thinks that in philosophy, as he conceives it, one cannot try to advance theses as such, because if one did, "everyone would agree to them" (PI, 128).

1. Grammar

In order to begin to interpret Wittgenstein's expression, let us first discuss the meaning of the term *grammar* in the *Philosophical Investigations*. This question is not an easy one because, although Wittgenstein does not automatically adopt the technical sense of the word *grammar* – as a set of rules defining a linguistic system – we cannot say, however, that he either ignores, or opposes, this technical sense when he uses the term. In fact, for Wittgenstein, the word *grammar* does not only designate a phonetic sound, or a syntactic structure, but rather the whole behaviour of an expression in language, or even *the whole life* of an expression in language. Wittgenstein himself confirms this interpretation in a passage from another manuscript, when he refers again to theology in a similar context: "How words are understood is not told by words alone. (Theology)" (*Zettel*, 144). It is clear that Wittgenstein is saying here that we can only understand the meaning of words not through the words themselves, but through the use or uses with which they are endowed in any given context.

For Wittgenstein, the function of grammar is to describe the use of words in language. In this sense, grammar bears the same relation to language as the rules of a game to the game itself, for grammar is the description of a particular language game. Another image will illustrate this point: grammar explains the real transactions of language, what is really happening in language. In the same way as there are games in the language of love, or in the language of the administration of justice, there are also language games that speak of god, or that speak to god. Theology studies these language games, and in so far as it clarifies, specifies, explains and expounds on these subjects, theology is presented as the grammar of the language of faith.

The main advantage of stressing the objective and public nature of grammar, and more specifically of theological grammar, is that the two particularly awkward, paradoxical and controversial difficulties of psychologism and essentialism can be simultaneously overcome. Wittgenstein was always strongly critical of both these theories of meaning. However, since neither theory has been abandoned and both still exert influence and carry a good deal of their original weight, in theology and elsewhere, we will now submit them to a brief examination.

According to *psychologism*, "what the speaker *wishes to say*" is what confers meaning on language. What is meant is what the speaker *thinks,* what the speaker *intends* to say, or the *mental* content he gives to words. In psychologism, language and reality are cold, inert elements. Language is vivified, given life and strength, and *connected* to reality by the mental action of *meaning* the words that we pronounce. This meaning fills the words with content. Psychologism is often present in the language of theology and religion: for example, in casuistry on the subject of the concept of "intention" in the administration of the sacraments or in prayer, or on the subject of debates concerning the will, the self-awareness or the knowledge of Jesus, or on the subject of religious experiences or on the acceptation of sentiment as a symptom of faith.

According to *essentialism*, "what *can be said*" or "what *can be understood*" is what confers meaning on language. What can be said is the real content of a word or a sentence, but in fact this content hides *behind* the words and is only *partially* expressed through what is actually said. An expression can always say much more than what it actually says. What an expression *can* mean – the *essential* meaning of the expression – is what in the last analysis gives meaning to that expression, beyond the partial meaning that anybody is capable of transmitting. This vision is also to be found in theological reflections: for example, in certain conceptions of transcendence, or when form and content are rigidly separated, in the tendency to internalisation, or in questions about the true essence of faith or about the real, or essential, meaning of fasting, praying, etc.

In the face of these two conceptions, Wittgenstein wishes to emphasize something very different. What confers meaning on language is not to be found *outside* or *apart* from language – neither in the mind of the speaker, nor in any deep, hidden essence – but rather *within* the grammar of what is actually being said *within* the grammar of the language game that is being played as we speak. We do not understand language by understanding, decoding, or grasping the intentions of the speaker – as claimed by psychologism – and neither do we understand language by seizing upon the hidden essence of the meaning behind the words – as claimed by essentialism – but rather by seeing how grammar works in the expressions used by ourselves and by other people. In fact, we only understand the meaning of psychologism and essentialism precisely because we understand the grammar of psychologism and essentialism, which, like any other grammar, is open and accessible to all. Or in other words, we understand psychologism and essentialism because we understand the language games that they set in motion.

Thus, the grammar of an expression is recognized by the way that the expression is used, or brought into play. And to recognize the grammar of an expression is the equivalent of understanding that expression. Because, how could anybody know what an expression really "means" if not by observing the grammar – the use – of that very expression? Perhaps we sometimes need to have the use of an expression explained to us, but if we eventually understand the expression, it is because we have understood the use for our own part and we are able to command it at will. Or, to formulate it in another way, we will not accept that the person who explains an expression has a much better and more reliable way of understanding the meaning of that expression, than the way that is ultimately understood by the person to whom the expression is explained. The psychologist and the essentialist, on the other hand, think that the intention of the speaker or the deeper meanings of language carry a higher significance than the very fact of speaking and acting with language. Wittgenstein rejects both these theories.

Psychologists would defend their position as follows: "*I* know what the expression really means, because it is *I* who *meant* it!" However, this only means "I know what I meant" or "I understand the expression". Likewise, "I meant 'X'" obviously does not mean "I said 'X'", in the same way as "I understand the expression" does not mean "The expression is understandable". The point is that psychologists are always faced with the problem of proving that their meaning has got across. We cannot therefore assume that the content with which we wished to endow an expression has been effective.

On the other hand, essentialists will insist that the ultimate level of meaning is to be found in a *deeper* content than that offered by the mere superficial form of the grammar that is used. Essentialists, therefore, make a distinction between "surface grammar" and "depth grammar" and to support their theory, call upon the authority of Wittgenstein himself, who makes the same distinction in paragraph 664 of the PI. In this text, however, Wittgenstein does not wish to distinguish between a superficial *meaning* and a deep *meaning*. Let us remember that for Wittgenstein, grammar is *not* the meaning, but the description of the meaning. In this sense, to speak of depth grammar, or surface grammar, is not the same as speaking about deep or superficial meanings. In fact, Wittgenstein wrote his works precisely in opposition to depths of this kind. Thus, by "depth grammar", Wittgenstein is *not* referring to a supposedly original or primitive meaning of words, according to which, the words that we use would have a deep, basic, root sense from which we would extract the meaning to give to our expressions.

Contrary to this theory, Wittgenstein's distinction in paragraph 664 of the PI reiterates that we should not jump to hasty conclusions as to the sense of the expression from its mere apparent form, for example, from its syntactical form. The reason for this is that the syntactical form, for example, is only a part of the grammar of the expression. In order to fully understand the sense, we have to give our attention to the *whole* grammar of the expression and, therefore, to the effective use of the expression. (For example, we could use an interrogative in the sense of an imperative, as when we say, "Would you close the door?" in the sense of "Close the door!") The mere superficial form of the expression, with its apparent similarity to other expressions, can lead us into all sorts of false analogies and misconceptions. Wittgenstein uses the term *depth grammar* to describe this *effective* use of expression. In order to understand an expression, however, it is not necessary to go "deeper" than the expression itself. Depth grammar does not therefore refer to a nucleus of deep, hidden meaning – to be found beyond and in spite of the words themselves – but rather refers to the effective working of words in language. Thus, those who believe that there is a depth grammar of the word of faith, an essential, unchanging and unchangeable grammar, lying beyond all linguistic practice of expression of faith, are defending a position that is in open contradiction with the Wittgensteinian sense of "depth grammar".

2. Theology and ontology

It is now easier to understand that paragraph 373 of the PI belongs to the very heart of Wittgenstein's ontology. Wittgenstein maintains that grammar itself always says – and demonstrates – what it is speaking about. Given that essence is expressed by grammar, we can tell from the real use of grammar what kind of object we are up against. Wittgenstein refers to theology as a clear example of the foregoing, since the grammar of theology tells us what theology is all about and in doing so, shows the enormous difference that exists between the object of theology and, for example, the object of physics or mathematics.

It is true that philosophers cannot venture to say what the grammar of theology is, and even less, what it *ought* to be. Nevertheless, it is interesting to note that not even theologians themselves can say this. Only the grammar of theology can tell us, innocently and without prejudice, what it is, what it is all about. Grammar must always introduce itself and grammar must always speak for itself. Of course, theologians may reflect on the grammar that they use and make valuable observations on that point. However, this in no way changes the grammar that theology actually uses.

For this reason, as opposed to the psychologistic and essentialist conceptions, it is always appropriate to distinguish between what *is intended* to be said, what *can* be said and what in fact *is said*. The place that shows what is said and what is meant is the grammar of the corresponding language game. This is not by any means to claim that what happens in grammar is always, or even often, something absolutely clear, coherent and well rounded. Expressions insinuate some things, silence some other things and leave some things open-ended. In a language game, when these insinuations and possibilities in the use of an expression are made patent, then they become incorporated in the grammar of the expression, but always just as what they are, that is, as insinuations and possibilities. Only a clumsy mixture of categorical differences would claim that an expression "really" *meant* this or that, simply by virtue of the fact that it *could* mean this or that.

The characteristics of theological, or religious, language should not be sought at any special depth which could only be reached by going through grammar to a place beyond grammar. The characteristics of theological language, or of theology itself, must be deposited *within* the grammar of theology. All this, however, only applies to the grammar of theology, not to the theology of grammar. In the theology of grammar – towards which the essentialist vision precipitates – theology is *about* language and *about* grammar. When we refer, on the contrary, to the grammar of theology, we are *not* claiming a grammar *about* theology, but rather considering the grammar that has been developed by theology itself, the grammar that is expressed in theology.

What is relevant for faith, or for reflection on faith, is also seen in the way that faith is shown, or in the way that reflection is manifested. The relevant experiences, the feelings, associations and expectations are also shown in the grammar. And if they are not shown in some way, then theoretically there is no reason to accept that they still play a hidden but important, or maybe even decisive, role. In such a case we should ask what, if anything at all, is meant by the fact that something that is not shown in any way in a language game is, nevertheless, *relevant* for *this* language game.

For theology it is of the greatest importance to emphasise the public character of grammar, especially in view of the importance – according to 1Pet 3,15 – of accounting for faith, both to others and to oneself. And accounting for faith means accounting for the grammar of faith, not just for the word "faith". At this point an important distinction appears between knowledge of the grammar of faith and faith itself. What is essential in faith is, of course, believing, that is, *applying* the grammar of faith and not merely *knowing* how to apply it. (Likewise it is the person who applies the grammar of counting who is said to be counting and not the person who merely knows this grammar.) Those who accept what believers accept, who show certain characteristics in their speech, in their silences and in their behaviour, while forsaking other characteristics, that is, those who consciously apply the grammar of faith – by accepting the consequences and emitting judgements, etc. – these are believers. There is no need for a decisive act expressly *in favour* of this grammar. The personal act of faith does not consist of a personal *decision in favour* of faith, but rather of the very fulfilment of faith, of the effective application of the grammar of faith. An explicit, pondered decision only occurs in very specific circumstances. In other circumstances, this level of reflection is not even considered; this is clearly seen, for example, in the absolutely evident, unreflective faith of a child or that experienced by a community where Christianity is a straightforward way of life.

The language of faith must thus be learned just like any other language, and can be learned, of course, in many different ways. It is not *necessary*, however, to have reflected on one's faith. That is to say, theological reflection on faith is not necessary for everybody's faith, although it must be admitted that all believers, *on being asked* about their faith, will show that they *have* some type of theology. However, the question about the reasons for belief is not primarily a question about the theology – or theoretical superstructure – that is held, but rather a question about the clarification of the grammar of faith. Thus the question on the justification and understanding of theology is not a question on meta-theology, but on the grammar of theology. When the grammar is made manifest, the foundations of the underlying language game also become manifest.

The fact that, following Wittgenstein, we emphasize the consideration of *existing grammar* should not make us forget that Wittgenstein proposes a method, which although not dogmatic, is not neutral. The method is not dogmatic because it does not require the adoption of any theses or results which are not given in grammar itself. The method is not neutral either, however, because its aims and purpose contain a whole philosophy. In this sense it is clear that the application of this method to theology, although it does not change the *existing grammar* of theology, does, however, really influence the way that we continue to do theology. Theology pays attention to new aspects, ponders over significant consequences or inconsequences, decides to raise different issues, etc.

To speak of *the* grammar of theology cannot lead to error as long as we bear in mind that there is not just *one* theology. Given this, it follows that there is not just *one* grammar of theology, but rather theological grammars. The clarification of the language of theology – or the language of faith – is also the clarification of theological propositions, situations, mental schemata, language games, with the help of which we can perceive the similarities and differences between different theological positions – or between different positions on faith – and moreover, of course, in relation to non-theological or non-religious language games. We can never assume that the gap between language games has to be rigid or clean-cut, but, on the contrary, we can often find transitions between seemingly different uses of language, or between different language games, and these transitions help us to understand that the players in dissimilar language games can in fact understand each other in spite of everything. The immense field of language, with its infinite range of possible games, is a field of very fine contacts, difficult boundaries and surprising reverberations.

Indeed, although we cannot assume that there are words with an *exclusively* theological meaning, we can, nevertheless, state that some words and expressions have acquired and consolidated a strongly religious, or theological, primary meaning. In this sense, the word "god" is a term of deep religious import. But this term can also have very different functions – for example, as a concept referring to any divinity or as the proper name of the god of a given religion – and can be used in many different grammatical senses. Thus, in a theology that uses an anthropomorphic image of god, the proposition "god has two arms" can make sense, but so can the proposition "god has four arms". In this theology it would also make sense to debate which of the two propositions is true. These propositions, however, are not refuted by the proposition "god *cannot* have arms", because this latter proposition only expresses a different grammar of "god", a different, non-anthropomorphic theology, for which it is senseless to speak about the arms of god in a literal sense or to debate how many arms god has. In fact, the theology that wishes to avoid, for example, being able *to possess* god or *use* god, has already partially determined the concept "god" and, therefore, god as well. The religions in which believers can use their god do not hold a worse image of god than that held by others. They have a completely different image of god, a completely different god, above all by virtue of the fact that, at least at a fundamental level, they already have a different grammar of "god".

It is true that, in some religions, the understanding of god is not aided by the attempt to point to god, simply because in these religions, god is not a physical object and has no correspondence with any physical object. (For this reason, the Christian statement that "Jesus is god" raises new – Trinitarian – difficulties for the language game with which believers refer to god, because this must be reconciled with another statement: "Nobody has ever seen God", Jn 1, 18.) This also confirms that the grammar of each theology is that which says what kind of object god is. And the fact is, that the object itself appears within the grammar that is used. This avoids the dangers both of a theology created "from the selfsame god" – which seems hard to defend – and of a theology as an image of the god that is known – which seems very vulnerable to any Feuerbachian-based criticism.

If it is grammar that tells us what kind of object anything is, then *god* is not a being outside faith, a being that must be reproduced by faith – or by theology – as well as possible, but rather fully belongs to the language game of faith. The god that is spoken about by the grammar of faith is the god that is adored by the believer. In their faith, believers do not only relate to a – true or false – image of god, but also to the selfsame – true or false – god. However, the incorporation of god into the language game of faith need not *necessarily* deny the independence, or transcendence of god. Whatever is meant by the "independence of god" or by the "transcendence of god" has to be *shown* by the independence or transcendence that is attributed to god within the grammar of faith. A transcendent god is shown, among other things, by the fact that *false* gods can be discovered *within* the grammar of faith itself. The grammar must permit contradictory visions of god, unsatisfactory statements about god, principles which can no longer be upheld or actions which must no longer be carried out. It is through such things that we realise that something does not work with a certain concept of "god" or with a certain god.

In fact, an essential characteristic of Christian theology is constituted by the fact that its representation of god can never be *totally* correct *on principle*. However, theology does not *know* that it cannot achieve any perfectly correct representation, because where could it have got this knowledge from? Or maybe it could achieve a perfect representation of god one day, in the future? But then, how could theology *know* that its representation of god was fully correct at last? However, if theology cannot know *that,* then neither can it *know* that it cannot offer any fully correct representation. This question of principle has nothing to do with "knowing". Theology does not know that, but rather assumes it. And this premise decisively determines the activity of theology, which will strive to constantly correct its own grammar. And if some essential characteristics of this grammar are not corrected, it is because theology also assumes, at the same time, that its grammar is, nevertheless, correct *in principle*. The *type* of constant perfectibility of theology demonstrates, therefore, something about its grammar and about the grammar of "god": among other things, the meaning of "god's transcendence".

It is obvious that a grammatical consideration does not consist of a subjective projection. It is clear that it is *humans* who conceive of god, but, in so doing, we present the conception which we hold of *god*, not that which we hold of ourselves. Formulated in grammatical terms: we know the difference between "us" and "god". All philosophical or psychological attempts to show that by "god" we are not really referring to god cannot contradict the real grammar, which *shows* that by "god" we certainly are referring to god. We can thus say that, by speaking of god as an object of faith, we do not have god *before us*, but that, on the other hand, grammar really does speak about *god*, as we understand god. When god is spoken about, each person does not only speak about himself or herself or about the word "god", but about god. (And this god can be a projection of oneself or the unexpected object of a revelation: whatever it is will be discovered within the grammar that is adopted to describe it.)

3. Theological grammar: principles and rules, versus hypothesis

Theological propositions can be, by their content, very varied: we can refer to historical, ethical, liturgical, dogmatic or juridical propositions, and so on. In order to exemplify the foregoing, I shall merely make a couple of observations on basic structures of theological grammar. A distinction will be made, above all, between principles and rules and these will then be shown in relation to hypotheses.

We can call theological *principles* those propositions that constitute the foundation of a theology and, therefore, essentially determine the nature of a theology. These principles make up a definite theological position. They are not, however, theological theses as such: theses are that which, *within* the grammar, can be debated; on the contrary, theological principles can be debated from outside the theological grammar – simply because they are not accepted – but not from within; theological principles, thus, are not theses, but rather premises, accepted things, that belong to the *dictionary* of theological grammar and which are *shown* by the very way in which theology is developed. It is absolutely essential that theological principles – or principles of faith – should be recognizable as such and should not be confused with other grammatical forms. For example, propositions like "god is love", "god can do no evil", "god is the goal of all human beings" do not state *fortuitous* properties of god, properties that god might be without, but rather essential properties of the concept that is held of god. This is why it is so disorienting when these grammatical propositions are formulated in such a way as to appear as experimental propositions, or as hypotheses that can be controlled, confirmed or refuted. Let us take the case, for example, when propositions of the type "Lord, bless this day!", "Give thy love to all human beings", "Oh God, may all thy works come to fulfilment" are formulated as prayers, the believer must bear in mind that they are prayers of faith, not prayers of petition, because otherwise the impression will be given that the alternative is possible and that, therefore, it is possible that what is asked for may not happen. Nonetheless, it is clear, according to the conception held by the believer, that *in any case* god blesses every day, that god loves all human beings and that god's own work will be carried out until the very end. Thus it is not only unnecessary but also impossible to pray *for that.* I do not mean that it is physically impossible to do this – in fact, many people do – but that it is not possible in theological grammar: indeed, those are *not* prayers in theological grammar, despite the fact that at a superficial level or as a subjective experience they may seem to be.

In like manner, the proposition "We can affirm that the Holy Spirit acts" could not be an affirmation because in the Christian tradition it is not possible to affirm or not to affirm that the Holy Spirit acts, but only to assume that it does or it does not act. If we assume that the Holy Spirit does act, then, in the definite case of the Holy Spirit acting ("You see? That was the intervention of the Holy Spirit!"), we are not so much pointing out *an* intervention by the Holy Spirit as the very fact of its *intervening*. And this intervening of the Holy Spirit can be pointed out in *all* the situations in the life of a believer, even in those where *no* intervention can be *seen.* At this stage, the believer is not making an affirmation but a profession of faith.

Certain characteristics of theological grammar that seem to be legitimate and even familiar in their surface structure in fact stem from an illegitimate use of theological grammar and have very disorientating consequences: theological grammar allows believers to ask god, for example, to spare their lives, maybe because they fear the possibility of a sudden death, and, for whatever the reasons, do not wish to die. Believers may pray that they be able to recognize god's love, but on the contrary, cannot pray for *god* to love them, because god cannot do otherwise than love them. This last sentence, however, does not express an empirical limitation to the omnipotence, or to the freedom of god, but is rather a logical determination – that is to say, a grammatical determination – of "god". And that means that the concept of "god" is used in connection with the concept of "love", but not in connection with that of "hatred" or "indifference". The non-realization of this very important distinction between empirical predication and logical determination is often the source of many far-reaching popular and theological paradoxes. (Let us remember, for example, the theological paradoxes related to the concepts of "omnipotence", "omniscience", "love", and "freedom" and to the problem of evil in the world or to predestination. If the very definition of "god" clearly excludes any link or connivance with evil, then no pernicious or harmful act can exist that can question the acts of god; in the same way if it has been excluded that god is anthropomorphic, no serious debate can take place on the relationship between the physical appearance of human beings, whether real or possible, and that of god.)

Thus, the grammatical principles of theology are obvious truths – or postulates – of theological grammar. I should now like to point out another grammatical form which, although also acting as a postulate, is not in fact a theological principle in the sense that have just been set out. I refer here to theological *rules,* which have an enormous theoretical and practical importance in any theology, and as a case in point, in Catholic theology.

Theological rules differ from theological principles in the sense that these rules do not belong to the premises of theology, but rather are actual theological *theses*. Nevertheless, the rules are not mere hypotheses but theses with a peculiar strength. Once these rules have been adopted as such, their solidity is no longer put to the test and they cannot be relinquished. On the contrary, they are presented as fixed, compulsory norms of grammar. A good example of these rules is to be found in the expressly formulated and well-defined ecclesiastical dogmas, or "dogmatic definitions", of Catholic theology. It is not always clear, however, where the boundary between rules and principles lies. Obviously, it cannot be seen by contemplating the expressions themselves but rather by looking at the overall role that they really play in theological grammar. This role, moreover, can change with the times. Some theological formulations only become basic principles after many years or even centuries, as is the case, for example, with some Trinitarian formulae. There are also some expressions that oscillate between the hypothesis and the rule, as for example, the classic distinction between dogma and the interpretation of dogma that attempts to maintain the separation between these two grammatical forms. There are also some expressions which can change from rules to principles.

Nevertheless, we can point to one essential characteristic in the physiognomy of theological rules – rules that are not reduced only to dogmas. These are considered to be, and are, true rules, not because they have been *proved* to be true, but because, for believers, they *cannot* be false. They are propositions that cease to be hypotheses not by having been confirmed as true hypotheses, but rather because in this respect it obviously makes no sense to speak in terms of confirmation or falsification. Thus, rules are unconditionally true propositions. They are not, on the contrary, analytical propositions. We are not speaking here about propositions that are necessarily true – in other circumstances they might not have been recognized as rules – but rather about propositions recognised as *unconditionally* true. For believers, these become rules among the many other rules that exist in their vision of the world. Given that the confirmation or falsification of these rules is not an issue, believers can thus say that they cannot be mistaken and this means that the term "error" has no place and no space in these rules. Thus, for example, the Catholic formula "The Pope is infallible when he speaks *ex cathedra*" can seem acceptable or unacceptable, meaningful or meaningless, adequate or inadequate, appropriate or inappropriate, but whether it is true or false cannot be debated because it is a *rule*. Thence the proposition "The Pope is *not* infallible when he speaks *ex cathedra*" is merely the *formal* negation of the first proposition. The speaker, however, is not really putting forward an antithesis to the first proposition (as in "The Pope *is* fallible when he speaks ex cathedra"), but expresses a rejection of the first proposition, a rejection of accepting that proposition *as a rule*.

Nevertheless, the debate on this type of proposition is often carried out in such a way that it appears to be about predicative principles, or about experimental propositions. To do this is to underrate the distinction between a theological proposition based on experience and a theological rule. In this sense, the expression "The Pope is infallible" is not a proposition that attributes any extraordinary quality to the Pope but rather a proposition that attributes a peculiar role to the Pope within the Church. The apparent similarity of the rule "The Pope is infallible" with the proposition "Mr X is extraordinarily punctual" – which is, effectively a proposition based on experience – can often cause confusion among speakers. In fact, the grammars of both expressions are quite different; that is to say they work in quite a different manner in both expressions. The statement "Mr X is extraordinarily punctual" is a prediction which can be proved to be true or false: it can just as easily be affirmed that Mr X is indeed very punctual as it can be concluded at any given moment that Mr X is no longer as punctual as he used to be. On the other hand, with the proposition "The Pope is infallible" there is no prediction being made of which the truth or falsity can be proved. This latter sentence is not affirming that, having taken into consideration all the dogmatic proclamations of the future, it will be stated that the Pope will have never made a mistake. The proposition says rather that there is no need to wait for any future experience, because such experience could neither confirm nor contradict the proposition. The proposition does not say that the Pope *will not* err, but rather that he *cannot* err. Error is thus not excluded by experience, but by logic, that is, by grammar.

Let us now fall back on an example that Wittgenstein himself proposes in page 67 of *The Blue and Brown Books*: when we play chess, a pawn cannot be promoted to a king, not even by mistake; whoever accepts this movement is not saying that the game of chess is wrong, but only that other rules and another game are preferred and that these may be more interesting than chess. Likewise, believers can abandon, at any given moment, a rule that they had previously accepted. They will do this, for example, if they value certain things as a refutation of the rule. By doing so, however, they are conferring another value and a different status on the former rule. Then the rule no longer serves for these believers as the ultimate orientation in the grammar of faith, but has become a proposition based on experience – or maybe a hypothesis – that seeks its place within the system. A change of status like this is produced when certain rules lose their force – perhaps not in theory but certainly in practice – or when they are forgotten or when they lose their relevance as rules.

4. Inconclusive epilogue

From this Wittgensteinian perspective – outlined from paragraph 373 of the *Philosophical Investigations* – theology is the grammar of speaking about god. This grammar, like any other grammar, tells us about the objects that we speak about, how we see them, how we want to treat them. However, as grammar is not the language game that is played, but rather the description of the language game, theology does not become confused with faith. The complex relationship between theory and practice is then once again shown. Language games are not played in any prescribed way but neither are they played arbitrarily. In this case, faith not only always has a language with which to express itself, but also needs grammatical (theological) formulae in order to express itself. In the same way as it does not seem possible to separate thought from language, it does not seem possible either to separate faith from the grammar of faith.

However, since there is not just one language game of belief, since not even every believer adopts the same – or the only – language game, it is as well to bear in mind that theological grammar is in constant contact with infinite other grammatical forms that are present in the lives of believers and non-believers. It is true that Wittgenstein has no interest in detaching and isolating grammars but rather wishes to compare and relate them. "The language-games are rather set up as *objects of comparison* which are meant to throw light on the facts of our language by way not only of similarities, but also of dissimilarities" (PI, 130).

And it is true – as Wittgenstein also says in his *Remarks on Frazer's Golden Bough* – that, in order to understand and be understood, we always "must plow through the whole of language"[2].

---

[2] Rush Rhees (1967), *Bemerkungen über Frazers* The Golden Bough, Synthese 17, 240.

ALEJANDRO TOMASINI BASSOLS

Wittgensteinian Considerations about Time

I. Time and Conceptual Chaos

Philosophical puzzles may be classified from different points of view, one being, I suggest, their degree of difficulty. From this perspective, time strikes us as a philosophically frightening subject. Indeed when for the first time we approach the subject and try to grasp its essence or nature, we can't help shuddering. A way of showing that time does have a highly complex character is to point to the huge variety of metaphors, puzzles and theories it has given rise to. This in turn would explain why the views about time advocated by classical philosophers may be both attractive and mutually incompatible. The diversity of conceptions and theses produced in connection with time is indeed amazing. The idea of time has been understood as directly got from experience, but also as a construct or as pointing to something unreal, to a mere illusion; time has been visualized as a special kind of fluid, a sort of container in which objects lie, as an epistemological structure and therefore as something mental in character, and so on. Thus it is understandable that in a first approach we should feel completely lost as to how to take it and what to say about it. Let us recall the much quoted passage by St. Augustine: "What, then, is time? If no one asks me, I know: if I wish to explain it to one that asketh, I know not".[1] This is unmistakably a clear sign that the notion of time is a marvelous source of philosophical confusion.

In this essay I shall assume that any philosophical theory, regardless of its subject matter, is the outcome of a confusion, of a misunderstanding. Indeed, the fact that no universal agreement with respect to a particular philosophical topic has been reached reveals that so far it has turned out impossible to state clearly the rules of use for the term in question. The general situation may be presented as follows: the more complex the rules of use of a given term are, the easier it is to privilege one particular aspect of the relevant concept and, accordingly, the more will philosophical theories proliferate, all of them being of course mutually incompatible. Metaphors concerning time privilege one particular aspect of the concept and by employing them speakers show which particular aspect strikes them as the most representative, as the decisive one. Thus if we speak of time as a river, we may be willing to emphasize the continuous character of our tempo-

---

[1] St. Augustine, *Confessions*, Book XI, sects. X-XXXI, in: *The Philosophy of Time*, edited by Richard M. Gale (New Jersey: Humanities Press, 1968), p. 40.

ral measurements or perhaps the idea that with respect to temporal series it makes no sense to point to a beginning or to an end. Nevertheless, it should be clear that no image or metaphor, however fortunate, is tantamount to a conceptual elucidation. They are rather an easy linguistic mechanism to grasp or express in a plastic way a sector of the total meaning of a term. On the other hand, it is obvious that what many philosophers do (in particular those more influenced by the natural sciences), *i.e.*, to try to explain time by having recourse to the latest and most sophisticated scientific theory (*e.g.*, a physical one), is from a methodological point of view utterly unacceptable.[2] It is evident that in order to solve the usual puzzles connected with "time" theories like those are, in spite of their mathematical and technical structure, simply useless since they presuppose an intuitive or natural concept of time ("natural" in the sense of "belonging" to natural language), a concept elaborated prior to the concept constructed by, for instance, physicists. Therefore, the latter can be of no help for the clarification of the former.

The kind of elucidation we strive after springs not from a theory, however formalized it might be, but from an analysis and this can only consist of an examination of the use of the term, that is, of its actual application. The description of its application is what enables us to grasp its *grammar* and through this its "essence" or nature. Seen in this way, the original feeling of intellectual terror mentioned above now appears to us understandable but basically unfounded. In Wittgensteinian terms, the diagnosis is rather simple but nonetheless hits the target: it is the lack of a perspicuous representation of the grammar of the word 'time' (and of words that logically derive from it) which lies at the bottom of all the philosophical knots that trouble us. In other words, the rules of grammar for 'time' form a very complex structure, which cannot easily be visualized or grasped as a whole. That is why the concept of time is so easy to misunderstand. It is quite obvious that the grammar of 'time' is much more complicated than that of, say, 'table' and, accordingly, it is much easier to explain what tables are than to explain what time is. Incidentally, this shows that what are usually taken as "substantial" difficulties do get resolved by conceptual ones, since to understand what "things" are is something which emerges from our apprehension of the grammar of their respective concepts. Now all concepts, *qua* concepts, have exactly the same status, that is, they are all the same kind of thing, *viz.*, concepts. Therefore, they all have to be investigated in the same way. So philosophical troubles concerning the essence or nature of things are due to the fact that till Wittgenstein we just lacked a well characterized method of conceptual clarification and of the way it has to be applied since, as I have already said, the clue to the understanding of what the "thing" which interests us "really" is is precisely

---

[2] Hans Reichenbach, I believe, is a good example of this. See his *The Philosophy of Space and Time* (New York: Dover Publications 1958).

conceptual research or, in Wittgenstein's words, grammatical investigation. "Essence is expressed by grammar".[3] Obviously, Wittgensteinian grammatical investigation (in this case, about the concept of time) sharply contrasts, as we shall see in a moment, with conventional philosophical theories about time.

II. Some Puzzles concerning Time

Before attempting to exhibit and criticize, in the spirit of a mature Wittgensteinianism, some sources of difficulties concerning time, it will be useful to present briefly some of the well known enigmas about it. It is not my aim here to carry out a particular detailed description of the problems, but simply to illustrate the sort of complication this concept generates in order to contrast it with Wittgenstein's novel approach and diagnoses.

A) *Saint Augustine*. Perhaps the most perplexing of all puzzles connected with time is the one St. Augustine explicitly raises, namely, that of its unreality and (as a consequence) of its essentially mental nature, *i.e.*, its being an affection of the mind or, in his terminology, of the soul. There is a sense in which in this view time unavoidably becomes something unreal: since future is not yet and past is no longer, the only temporal reality has to be the present and, if we take the reasoning one step further, only the specious present. To talk of measuring time can therefore only mean to speak of a capacity of the mind to retain (thanks to memory) past events. Needless to say that the idea of the world associated with this view of time is absolutely unintelligible. The problem is: how to get rid of it?

B) *Kant*. The Kantian conception of time is well-known and has been (and probably will always be) the object of all sorts of analysis and discussions, although it is worth observing that at least in so far as the nature of time is concerned practically nobody has ever considered himself a Kantian. With respect to time, Kant makes two important claims:

   a) that (together with space) time is the pure form of intuition, and
   b) that time is the form of inner sense.

Kantian transcendental idealism, on the other hand, commits him to the view that we simply cannot know whether or not time is objective, in the sense of being real of things in themselves and not only of objects of possible experience. The only thing we can be sure of is that time is a necessary presupposition for

---

[3] L. Wittgenstein, Philosophical Investigations (Oxford: Basil Blackwell 1974), sect. 371.

the possibility of experience. Clearly this is alarmingly ambiguous. If what Kant holds is that the idea of an object, and hence of the world, is unintelligible if we are unable to establish temporal connections, although debatable his position is understandable. But if, as some seem to believe, the thesis Kant advocates is that had there been no minds then there would have been no time (as well as no space), then his stance is utterly unacceptable. On the other hand, the idea of time as the form of inner sense makes him fall into the grave mistake of trying to start from "the given" in order to construct public time out of it. Why and how should all individual minds coincide is something his philosophy never sufficiently explains.

C) *McTaggart*.[4] In order to maintain his astonishing view that time is unreal, McTaggart conjoines several thesis, all of them quite problematic. First, he assumes that time implies change and that change cannot be explained without the categories of past, present and future, as opposed to "earlier than" and "later than". Secondly, there is the idea that the categories of present, past and future are both essential to time and "unreal", since they lead to contradictions; it is also interesting to note, thirdly, that he makes use of an important metaphysical principle, called by Russell the 'axiom of internal relations', according to which relations are essential to their *relata*. That is why McTaggart feels justified in making picturesque assertions like "The sand of a sand-castle on the English coast changes the nature of the Great Pyramid".[5] All his claims and analysis can of course be criticized, but it is not our purpose here to discuss in detail his arguments but simply to state the core of his conception of time.

D) *Russell*. Russell holds different things at different moments, so that it seems impossible to get from his writings a single, coherent doctrine. In some texts, for instance, temporal relations as "before" and "after" are said to be known by acquaintance. "Thus we must suppose that we are acquainted with the meaning of 'before', and not merely with instances of it".[6] When we know a truth like 'a is before b' we of course are acquainted with both a and b, but we also know by acquaintance (although of course not in the same way, that is, through the senses) the abstract relation "being before than". This suggests that the categories "before" and "after" are more fundamental and logically prior to other temporal relations, like "past", "present" and "future", which apparently can be constructed out of them.

---

[4] J. M. E McTaggart, "Time", en: *The Philosophy of Time*, edited by Richard M. Gale (New Jersey: Humanities Press, 1968), pp. 86-97.

[5] J. M. E. McTaggart, Ibid., p. 89.

[6] B. Russell, *Mysticism and Logic* (London: Allen and Unwin, 1976), p.155.

This immediate knowledge by memory is the source of all our knowledge concerning the past: without it, there could be no knowledge of the past by inference, since we should never know that there was anything past to be inferred.[7]

However, in a slightly previous essay, Russell advocates exactly the opposite view. There he maintains that "before" and "after" are so to speak secondary or derivative categories, the fundamental ones being precisely "present", "past" and "future". The latter have to do with the relations between the subject and things outside him. Thus Russell introduces the dichotomy "physical time – mental time" and reserves 'mental time' to speak of past, present and future. His view is then that

> Although, in the finished logical theory of time, physical time is simpler than mental time, yet in the analysis of experience it would seem that mental time must come first.[8]

So which are the fundamental temporal categories is something very difficult to be clear about. The truth is that were we asked what is Russell's concrete position with respect to time, we would not know what to answer.

Of course, difficulties and contradictions like those just mentioned can be found not only in the thinkers just quoted, but in practically every philosopher who has dealt with the subject of time. I believe however that, thanks to his quite original method of dissolving philosophical puzzles, the mature Wittgenstein not only avoids the traditional kind of philosophical error, but gives us the elements to get rid of philosophical enigmas in a definitive way. It is debatable whether or not the same thing holds of the view advocated in the *Tractatus*. Let us first have a look at what young Wittgenstein had to say about time in his famous first book.

III. The solipsist view of time

This is not the right place to develop in detail an argument in favour of my interpretation of the *Tractatus* but, for the purposes I set myself, I think that a good test or way of showing that the interpretation in question is right is that as a matter of fact it enables us to give a satisfactory account of the passages of the book and especially of those concerning time. My view is the following: the *Tractatus logico-philosophicus* contains the best possible expression of the solipsistic picture of the world. That is, the book offers the best possible view of

---

[7] B. Russell, *Problems of Philosophy* (Oxford: Oxford University Press, 1980), p.26.
[8] B. Russell, "On the Experience of Time" in: *The Collected Papers of Bertrand Russell*, Vol. 7 (London: George Allen and Unwin, 1984), p. 64.

factual reality, logic, mathematics, science, values, knowledge, the meaning of life, etc., which could be elaborated *from the subject's perspective*. Clearly, in the philosophy of the *Tractatus* there is no place for others, just as history and the social character of language are simply ignored. Wittgenstein simply assumes that he speaks for the rest of us and that once we have grasped his meaning, we shall all agree with what he says for, putting ourselves in his place and repeating the sentences he wrote, we could easily confirm that what he says is true. There are multiple passages which confirm that the solipsistic *Weltanschauung* was indeed Wittgenstein's goal. In this respect, the *Notebooks* are particularly revealing too. He explicitly states there for instance: "I want to report how *I* found the world",[9] a pronouncement which doesn't allow any ambiguity at all; and, more brutally perhaps, he also says: "What has history to do with me? Mine is the first and only world!".[10] On the other hand, the explicit acknowledgement in the *Tractatus* that what the solipsist wants to say but cannot say is in this respect just as conclusive.[11] We all know, of course, that given the interpretative richness of the book, alternative interpretations will always be possible, but it can be argued that they will either leave unexplained many passages of the book or probably be incoherent or simply unconvincing. For the time being, I shall just point out, first, that my view fits perfectly well with some of the exegetical work which, in my opinion, belong to the best of all, *viz.*, Jaakko Hintikka's[12] and, secondly, that the solipsistic interpretation of the book enables us to give a much clearer account of what Wittgenstein says about time than alternative interpretations and that it does contribute to a coherent reading of the book as a whole. I shall try now to show that this is indeed the case.

The first thing to be said is that in the *Tractatus* Wittgenstein has not one but two different notions of time; accordingly, he distinguishes between what could be called 'objective time' and 'subjective time'. If, regardless of the way we characterize them, we accept this distinction, the solipsist's project with respect to time becomes immediately clear. Curiously enough, his goal is to establish the reality of objective time while rejecting that of subjective time. What Wittgenstein does is to argue in favour of the reality of time with respect to objects (since time, like space and color, are formal properties of objects, which are the elements of all possible worlds), while rejecting the idea of time as something we can have experience of. Subjectively time is unreal. His stance, as I shall try to make clear, is perhaps not as absurd as it could be thought of at first sight.

---

[9] L. Wittgenstein, *Notebooks 1914-1916* (London: Routledge and Kegan Paul, 1978), p. 82e.

[10] L. Wittgenstein, Ibid., p. 82e.

[11] L. Wittgenstein, *Tractatus logico-philosophicus* (London: Routledge and Kegan Paul, 1978), 5.62 and 5.621.

[12] See especially his book (written in collaboration with Merrill B. Hintikka): *Investigating Wittgenstein* (Oxford: Basil Blackwell, 1986).

In a passage filled with clear anti-realist intentions, Wittgenstein asserts that

> We cannot compare a process with 'the passage of time' – there is no such thing – but only with another process (such as the working of a chronometer).
> Hence we can describe the lapse of time only by relying on some other process.[13]

It is difficult to say whether or not this pronouncement implies that time as such is unreal, but what is clear is that for Wittgenstein it is not an object of experience. Surely for us as knowing subjects there is no such thing as time in the sense in which there are, say, tables or lions or, more generally, "objects" (whatever they are). The world has nonetheless a coloured-spatio-temporal structure. The point seems to be that the idea of a world would be utterly unintelligible were we unable to make temporal measurements ("after than", "future", "right now" and so on). So Wittgenstein seems here to be surprisingly near to philosophers like Aristotle, for whom time is basically the measure of change. Thus for Wittgenstein the concept of time serves solely to determine, calculate, manipulate, etc., the change processes of objects we meet with in experience; moreover, it is always to be understood by reference to some special, arbitrarily chosen, process. As a purely empirical hypothesis, it could affirmed that most probably the original process in the construction of the concept of time was the movement of the sun. In view of the latter's obvious importance for life, it had to be (and in fact it still is) by reference to it that the rest of processes and activities had to be measured. But whether or not it was like that it is completely irrelevant and, moreover, the object or process which functions as the axis of temporal reference may change. If, for instance, we wish to determine who won a race the framework of reference will no longer be the movement of the sun across the sky, but a watch or a chronometer. What could be called 'parameter processes' may be improved in order to meet the speakers' practical requirements. But all this seems to imply that the idea of time as something objective, composed of an ordered infinite set of real entities (instants), something *in* which objects are, has to be discarded. Contrary to Newton's assumptions, for whom time was a substance, for Wittgenstein the idea of time is rather the idea of a mechanism which is however necessary for the world to have a structure and to be intelligible. It could be thought that this is all that could reasonably be said about it. The solipsist Wittgenstein, however, has still something important to say.

Jacques Bouveresse has brilliantly stated the solipsistic idea of the world put forward in the *Tractatus*:

> For us it will suffice to note that the universe of the *Tractatus* is anyway that of a completely atomized one, not only spatially but temporally as well, in which there is no place for continuity and movement, a universe without events and history. [Translation mine, ATB][14]

---

[13] L. Wittgenstein, *Tractatus logico-philosophicus*, 6.3611 (a) (b).
[14] J. Bouveresse, *La Rime et la Raison* (Paris: Les Éditions de Minuit, 1973), p.47.

It is evident that for the solipsist the world is or rather *has* to be *now* the totality of facts, that is, the world includes now *all* the facts, *i.e.*, the facts that were, those are and those that will be. In this sense, to speak of past or future is to have recourse to mere linguistic conventions, useful forms of speaking to impose a convenient order upon the whole of experiences. But the point is that, strictly speaking, from the subject's point of view there is simply no such thing as duration, temporal reality, apart from the eternal present each "I" lives in. So it is indeed the solipsist who speaks through Wittgenstein when he asserts that "The world is *my* world".[15] This world is, however, submitted to logic; there is an order in it. The world, regardless of its being mine, is not a mere chaos, a random or chaotic collection of experiences. My (the) world is organized: some experiences come after others, some come before, some are simultaneous to others, but at every stage I group them together, I order them and have them organized. "Time" is needed to state our view of the world, but the self is, so to speak, fixed outside time. Thus time cannot be something different and above the ordered sequence of experiences, that is, of *my* experiences. Now there is a sense in which, by making Wittgenstein reject a realist or objectivist conception of time, partially at least, solipsism forces him also to get rid of the notions of past and future, as applied to the subject himself. Here Wittgenstein seems to have been prey to the same confusion which befell St. Augustine. From their common perspective, so far as the self is concerned, real time, the only time there can be, is a permanent or eternal present. The solipsist might argue that, on a purely linguistic plane, there is no problem at all: the only thing that has to be done is to put systematically the expression 'now' before the usual discourse. For instance, to say that Napoleon died in St. Helen is to say that I learn now (I hear or read) what is expressed in what I call 'past tense', namely, that Napoleon died in St. Helen; to say that tomorrow it will rain is to say that I calculate now that an event (*i.e.*, raining) described in what I call 'future tense' takes place, and so on. In this sense, time can be nothing else than a mere ordering of *my* experiences, of the world, that is, of the world of objects I encounter. This makes clear the content of the important proposition to the effect that

> If we take eternity to mean not infinite temporal duration but timelessness, then eternal life belongs to those who live in the present.[16]

Thus although undoubtedly the world has a temporal structure, so far as the knowing metaphysical subject is concerned, real time can only be an eternal present, enriched by the data of memory and states like expectation and this is nothing but the vindication of atemporality.

---

[15] L. Wittgenstein, *Tractatus*, 5.62 (c).
[16] L. Wittgenstein, Ibid., 6.4311 (b).

An obvious manifestation of philosophical confusion is that it ends up in a thesis which, as all of its kind, is openly paradoxical, counter-intuitive, opposed to common-sense and to the normal modes of speaking. Such is, probably, the final position reached in the *Tractatus*. However, I also think that it was Wittgenstein himself who prepared the tools to refute what was there maintained. Without debating explicitly with the *Tractatus*, I shall rapidly present the elements thanks to which the mature Wittgenstein put himself in a position to free himself from the simultaneously hypnotic and misleading effect of certain metaphors and modes of speaking and could thereby "retrieve time". But we have first to carry out some kind of analysis of this important concept.

IV. Notes about the grammar of "time"

Before presenting Wittgenstein's final view about time, let us quickly examine some expressions in which the term 'time' is actually employed. Let us take, for instance, the idea of "wasting time". What is this expression used for? A possible situation is the following one: someone has his life organized in such a way that his day divides itself into previously programmed activities. He knows what he has to do during the whole day and let us suppose that he sticks very rigidly to his time-table and plans. Let us further imagine that a friend calls him up and invites him to the cinema. The answer could be: "Look, I've got no time to waste!" Every normal speaker would understand perfectly well the situation and what is being said. What is not transparent at all is the philosophical interpretation of what this fellow *meant*. According to me, he must have meant something like "I'm busy", "I've already scheduled my day", "I can't change my activities for today", "I'm more interested in doing what I'm doing right now than in going to the cinema", and so forth. At any rate, there is something clear: the only thing the speaker didn't mean is what could be the literal reading of the expression. It is not a question of losing or wasting a piece of something called 'time'. To interpret 'I have no time to waste' taking as a model 'I have no marbles to play with' would be just absurd. 'Time' doesn't serve in this case to designate something which could be lost or gained. In this case to speak of time is basically to allude to a set of organized activities.

A second example would be 'to have plenty of time'. Once again, its literal reading is palpably absurd, since normally 'to have' and 'to possess' are equivalent, but what would it mean to speak of "possessing time"? Nothing intelligible. 'To have time' is used to indicate that one can carry out activities which had not been previously considered. If someone asks a friend 'have you got some spare time to come with me to the university?', what he is asking is something like 'would it be possible for you to include among your activities going with me today to the university?'. This example reinforces the idea that 'time' is not the name for something special or particular.

Let us imagine now a teacher who begins his narration as follows: "A long, long time ago, ...'. What could he possible be saying by that? What would such an expression be useful for to him? I think the answer is both simple and clear: he is pointing to a certain order in the events of the narration, *i.e.*, the starting point. This example is connected with other linguistic considerations to which I shall return later on. At all events, it should be clear that, as long as what is at stake is, say, a tale, 'time' could not possibly designate anything real, otherwise we should then be capable of speaking of a fictitious time, as opposed to a real one, and what on earth could that be? A sort of pragmatical reading of the expression is by far the most reasonable one.

Let us consider a final example. Let us suppose that during a political debate a member of a party says to a colleague: "Don't worry. Time is on our side". I don't think that, were we forced to impose upon this sentence a direct or literal reading, we would be able to say something sensible about its meaning and, *a fortiori*, it could not be possibly said of us that we did understand what was said. We would have to assume that there is a kind of medium in which objects and persons lie and that that medium would move in such a way (*e.g.*, as a pendulum) that the balance would incline in favour of someone. It is evident, I suppose, that to interpret in this way what is being said would just be crazy. What is meant is that certain events or changes will take place such that it will be possible for the common ideals to materialize, that sooner or later the efforts to achieve previously fixed goals will be fruitful, that the decisions taken were the right ones, and so on. That and not any other thing is what is meant by someone who uses the expression 'time is on our side'. Notice that it could also be used as a threat or as a warning. This, however, is not incompatible with his other, colloquial meaning, which is the one we are interested in here.

What can we infer from what has been said up to now? Several consequences, whose importance are worth taking into account. First, the examples suggest that *the concept of time is not a concept of experience*. 'Time' is not used to allude or to give expression to a particular, special experience. Against what was held by Bergson and others, I wish to maintain that *there is no such thing as the experience of time*. Here we certainly can accept what is said in the *Tractatus*. Secondly, the examples indicate that the concept of time is above all what could be called an *'organizational'* or *'classificatory'* concept. What does it help to organize or classify? Basically, our activities. The concept of time enables speakers to coordinate their activities, both potential and real. This seems to be, if not the fundamental one, at least one of the most important functions of this concept. Along with it another idea that comes in is that the core of the notion of time has to do with something public and that if there is another concept of time, a purely mental or subjective one, it will have to be taken as a merely derivative one. In summary, the concept of time is basically an operative one, characterized by a huge functionality, since it serves to coordinate no more and no less than the *whole* of activities and experiences of the totality of speakers. It is only on such a basis that it becomes possible to retrieve all sorts of times (mental time and physical time, past and before, biological and imaginary times, etc.), for all of them spring in one way or another from our natural concept of time.

V) The retrieving of time

A solipsist that, as Wittgenstein in the *Tractatus*, acknowledges the reality of the world, would be quite satisfied with a twofold conception of time: on the one hand the idea of an objective structure for objects and, on the other hand, the idea of an eternal present, of timelessness, for the knowing subject. The trouble is that this does not seem to be a coherent global position. It is perhaps true that if the world is "my" world, temporal notions like before or after suffice to organize the whole of my experience, but if I take into account (as it seems I should) that there are other sentient beings, beings who think, reason, have intentions, desires and so forth just as I do, then the solipsist's time (call it 'mental', 'phenomenological', 'subjective' or 'experienced') will be very difficult to accommodate with all these private times in a coherent way and, most probably, such time will turn out to be nothing else than a philosophical myth. Moreover, such time seems to be logically and factually independent of common time and thus we are left with two independent sets of temporal notions. Indeed, the problem with the solipsist's time is exactly the same as the problem of trying to reconstruct the external world starting from one person's perceptions, memories and so on (together with the laws of logic). We nowadays know that such programs are a complete failure and this applies to time as well. What is needed is a concept of time which from the beginning would embrace in a single whole, among other things, other people's times. We need, therefore, one temporal net which would contain both the time of objects and the time of persons. In other words, we need an all-embracing objective concept of time. Now from my point of view, this shared structure is actually given by language and, in particular, by the verbs and their tenses. This concept of time is rather a kind of metrics, with different aspects, whose main point is to organize in a non-spatial way the shared system of speakers' activities and of facts identified by reference to those activities. In both cases we need all temporal notions ("before", "now", "past", "future" and so on). Let us see why.

Wittgenstein dealt in different stages of his thinking with the subject of time and, as Hintikka[17] rightly points out, his views are a function of his evolution concerning other subjects (object, meaning, rules, etc.). In particular, the

---

[17] J. Hintikka, "Wittgenstein on being and time", *Theoria* 62 (1-2), 1996, pp. 3-18.

changes in his conception of language did alter his conception of time and contributed to its improvement. He was aware that the concept of time is an extremely elusive one. "'Time' as a substantive is terribly misleading",[18] but his new techniques of philosophical analysis automatically put him in a better position to dissolve the puzzles our complex concept of time very easily gives rise to. Before considering in detail what I take to be his final conception, let us quickly see how he draws the distinctions I mentioned above. From notes of his classes we have the following statement

> We have here two independent orders of events (1) the order of events in our memory. Call this memory time. (2) the order in which information is got by asking different people, 5 – 4 – 3 o'clock. Call this information time. In information time there will be past and future with respect to a particular time. And in memory time, with respect to an event, there will also be past and future. Now if you want to say that the order of information is memory time, you can. And if you are going to talk about information and memory time, then you can say that you remember the past. If you remember that which in information time is future, you can say "I remember the future".[19]

According to Wittgenstein, we need two concepts of time, one which serves basically to order experiences and another one to order events. In the first case no particular date is involved. Dates appear with the second one, that is, with the inter-subjective notion of time, thanks to which the activities of the community of speakers can be coordinated. Now it is important to understand that we don't have here two applications of one and the same concept (as in the case of "pain") but two different concepts of time and also that they are nevertheless related to each other and could not possibly exist in isolation, as Wittgenstein had believed in the *Tractatus*.

In his masterful paper, "Wittgenstein on being and time", Hintikka shows that Wittgenstein's criticism of the *Tractatus*' conception of time was due to his abandoning of the notion of pictoriality (that is, the pictorial character of propositions). Soon after his return to philosophy, Wittgenstein very quickly got rid of the *Tractarian* idea that a proposition is simply something that is directly compared with reality. Wittgenstein was at the time increasingly recognizing the importance of the application of language and this in turn led him to confer on propositions a more practical or pragmatical or even praxiological character. But this change brings along with it the idea of a physical world and, therefore, the idea of public time. For Wittgenstein, from 1929 onwards, it was therefore more and more difficult to go on advocating the idea of a purely phenomenological time, *i.e.*, the solipsist's concept of time. Moreover, his emphatic rejection of the

---

[18] L. Wittgenstein, "Philosophy" in: *Wittgenstein's Lectures. Cambridge 1932-1935*, edited by Alice Ambrose (Oxford: Basil Blackwell, 1979), p.15.

[19] L. Wittgenstein, Ibid., p.15.

philosophical idea of privacy forced Wittgenstein to get rid of any idea of time about which we simply could not possibly speak in public language. "Ergo", Hintikka concludes,

> the time we live in is memory-time, but the only time we can directly speak of in our language is information-time. Thus Wittgenstein's change of mind had clearcut implications for his conception of time. It meant a total victory of physical time.[20]

Before raising a couple of objections to Hintikka's reconstruction of Wittgenstein's ideas about time, we have to finish the overall picture he elaborates for us. According to him, the Wittgensteinian dichotomy "memory time – information time" is "a special case of two different general distinctions. They are the distinction between perspectival vs. public identification and between phenomenological and physicalistic language systems".[21] In fact, Hintikka identifies Wittgenstein's dichotomy "memory time – information time" with his own distinction between "perspectival identification" and "public identification". In this respect, Hintikka says something which, in my view, leads him in a quite different direction than Wittgenstein's. According to Hintikka, we have to take into account the contrast

> between two kinds of discourse, involving two different kinds of objects identified. Very briefly, in our actual thinking and speaking we are tacitly using two different cognitive systems. The difference does not lie in a difference between different cognitive attitudes, for instance between two different kinds of knowledge or two kinds of memory. It lies in the way we identify the objects of our perception, knowledge or memory.[22]

Thus, in Hintikka's interpretation, the objects of memory time are identical with phenomenological objects and since Wittgenstein rejected the latter, he had to give way to the public mode of identification *at the expense of the perspectival identification* one. It is worth noticing that Hintikka accepts that the perspectival identification is simply a variety of physicalistic language, that is, natural language, but does not draw out the consequences of this rather important fact. For him the problem is the relation between the two systems of identification and natural language.

> But what is the relationship of the two kinds of frameworks to ordinary language and to its semantics? Here Wittgenstein reached an important insight. Wittgenstein realized that the 'grammar' we use in describing our immediate experiences is different from the 'grammar' (semantics) of ordinary discourse. The world we live in may in some sense be a world of phenomenological objects, but the world

---

[20] J. Hintikka, "Wittgenstein on being and time", p.11.
[21] J. Hintikka, Ibid., p. 11.
[22] J. Hintikka, Ibid., p. 11.

we speak of in our ordinary language is indeed the world of physical objects. Speaking more generally, he in effect realized, even though he expressed his point in a different terminology, that almost all of *the semantics of our language relies in its operation on the public mode of identification.*[23]

Now I think that, although there is plenty of elucidatory observations in Hintikka's paper, he nevertheless is seriously wrong on certain points. Roughly speaking, it can be objected, first, that there is nothing more alien to Wittgenstein's perspective than Hintikka's rather vague and inexact way of speaking about language (*e.g.*, "almost all the semantics": how much of it?); secondly, and more importantly, I think that it is implied by Hintikka's reconstruction that Wittgenstein aimed, with respect to verbs like 'remember', at privileging the third as opposed to the first person and this must be wrong. And, thirdly, I hold that for Wittgenstein the issue of the connection between those two identification systems and natural language was senseless, since for *him both of them were a part of or belonged to it*. Therefore it seems to me a sheer mistake to ascribe to Wittgenstein the idea that memory time *has* to be conceived as a time of phenomenological objects. I shall presently try to make clear why what Hintikka asserts under this heading is wrong.

Hintikka seems to advocate the idea that Wittgenstein was trying to reduce one identification mode (the "perspectival" one) to another (the "public" one). In my view, *both* modes are not only irreducible to each other but indispensable. Wittgenstein himself introduces the notions of "memory-time" and "information-time". So from his point of view the memory-time language-game is as objective as the information-time language-game. In both cases we can speak of past, present or future and of earlier than or later than, but in one case I speak of what really happened and in the other case I speak of what I remember. What I remember may coincide with what happened, but it may also be false. In this sense, "private" time is as objective as "public" time, although of course the concepts are applied in accordance with different rules. For instance, they are not verified in the same way. Anyway, the crucial point is that it is only if both are used that we can draw the contrasts we usually need. This is so for, as a matter of fact, we just don't stay at a fixed position, but are constantly moving around a set of objects which are incessantly moving too. Thus we need not one but two different modes of identifying and coordinating them in a single homogeneous whole. Something similar happens with the personal pronoun 'I': it's not because we discovered that there is no such thing as an "I", a self, that 'I' becomes meaningless or that we have to forget about it. After all, there is the use of 'I' as "object" and its use as "subject". What we have to grasp and understand are its different sets of rules, to understand, *e.g.*, that the denotation of 'I' changes depending upon who occupies the center of language. It would be very

---

[23] J. Hintikka, Ibid, p. 14.

strange if the grammar of words like 'I' or 'time' were not significantly more complex than that of a simple noun like 'chair'.

So as a matter of fact we need not two but four temporal series, that is, the series <"earlier than"-"now"-"later than"> and the series <"past"-"present"-"future"> applied in two different ways. They are first needed to identify events, but they are also needed to give expression to our memories. Were we to lack the information-time language-game, we would be unable to describe the world and were we to lack the memory-time language-game we would be unable to speak of remembering anything whatever; we would be unable to explain, *e.g.*, memory errors. Let us consider one example to justify our claim.

Let us suppose that we want to speak of, say, the battle of Austerlitz. We may wish to do, first, two different things. If I say that the battle of Austerlitz is a past event, the only thing I'm doing is to locate it within a particular set of events. But then I cannot identify it, for such a set includes countless other objects or events which will all have the same property, *viz.*, being past items. If I want to identify the battle of Austerlitz and distinguish it from, say, the battle of Eylau, both being past events, then I shall have to use the notions of "before" and "after", since these words introduce asymmetrical relations and with them the idea of order, which can then be applied to groups of events. In other words, these categories enable us to structure them; in fact that is what they were created for. So it would be impossible for us to forgo any of the two series: in one case I locate the battle of Austerlitz within a group which has as an axis my present, and if I wish to point to it I shall have to employ the "before" and "after" categories. Only then shall I be able to locate at a precise point the first of the above mentioned battles and to distinguish it from the second one. The truth is that it makes no sense to ask which set of temporal categories has priority, since my interests may change. On some occasions, when I already know that an event is previous to another one, what I may wish to know is whether they are future, present or past events. What would happen if we had only one temporal series? Clearly there would be many things we just would be unable to express. If the only thing I can say is that x is before or after y, I won't be able to answer questions like 'when ...?', and if I only have the "past-present-future" categories I will be able neither to order them in a sequence nor to identify each element of the group. The two systems are independent of each other, in the sense that they are irreducible, but that does not make them dispensable. It could perhaps be argued that the notions of past, present and future are more basic than "before" or "previous to" and "after" or "later than", since the former enable us to group together huge blocks of events, while the latter put an order on already conformed blocks of them. For my part, I take the issue of priority as both irrelevant and trivial. What we have to understand is that both are necessary, but not sufficient temporal systems.

Now this cannot be the end of the story, for I may speak of what I remember or do not remember, but how are we going to account for memory mistakes? Anybody may be wrong in making a memory claim, we may remember something more or less vaguely, we may confuse the order of events or even memories with fantasies or hallucinations. Thus memory-time is simply not reducible to information-time. What has to be avoided, therefore, is not the idea of memory-time itself, but its solipsistic interpretation. When I say that something happened, I imply that I remember it, that is, I locate it in the set of my memories at such and such point, *i.e.*, as present as opposed to future and as earlier than some event and later than another one. But my memory may or may not correspond exactly to the actual happening of events and thus my memory-time statement may or may not correspond to the information-time proposition. On the other hand, it is clear that memory claims are public statements, moves in a particular language-game and not the expression of something only the subject has access to. The idea of memory-time, therefore, does not compel us to accept anything connected with the philosophical notion of privacy.

If what I have said is right, it follows that it is a mistake to link, as Hintikka does, the Wittgensteinian notion of memory-time with the solipsistic pseudo-concept of time and, therefore, with phenomenological objects, private objects of "immediate experience" and so forth. The "total victory" of physical time does not imply the abolition or the transformation of memory-time. After all, few things are as alien to Wittgenstein's way of thinking as the idea that there is a world in which we live and another world we speak of, an idea that Hintikka does ascribe to Wittgenstein. It would be quite useful to carry out an analysis of expressions like 'I remember that' or 'he remembers that'. For obvious reasons I cannot do that in this paper and so I will not be able to show in detail why the idea of memory in the first person does not commit us to internal, private and mental objects. I think we can now go on to present, although in a rather sketchy way, what could be said from a Wittgensteinian point of view about traditional philosophical theories concerning time.

VI. Diagnosis of puzzles

It would be extremely dogmatic (and rather clumsy) to state in a categorical way that all the puzzles concerning time and which have worried the most brilliant minds throughout history have been solved once and for all. Nevertheless some progress has been realized and, I hold, mainly thanks to Wittgenstein's insights and conceptual apparatus. We have to bear in mind that our study has not an empirical character and thus it is not meant to have genetic implications or connotations. We are describing no phases of mental evolution, just as we are not interested in establishing any kind of temporal or cognitive hierarchy or primacy. Still less is our aim to "reduce" one concept of time to another. There have been, however, throughout the history of philosophy, thinkers who have tried to develop "programs" which instantiate one or other of the above mentioned options. For us, the concept of time emerges from natural language and is in this sense indisputable. What we ask is above all: which use do we make of the concept of time? After all what was this concept coined for? Questions like these indicate that what really matters is in the end the language of time.

With this in the back of our minds, let us face first the intriguing puzzle of the unreality of past and future and, correspondingly, the sole reality of the present. The truth is that any speaker is capable of feeling tempted into saying that only the present is real. Here the interesting question is: why is it that, occasionally at least, we all feel like saying things like that? The diagnosis is, I think, clear: the speaker's trouble is similar to the problem that someone has who believes that "experience" is only what he has, what happens to him; other people just behave like he does when he feels pain, but the experience of pain is something that only he can have. What such people don't seem to understand is that the concept of experience has two different modes of application and that what is absurd is to try to explain its use in the first person in terms of its use of the third person, or the other way around. What has to be done is to recognize both uses. So in the case of past, present and future, what has to be understood is that there are true propositions in present tense as well as true propositions in past tense. Both may be true and false and both have their peculiar or *sui generis* mode of being verified, refuted, contrasted, accommodated with others and so on. It could even be admitted that there is a sense in which all of them are verified in the present. This, however, doesn't matter, since they are not verified in the same way. 'My neighbour is having a party right now' is not verified in the same way as 'Napoleon died in St. Helen in 1821', even if there is a sense in which both are verified in the present. Thus whoever rejects the reality of the past must be someone who thinks that the only possible way to verify propositions is to verify them as sentences in the present tense are. Indeed, he must be in a serious state of confusion. This diagnosis is interesting, I think, because if accepted, that is, if one accepts the point made by it, then we no longer feel like saying what we were tempted to say. Once we understand that we may have different classes of true propositions we shall no longer try at all costs to reduce the tense of some of them to the tense of others; we then shall no longer wish to state that only the present is real.

The empiricists exemplify quite well another sort of philosophical error, namely, 'psychologism'. I must say that in general, and in particular with respect to time, to link conceptual analysis to psychological and introspective exercises seems to be something dangerously misguided. Locke and Russell, to quote just two of the greatest representatives of empiricism, are good instances of it. To explain time both of them appeal to introspection, to the powers of the mind, to memory and so on, without realizing that all that is wholly irrelevant for the understanding of the common or normal meaning (*i.e.*, non technical meaning) of, say, 'remembering', 'memory', 'before', 'instant', etc. Their approach is similar to somebody's approach for whom in order to determine the meaning of 'eating' it would be necessary to speak of gastric liquids. This is obviously wrong, because although empirically it is a fact that the act of eating is linked to the action of gastric liquids, this is a *datum* known *a posteriori*, an empirical discovery which logically presupposes that the meaning of 'eating' has already been grasped. So we can infer that the notion of gastric liquid is not included in the meaning of the verb 'to eat' and that, therefore, it is irrelevant for its clarification. The same happens, *mutatis mutandis*, with the ideas of time and, say, memory. Locke, for example, tries to get the idea of time out of the idea of succession of experiences, images, thoughts and so on, not realizing that the very idea of succession is already a temporal idea. For his part, Russell pushes forward the same idea to its last consequences and so he holds that what we know by acquaintance can only be the specious present, that is, what has just passed but still remains in consciousness and that it is thanks to this peculiar experience that we can know what the past is. Few thesis seem to me as absurd as this one. Nevertheless, his system requires it, for otherwise there would be a kind of empirical knowledge which would not be founded on acquaintance.

As a matter of fact and very broadly speaking, philosophical theories incorporate or take shape in myths, which clearly have their source in deep misunderstandings of certain forms of speaking, of certain ways of expressing ourselves. In the end, such myths turn out to be very pernicious. Myths like that are, for instance, the myths of the self, of intentionality, of pure temporal succession apprehended in introspection, of eternal truths, etc. The great advantage (and indeed, superiority) of the Wittgensteinian approach is precisely that it enables us to avoid such myths, to get rid of them, freeing us from their hypnotic spell. The case of time, if I'm not mistaken, shows that it is so. From this perspective, as some philosophers have asserted it, *e.g.*, that time is not real amounts to asserting that 'time' has no regular, objective, socially sanctioned use. This is impossible to accept and, accordingly, the corresponding philosophical thesis *must* be utterly misguided.

VII. Final comments

I would like to end this essay by presenting in a somewhat compact way the central features of the concept of time, features milked from an examination of its application. Thus perhaps the first thing we have to say is to recall that 'time' denotes neither something external nor something internal to us. The concept of time has nothing to do with "immediate experience". In other words, to speak of the "experience of time" is to create one more philosophical myth. It is the natural outcome of a grammatical illusion. This, however, does not imply that the concept of time is not an empirical one, as opposed to a, say, mathematical concept. It is obviously a concept which applies to the world. But if it is empirically applicable and is not a concept of experience, what kind of concept it is then? My view is that it is basically an organizational and coordinating concept. Thanks to it the users of language may coordinate their activities and organize their lives with respect to the constant change of both objects and speakers. This explains why the language of time takes shape in the first place in the lexicon of dates (months, years, days, hours, etc.). In this sense, the concept of time is not only unavoidable but needed and, given the importance of its role, it is even understandable its having been labeled '*a priori*'. It follows from what I have been saying that the idea of an objectless world is the idea of a timeless world. But what sort of idea is the idea of a objectless, completely empty world? Surely it is an unintelligible idea. Therefore, the idea of a timeless world is utterly nonsensical. Now what all this entails is that philosophical discussions like those concerning the reality or the irreality of time are not only sterile but cognitively useless, completely lacking sense. And finally, I wish to point out that, just as happens in psychology with concepts which emanate from natural language,[24] the "mother" or source concept, that is, the natural concept of time, may give rise to a technical one, which will turn out to be a function of the theoretical and practical requirements of disciplines like biology, psychology or astrophysics. There is a legitimate sense for expressions like 'biological time', 'psychological time', 'physical time' and so on. This natural conceptual transfiguration does create, as is to be expected, new philosophical puzzles about which, however, I will not even try to occupy myself in this essay.

Bibliography

St. Augustine, *Confessions* in *The Philosophy of Time. A Collection of Essays*, edited by Richard M. Gale (New Jersey: Humanities Press, 1978).

Bouveresse, J., *La Rime et la Raison* (Paris: Les Éditions de Minuit, 1973).

Gale, R. M. (ed.), *The Philosophy of Time. A Collection of Essays*. (New Jersey: Humanities Press, 1978).

Hintikka, J. & M., *Investigating Wittgenstein* (Oxford: Basil Blackwell, 1986).

Hintikka, J., "Wittgenstein on being and time", en: *Ludwig Wittgenstein: Half-Truths and One-and-a-Half-Truths* (Dordrecht/Boston/London: Kluwer Academic Publishers, 1996).

---

[24] See my "Materialism, Interactionism and Grammatical Analysis" in my book Essays in the Philosophy of Psychology (Guadalajara: Universidad de Guadalajara, 1994).

McTaggart, J. M. E., *The Nature of Existence*, Vol. II (Cambridge: University Press, 1927), in: Richard M. Gale, *op. cit.*

Reichenbach, H., *The Philosophy of Space & Time* (New York: Dover Publications, 1958).

Russell, B., *Problems of Philosophy* (Oxford: Oxford University Press, 1980).

Russell, B., *Mysticism and Logic* (London: Allen and Unwin, 1976).

Russell, B., "On the Experience of Time", in: *The Collected Papers of Bertrand Russell*, Vol. 7 (London: George Allen and Unwin, 1984).

Smart, J. J. C. (ed.), *Problems of Space and Time* (New York: Macmillan Publishing Co, 1964).

Wittgenstein, L., *Notebooks 1914-1916* (London: Routledge and Kegan Paul, 1978).

Wittgenstein, L., *Tractatus logico-philosophicus* (London: Routledge and Kegan Paul, 1978).

Wittgenstein, L., "Philosophy" in *Wittgenstein's Lectures. Cambridge 1932-1935*, edited by Alice Ambrose (Oxford: Basil Blackwell, 1979).

Wittgenstein, L., *Philosophical Investigations* (Oxford: Basil Blackwell, 1974).

JESÚS PADILLA-GÁLVEZ

Spanish Wittgenstein Bibliography (1986 - 2001)

Abreu e Silva Neto, N. (1995), "Resignation of feelings and will", in: K. S. Johannessen/T. Nordenstam (eds.), *Culture and Value* (ÖLWG), Kirchberg am Wechsel, 453-458.

Abreu e Silva Neto, N. (1998), "Maurice Drury and the psychiatric vocabulary", in: P. Kampits/K. Kokai/A. Weiberg (eds.), *Applied Ethics* (ÖLWG), Kirchberg am Wechsel, 13-20.

Abreu e Silva Neto, N. (1998), "The Knowledge of Other Minds: Wittgenstein and Carnap", in: J. Padilla-Gálvez/R. Drudis Baldrich (eds.), *Wittgenstein y el Circulo de Viena. Wittgenstein und der Wiener Kreis*, Cuenca, 49-60.

Abreu e Silva Neto, N. (2001), "Facing the unavoidable metaphysics: Notes on the work of Maurice Drury", in: W. Lütterfelds/A. Roser/R. Raatzsch (eds.), *Wittgenstein-Jahrbuch 2000*, Peter Lang, 63-87.

Acero, J. J. (1990), "Significado y necesidad en el *Tractatus*", *Daimon*, 2, 5-41.

Acero, J. J. (1993), *Lenguaje y filosofía*, Barcelona.

Acero, J. J. (1999), "Wittgenstein, la definición ostensiva y los límites del lenguaje", *Teorema* XVIII/2, 5-17.

Aguirre, J. (1991), "¿Cómo hablar de Dios hoy? La meditación religiosa en Wittgenstein", *Analogía*, (5:1), 79-105.

Alemán, A. (1994), "La noción de convención en Wittgenstein", *Revista de filosofía*, (7:12), 369-381.

Alemán, A. (1995), "Wittgenstein: lógica, matemáticas y convención", *Revista de filosofía*, (8:14), 57-75.

Alemán, A. (2001), *Lógica, matemáticas y realidad*, Madrid.

Almeida Marques, J.O. de (1995), "Espaço e tempo no 'Tractatus' de Wittgenstein. Espaço e tempo". Guas de lindoia, 14.-17.10.1993. Ed. by F.R.R. Évora. Campinas: Centro de logica, Epistemologia e Historia da Ciencia.

Álvarez Ortega, F. (1990), "Dos nociones wittgensteinianas en torno a la filosofía", *Revista de Filosofía*, (23-69), 375-381.

Aranzueque, G. (1995), "Realidad y mundo en el *Tractatus* de Wittgenstein. Notas para una ontología integral", *Revista de Filosofía*, (8:14), 45-56.

Arregui, J.V. (1992), "Wittgenstein on voluntary actions", *International Philosophical Quarterly*, (32:3:127), 299-311.

Arregui, J.V. (1994), "'Yo pienso' y 'yo quiero'. Razones de una simetría", *Anales del Seminario de Metafísica*, 28, 211-226.

Arregui, J.V. (1996), "Descartes and Wittgenstein on Emotions", *International Philosophical Quarterly* (36/3), 319-334.

Arregui, J.V. (1996), "On the Intentionality of Moods: Phenomenology and Linguistic Analysis", *American Catholic Philosophical Quarterly* (70/3), 397-411.

Arregui, J.V. (1997), "¿Fue Wittgenstein pragmatista? Algunas observaciones desde Vico", *Anuario Filosófico* (30/2), 353-360.

Aurrekoetxea Olabarri, M.[et al.] (1999), *Filosofiaren historia. Español / Historia de la filosofía: 2° ESPO: Bachillerato. Wittgenstein.* [traductores, Mikel Gillenea Mujika, Idoa Gillenea Mujika], Euba (Vizcaya).

Aurrekoetxea Olabarri, M.[et al.] (1999), *Filosofiaren historia 2. DBHO: Batxilergoa. Wittgenstein*, Bilbao.

Ayestaran Uriz, I. (1995), "Tecnologias del apartheid: Foucault, Wittgenstein, Negri", *Daimon,* (11), 47-59.

Ayuso Díez, J. M. (1991), "El ahogo del lenguaje. Sobre el carácter místico de la ética de Wittgenstein", *Cuadernos Salmantinos de Filosofía,* (18), 37-50.

Balderas Rosas, G. del C. (1996), "La concepción de 'leyes de la naturaleza' en el 'Tractatus' de Ludwig Wittgenstein", *Analogía* (10/2), 259-265.

Barceló Aspeitia, A. (2000), *Mathematics as Grammar. 'Grammar' in Wittgenstein's Philosophy of Mathematics during the Middle Period.* (Accepted by the Graduate Faculty, Indiana University, in partial fulfillment of the requirements for the degree of doctor of Philosophy), Bloomington.

Bermúdez, J.L. (1995), "Skepticism and Subjectivity: Two Critiques of Traditional Epistemology Reconsidered", *International Philosophical Quarterly* (35/2), 141-158.

Blanco Estellés, J.L. (1993), "La teoría del conocimiento en el 'Tractatus'", in: V. Sanfélix Vidarte (ed.), *Acerca de Wittgenstein*, Valencia, 21-29.

Boero Vargas, M. (1991), "Retrato de Wittgenstein", *Cuadernos Hispanoamericanos: Revista Mensual de Cultura Hispánica* (490), Madrid, 131-138.

Boero Vargas, M. (1994), "Wittgenstein: espiritualidad y mística en su biografía", *Logos,* (22:64), 39-81.

Boero Vargas, M. (1994), "La homosexualidad en Wittgenstein. Críticas y contribuciones", *Studium,* (34:3), 409-436.

Boero Vargas, M. (1996), "¿Qué pasa con Wittgenstein?", *Claves de razón práctica,* (63), 64-67.

Boero Vargas, M. (1996), "Wittgenstein y 'la palabra redentora'", *Logos,* (24:71), 43-49.

Boero Vargas, M. (1998), *Biografia y mística de un pensador*, Madrid.

Boero Vargas, M. (1997), "Bibliografía sobre Wittgenstein", *Cuadernos Hispanoamericanos: Revista Mensual de Cultura Hispánica* (561), Madrid, 137-141.

Boero Vargas, M. (1997), "Bataille y Wittgenstein: Aproximaciones místicas (En el centenario del nacimiento de Georges Bataille)", *Cuadernos Hispanoamericanos: Revista Mensual de Cultura Hispánica* (563), Madrid, 93-106.

Boero Vargas, M. (1997), " '¡Vive feliz!' Influjo de William James en el status de la felicidad wittgensteiniana", *Studium,* (37:3), 489-497.

Boero Vargas, M. (1998), "Lo indecible y el Zen en la vida de Wittgenstein", *Logos,* (26:77), 35-66.

Boero Vargas, M. (1999), "El 'comunismo' de L. Wittgenstein", *Claves de razón práctica,* (92), 68-71.

Bonín Aguiló, F. (1993), "Lenguaje, signos y realidad en el *Tractatus* de Wittgenstein", in: *Actas del I. Congreso de la Sociedad de Lógica*, Madrid, 151-155.

Bonín Aguiló, F. (1997), "Análisis de interpretaciones sobre realidad y mundo en el Tractatus de Wittgenstein", in: *Actas del II. Congreso de la Sociedad de Lógica*, Barcelona, 7-11.

Bustos, E. de (1995), "Wittgenstein y la evolución de la filosofía analítica", *Arbor: Ciencia, Pensamiento y Cultura* (150/589), 73-101.

Cano Cuenca, G. (1994), "La cárcel del lenguaje. Un comentario sobre el tema wittgensteiniano de 'Das Mystische' en el Tractatus logico-philosophicus", *Anábasis*, (1:1), 59-81.

Castany i Magraner, B. (1990), *Lectura de Husserl, Kant, Wittgenstein*, Barcelona.

Castilla Lázaro, R. (1990), "Wittgenstein, Hans Lipps y los supuestos de la predicación", *Diálogos*, (25:56), 123-133.

Cerezo, M. (1993), "La discusión acerca de la naturaleza de los objetos simples del 'Tractatus logico-philosophicus'", in: *Actas del I. Congreso de la Sociedad de Lógica*, Madrid, 32-35.

Cerezo, M. (1996), "Tractatus 2.013: An Essentialist Discussion Concerning Empty Logical Space", *Truth, Logic, Representation and the World* (Spanish), Santiago de Compostela, 177-192.

Cerezo, M. (1997), "Tractatus 4.221: la dificultad del Satzverband", in: *Actas del II. Congreso de la Sociedad de Lógica*, Barcelona, 12-17.

Cerezo, M. (1998), *Lenguaje y lógica en el* Tractatus *de Wittgenstein. Crítica interna y problemas de interpretación*, Pamplona.

Cerezo, M. (1998), "Nombrar kripkeano versus Nombrar tractariano: un intento de demarcación", *Theoria* (Spain), (13/33), 427-444.

Cirera, R./Ibarra, A./Mormann, Th. (eds.) (1997), *El Programa de Carnap: Ciencia, lenguaje, filosofía*, Barcelona.

Cordua, C. (1992), "Literatura reciente sobre Wittgenstein", *Diálogos*, (27:60), 197-217.

Cordua, C. (1992), "Wittgenstein y Heidergger, como críticos de la teoría", *Revista Agustiniana* (33/100), 383-305.

Cordua, C. (1993), "Literatura reciente sobre Wittgenstein, II.", *Diálogos*, (28:61), 169-193.

Cordua, C. (1993), "Explicación con ejemplos", *Diálogos*, (28:62), 1-30.

Cordua, C. (1994), "La claridad filosófica y cómo alcanzarla, según Wittgenstein", *Diánoia*, (40), 221-243.

Cordua, C. (1995), "Wittgenstein: Generalidad, Causalidad, Hipótesis", *Revista Latinoamericana de Filosofía* (21/2), 197-222.

Cordua, C. (1997), "La religiosidad de Wittgenstein", *Revista Agustiniana* (38/117), 789-825.

Cordua, C. (1997), *Wittgenstein. Reorientación de la filosofía*, Santiago de Chile, Dolmen.

Costa, J. M. (2001), "Wittgenstein, cincuenta años de silencio", *ABC, Cultura*, 29-4-2001, 44.

Cresto, E. (1996), "Algunas estrategias naturalistas contra el escéptico", *Revista de Filosofía* (Argentina) (11/1-2), 21-33.

Cruz, M. (2001), "Cincuenta años en la estela de Wittgenstein", *El País, Opinión*, 28. 4. 2001, 12.

Defez i Martin, A. (1990), *Wittgenstein i el problema del coneixement: una exposició crítica*, [tesis doctoral València: Universitat, Servicio de Publicaciones, 1990. - 8 microfichas (726 fotogramas): negativo ; 11x15 cm + 1 v. (5 p.). - (Tesis doctorales / Universitat de València ; n. 375-10)], Valencia.

Defez i Martin, A. (1994), "Dígales que mi vida ha sido maravillosa", *Isegoría*, 9, 154-163.

Defez i Martin, A. (1998), "Realismo esencialista y nominalismo irrealista: Acerca de la objetividad del conocimiento del mundo", *Pensamiento*, (54/210), 417-442.

Drudis Baldrich, R. (1992), *Bibliografía sobre Ludwig Wittgenstein: literatura secundaria (1921-1985)*, Madrid.

Drudis Baldrich, R. (1998), *Wittgenstein (1889-1951)*, Madrid.

Esparza Bracho, J. (1989), "El concepto de filosofía y conocimiento en Ludwig Wittgenstein", *Revista de Filosofía* (Zulia), 12, 55-65.

Esteban, J.M. (1993), "Argumentos wittgensteinianos en la filosofía de H. Putnam", in: V. Sanfélix Vidarte (ed.) (1993), *Acerca de Wittgenstein*. Valencia, 171-180.

Estela Gallach, A. (1995), "¿Es Wittgenstein un pensador antropocéntrico?", *Pensamiento*, (51:200), 269-281.

Fermandois, E. (1997), "Teoría, terapia, modo de ver: sobre la concepción wittgensteiniana de la filosofía", *Enrahonar*, 27, 75-101.

Ferrater Mora, J. (1949), "Wittgenstein o la destrucción", *Realidad* (13), 1-2; 14, 129-140.

Ferrater Mora, J. (1952), "Wittgenstein oder die Destruktion", *Der Monat* (4), 41, 489-495.

Ferrater Mora, J. (1953), "Wittgenstein, a Symbol of Troubled Times", *Philosophy and Phenomenological Research* (14), 89-96.

Ferrater Mora, J. (1954), "Wittgenstein, símbolo de una época angustiada", *Theoria (Spain)*, (7/8), 33-38.

García-Mauriño, J. M./Fernández Revuelta, J. A. (1992), *Historia de la filosofía*, Madrid.

García Picazo, P. (1998), "Viena roja: La ciudad oculta (1919-1934)", *Revista de Occidente* (207), 111-129.

García Baca, J. David (1933), *Assaigs Moderns per a la fondamentació de les matemàtiques*. Societat Catalana de Ciènces Fisiques, Químiques i Matemàtiques, Barcelona.

García Baca, J. David (1936), *Introducción a la lógica moderna*. Barcelona.

García Baca, J. David (1951), "Sobre las relaciones entre la lógica esquemática de Wittgenstein y la lógica axiomática de Hilbert", *Acta Científica Venezolana*, 2, 56-61, 103-105,144-147.

García Baca, J. David (1954), "Wittgenstein: Philosophical Investigations", *Revista Nacional de Cultura*, mayo-junio, 157-158.

García-Mauriño, J. M./Fernández Revuelta, J. A. (1988), *Wittgenstein Filosofía y Lenguaje*, Madrid.

García Norro, J. J. (1995), "La controversia acerca de las proposiciones sintéticas *a priori*. Reflexiones en torno a la proposición 6.3751 del *Tractatus* de Wittgenstein", *Anales del Seminario de Metafísica*, 29, 11-27.

García Selgas, F. J. (1986) *Aspectos fundamentales de las relaciones entre lenguaje y conocimiento: lenguaje y realidad: una investigación a partir de Wittgenstein*. Universidad Complutense de Madrid, (Colección Tesis doctorales; n. 51/86), Madrid.

García Suárez, A. (1972), "Cartesianismo fuerte y cartesianismo débil: A propósito de David Pears: Wittgenstein", *Teorema*, 8, 99-103.

García Suárez, A. (1972), "¿Es el lenguaje del *Tractatus* un lenguaje privado? ", *Teorema*, Número monográfico sobre el Tractatus logico-philosophicus, 117-130.

García Suárez, A. (1974), "Solipsismo y 'experiencia privada'", *Teorema*, (IV/1), 91-106.

García Suárez, A. (1976), *La lógica de la experiencia. Wittgenstein y el problema del lenguaje privado*, Madrid.

García Suárez, A. (1990), "Wittgenstein y la idea de un lenguaje privado", *Daimon*, 2, 87-98.

García Suárez, A. (1991), *Interpretaciones del pensamiento de Wittgenstein: lección inaugural del curso 1991-1992*, Oviedo.

Gil de Pareja, J.L. (1992), *La filosofía de la psicología de Ludwig Wittgenstein*, Barcelona.

Gil Velasco, A. (1989-90), *Filosofía*, Madrid.

Gómez Fernández, J.L. (1992), "Filosofía analítica: Wittgenstein y Ayer", *Diseño*, 32 pp.

Gomila Benejam, A. (1996), "La teoria de las ideas de Descartes", *Teorema* (16/1), 47-69.

González, W.J. (1995), "Strawson's Post Kantian Empiricism", Hintikka, J./Puhl, K. (eds.), *The British Tradition in 20th Century Philosophy (Proceedings of the 17th International Wittgenstein-Symposium, 14th to 21st August 1994, Kirchberg am Wechsel)*, Vienna, 249-257.

Grimaltòs, T. (1992), "Els fets negatius en el 'Tractatus Logico-Philosophicus'", *Theoria* (Spain), (7:16-17-18), 847-858.

Gutiérrez, E. (1997), "Lenguaje significativo y no significativo: 'El Kaspar' de Handke", *Revista Latina de Filosofía* (23/1), 153-167.

Hierro Sánchez Pescador, J. (1992), "La idea de mostrar en el 'Tractatus' de Wittgenstein", *Theoria* (Spain), (7:16-17-18), 859-874.

Hoyos, J. G. (1990), "Ética: acerca de la fenomenología de la regla para el análisis del problema de los fundamentos", *Daimon*, 2, 99-114.

Hoyos, J. G. (1992), "Wittgenstein: un concepto polémico de filosofía", *Revista de la Universidad de Antioquía*, (61:228), 23-37.

Iranzo, V. (1993), "Extensionalidad y proposiciones elementales en el 'Tractatus'", in: V. Sanfélix Vidarte (ed.) (1993), *Acerca de Wittgenstein*, Valencia, 31-41.

Jaramillo, J.M. (1989), "El 'Tractatus' y el Círculo de Viena", *Universitas Philosophica*, (7:13), 31-41.

López Baeza, C. (1993), "El análisis de las formas proposicionales de la psicología y la crítica del sujeto en el 'Tractatus'", in: V. Sanfélix Vidarte (ed.), *Acerca de Wittgenstein*. Valencia, 43-68.

López Cerezo, J.A. (1994), "La naturaleza de la ciencia en el *Tractatus*: Una lectura contemporánea", *Theoria* (Spain), 9, 75-88.

López de Santa María Delgado, P. (1986), *Introducción a Wittgenstein: sujeto, mente y conducta*, Barcelona.

López de Santa María Delgado, P. (1990-91), "'como nuestra vida'. Lo místico en el segundo Wittgenstein", *Er*, (11), 139-149.

López de Santa María Delgado, P. (1993), "'Pienso, luego no existo': la constitución del sujeto en Wittgenstein", *Anuario Filosófico*, (26:2), 261-269.

López de Santa María Delgado, P. (1998), "Wittgenstein: el mundo como voluntad y representación", in: J. Padilla-Gálvez/R. Drudis Baldrich (eds.), *Wittgenstein y el Circulo de Viena. Wittgenstein und der Wiener Kreis*, Cuenca.

Lorenzo, J. de (1998), "Criterios conceptuales para unas historias de la matemática", in: J. Padilla-Gálvez/R. Drudis Baldrich (eds.), *Wittgenstein y el Circulo de Viena. Wittgenstein und der Wiener Kreis*, Cuenca.

Marrades Millet, J. (1993), "Gramática y naturaleza humana", in: V. Sanfélix Vidarte (ed.), *Acerca de Wittgenstein*, Valencia, 97-111.

Martínez Freire, P. (1995), "Wittgenstein y Fodor sobre el Lenguaje Privado", *Anuario Filosófico*, (28/2), 357-376.

Marzal Melici, J.J. (1993), "Los cimientos de un castillo en el aíre. (El segundo Wittgenstein y la estética)", in: V. Sanfélix Vidarte (ed.) (1993), *Acerca de Wittgenstein*, Valencia, 161-169.

Meléndez Acuña, R. (1998), *Verdad sin fundamentos: una indagación acerca del concepto de verdad a la luz de la filosofía de Wittgenstein*, Bogotá.

Moros Ruano, E. (1991), "La concepción de los místico en el 'Tractatus Philosophicus' de Ludwig Wittgenstein", *Filosofía*, 3, 129-146.

Moya Espí, C. (1993), "Mente, sustancia y contexto", in: V. Sanfélix Vidarte (ed.) (1993), *Acerca de Wittgenstein*, Valencia, 123-135.

Muñoz Veiga, J. (1998), "Ludwig Wittgenstein y la idea de una concepción científica del mundo", in: J. Padilla-Gálvez/R. Drudis Baldrich (eds.), *Wittgenstein y el Circulo de Viena. Wittgenstein und der Wiener Kreis*, Cuenca.

Nieto Blanco, C. (1997), *La conciencia lingüística de la filosofía: Ensayo de una crítica de la razón lingüística*, Madrid.

Nubiola, J. (1995), "W. James y L. Wittgenstein: ¿Por qué Wittgenstein no se consideró Pragmatista?", *Anuario Filosófico* (28/2), 411-423.

Nudler, O. (1996), "Problemas filosóficos y filosofías del límite", *Cadernos de Historia e Filosofia Ciencia* (6), 85-96.

Ortiz de Landazuri, C. (1997), "La sociedad civil ante la ciencia", *Anuario Filosófico* (30/3), 627-658.

Padilla-Gálvez, J. (1986-87), "Review of: *Wittgenstein on Rules and Private Language. An Elementary Exposition. Saul A. Kripke*", in: *Theoria (Spain)*, (4), 207-210.

Padilla-Gálvez, J. (1990), "Review of: *Wittgensteins Philosophische Untersuchungen. Ein Kommentar für Leser, E. von Savigny*", in: *Theoria (Spain)*, (12-13), 282-286.

Padilla-Gálvez, J. (1990), "Review of: *Interpreting Wittgenstein: A Cloud of Philosophy, a Drop of Grammar. R. Suter*", in: *Theoria (Spain)*, (12-13), 295-299.

Padilla-Gálvez, J. (1991), "El origen de la controversia acerca de la noción de regla", *Arbor*, (543:138), 80-97.

Padilla-Gálvez, J. (1991), "Wittgenstein sobre la noción de regla en Frege", *Diálogos*, (57), 101-111.

Padilla-Gálvez, J. (1994), "Die spanische Rezeption des Wiener Kreises", *Nachrichten der FDÖP*, 5, 7-24.

Padilla-Gálvez, J. (1995), "Filosofía austríaca. Investigación y documentación", *Llull*, (18:34), 300-302.

Padilla-Gálvez, J. (1995), "Gibt es in der Sprache ein metaphysisches Subjekt?", *Culture and Value. Philosophy and the Cultural Sciences* (eds. K.S. Johannessen/T. Nordenstam), Kirchberg a. W.

Padilla-Gálvez, J. (1995), "Die Verwendung des Wortes 'Ich' bei Ludwig Wittgenstein – Eine sprachanalytische Skizze zur Selbstbezüglichkeit des Selbstbewußtseins", *Wittgenstein Studies*, 06-1-95.txt, Wien.

Padilla-Gálvez, J. (1996), "El Círculo de Viena, reconsiderado", *Arbor*, (CLV, 612), 9-13.

Padilla-Gálvez, J./Drudis Baldrich, R. (eds.) (1998), *Wittgenstein y el Circulo de Viena. Wittgenstein und der Wiener Kreis*, Cuenca.

Padilla-Gálvez, J. (1998), "Wittgenstein y el Circulo de Viena: Wittgenstein und der Wiener Kreis", in: J. Padilla-Gálvez/R. Drudis Baldrich (eds.), *Wittgenstein y el Circulo de Viena. Wittgenstein und der Wiener Kreis*, Cuenca.

Padilla-Gálvez, J. (1998), "Was trägt Wittgenstein zu der Carnapschen Metalogik bei?", in: J. Padilla-Gálvez/R. Drudis Baldrich (eds.), *Wittgenstein y el Circulo de Viena. Wittgenstein und der Wiener Kreis*, Cuenca.

Padilla-Gálvez, J. (2001), "Fremdverstehen, Spracherlernen, Horizonterweiterung", in: W. Lütterfelds/D. Salehi (eds.) *„Wir können uns nicht in sie finden". Probleme interkultureller Verständigung und Kooperation. Wittgenstein Studien*, 3, 87-101.

Padilla-Gálvez, J. (2002), "Nichts ist dunkler als das Licht. Das Problem der Farben bei Wittgenstein, Goethe, Rizzetti und Newton", *Philosophisches Jahrbuch*, 108, 259-273.

Palavecino, S.R. (1996), "La certeza fuera de la verdad", *Kriterion* (35/93), 184-194.

Pecellín, M./Reguera, I. (eds.) (1990), *Wittgenstein - Heidegger*, Badajoz.

Pérez Otero, M. (2000), "El argumento antiintelectualista de Wittgenstein sobre la comprensión del lenguaje", Theoria (Spain), (15/1), 155-169.

Pozo, A. del/Prades, J.L./Raga, V. (1981), *Historia de la filosofía/textos básicos: Platón, Aristóteles, Descartes, Hume, Kant y Wittgenstein [selección]*, Valencia.

Prades, J.L./Sanfélix, V. (1990), *Wittgenstein: Mundo y lenguaje*, Madrid.

Prades, J.L. (1993), "Epistemología del contenido y del significado", in: V. Sanfélix Vidarte (ed.), *Acerca de Wittgenstein*, Valencia, 83-95.

Quintanilla, (1997), "Significado y Verificación: Las Posibilidades de una teoría holista de la interpretación", *Ideas Valores*, 30-50.

Reguera, I. (1980), *La miseria de la razón: (el primer Wittgenstein)*, Madrid.

Reguera, I. (1994), *El feliz absurdo de la ética: (el Wittgenstein místico)*, Madrid.

Reguera, I. (1998), "Was heißt 'philosophieren' für Wittgenstein?", in: J. Padilla-Gálvez/R. Drudis Baldrich (eds.), *Wittgenstein y el Circulo de Viena. Wittgenstein und der Wiener Kreis*, Cuenca.

Reguera, I. (2001), "El destino de un genio: El filósofo Ludwig Wittgenstein", *El País, Babelia*, 28. 4. 2001, 4-5.

Rivadulla, A. (1998), "The Popperian Revolution in the Methodology of Science", in: J. Padilla-Gálvez/R. Drudis Baldrich (eds.), *Wittgenstein y el Circulo de Viena. Wittgenstein und der Wiener Kreis*, Cuenca.

Rivera, S. (1994), "Ludwig Wittgenstein: Entre paradojas y aporías", *Almagesto*, 145 pp.

Rivera, S. (1996), "Ludwig Wittgenstein: Matemáticas y ética", *Cuaderno de Etica* (21-22), 135-151.

Roche Ruiz, J. (1981), *Filósofos: Russell, Wittgenstein, Sartre: C.O.U.*, Valencia.

Rodríguez Consuegra, F. (1992), "El impacto de Wittgenstein sobre Russell: últimos datos y visión global", *Theoria* (Spain), (7:16-17-18), 875-911.

Rodríguez Consuegra, F. (1995), "Bertrand Russell and Bradley's Ghost (I): Evolution and Significance of Russell's Difficulties concerning Relations (1897-1905)", in: J. Hintikka/K. Puhl, (eds.), *The British Tradition in 20th Century Philosophy (Proceedings of the 17th International Wittgenstein-Symposium, 14th to 21st August 1994, Kirchberg am Wechsel)*, Vienna, 353-66.

Rodríguez Pereyra, G. (1993), "La anotación 202 de las Investigaciones Filosóficas de Wittgenstein", *Anales del Seminario de Metafísica*, (27), 25-37.

Rodríguez Sutil, C. (1991), *Wittgenstein y el problema de la mente en la psicología contemporánea*, [Editorial de la Universidad Complutense, 1991. - VII, 316 p. ; 22 cm. - Colección Tesis doctorales ; n. 211/91)], Madrid.

Rodríguez Sutil, C. (1998), *El cuerpo y la mente: una antropología wittgensteiniana*. (Prólogo, Nicolás Caparrós), Madrid

Rubio Marco, S. (1993), *La estética desde el pensamiento filosófico del segundo Wittgenstein*, [Microforma/Universitat de València, Servei de Publicacions, 1993. - 6 microfichas (V, 564 fotogramas): negativo ; 11 x 15 cm + 1 v. ([8] p.) / (Tesis doctorals en microfitxes, n. 375-20)], Valencia.

Rubio Marco, S. (1995), *Comprender en arte: (para una estética desde Wittgenstein)*, Valencia.

Sádaba, J. (1980), *Conocer a Wittgenstein y su obra*, Barcelona.

Sádaba, J. (1989), *La filosofía moral analítica de Wittgenstein a Tugendhat*, Madrid.

Sádaba, J. (1990), "Wittgenstein: ética y religión", *Cuaderno gris*, (7-8), 44-54.

Sádaba, J. (1992), *Lenguaje, magia y metafísica: (el otro Wittgenstein)*, Madrid.

Salas, de J. (2001), "El judío errante", *ABC, Cultura*, 29-4-2001, 44.

Salas, M. (1994), "Wittgenstein y la escalera – acerca de la proposición 6.54 del Tractatus", *Revista de Filosofía de la Universidad de Costa Rica*, (32:78-79), 181-188.

Salinas Moya, A. (1990), *El problema del lenguaje en la obra de Wittgenstein*, Córdoba.

Sánchez Cámara, I. (1996), *Derecho y lenguaje: la filosofía de Wittgenstein y la teoría jurídica de Hart*, La Coruña.

Sánchez-Mazas, M. (1954), "La ciencia, el lenguaje y el mundo según Wittgenstein", *Theoria (Spain)*, (7/8), 127-130.

Sanfélix Vidarte, V. (Ed.) (1993), *Acerca de Wittgenstein*. Valencia.

Sanfélix Vidarte, V. (1993), "Los límites de la lógica", in: V. Sanfélix Vidarte (ed.), *Acerca de Wittgenstein*, Valencia, 9-19.

Santianez-Tio, N. (1996), "Poeticas del modernismo: espíritu lúdico y juegos de lenguaje en La incógnita", *MLN*, Baltimore, MD, 299-326.

Tamayo Valencia, A. (1989), "Observaciones sobre el 'Cuaderno Azul' de Ludwig Wittgenstein", *Universitas Philosophica*, (7:13), 43-56.

Tamayo Valencia, A. (1992), "La ética de Ludwig Wittgenstein", *Cuadernos de Filosofía Latinoamericana*, (50-51), 145-157.

Tamayo Valencia, A. (1994), "Ludwig Wittgenstein: la filosofía como arte", *Cuadernos de Filosofía Latinoamericana*, 61, 5-15.

Tejedor Palau, M.A. (1996), "La crítica de Wittgenstein al escepticismo. Moore y 'Sobre la certeza'", *Anales del Seminario de Historia de la Filosofía*, 30, 287-296.

Terricabras, J.M. (1978), *Ludwig Wittgenstein. Kommentar und Interpretation*, Freiburg.

Terricabras, J.M. (1989), *A Wittgenstein Symposium: Girona*, Amsterdam.

Terricabras, J.M. (1990), "Els 'jocs de llenguatge' en la filosofia de Wittgenstein", *Enrahonar*, 16, 57-64.

Terricabras, J.M. (1998), *Teoría del coneixement*, Barcelona.

Terricabras, J.M. (1999), *Atrévete a pensar: la utilidad del pensamiento riguroso en la vida cotidiana*, Barcelona.

Tomasini Bassols, A. (1988), *El pensamiento del último Wittgenstein. Problemas de filosofía contemporánea*, México D. F.

Tomasini Bassols, A. (1992), "Heráclito y el 'Tractatus'", *Revista de Filosofía* (Universidad Ibero-Americana), (24:73), 42-53.

Tomasini Bassols, A. (1993), "Dos nociones de objeto en el *Tractatus*", *Analogía Filosófica*, (7:2), 101-114.

Tomasini Bassols, A. (1994), "Dos concepciones del lenguaje", *Analogía Filosófica*, (8:2), 37-72.

Tomasini Bassols, A. (1994), *Ensayos de Filosofía de la Psicología*, Guadalajara.

Tomasini Bassols, A. (1994), *Lenguaje y Anti-Metafísica. Cavilaciones Wittgensteinianas*. México D.F.

Tomasini Bassols, A. (1995), *Enigmas Filosóficos y Filosofía Wittgensteiniana*. México D.F.

Tomasini Bassols, A. (1999), *Nuevos Ensayos de Filosofía de la Religión*. México D.F.

Tresserras, M. (1995), "Wittgenstein: del silenci al llenguatge religiós", *Ars Brevis*, 1, 239-251.

Valcarcel, A. (1998), "Sobre la verdad de la proposición: La ética y la estética son una", in: E. Moya (ed.), *XIIe Congres Valencia de Filosofía, Casaban*, Valencia.

Valdés Villanueva, L.M. (1990), "Una mala comprensión de Wittgenstein", *Daimon*, (2), 217-227.

Vega, L. (1989), "Wittgenstein, un 'outsider' en lógica", *Contextos*, (7:13), 79-103.

Velázquez Jordana, J. L. (1992), *Wittgenstein y Ayer: la filosofía analítica*, Madrid.

VV.AA. (1990), "Aspectos de la filosofía de L. Wittgenstein", *Daimon*, 2, 5-41; 43-70; 87-98; 217-227.

Wankun, D. (1997), "La religión en Wittgenstein. Estudio de las 'Clases sobre creencia religiosa'", *Areté* (9:2), 271-292.

Zilhao, A.J.T. (1998), "A Sort of Philosophy Worth Only of Sancho Panza, who Had the Faculty to See Dulcinea by Hearsay", in: J. Padilla-Gálvez/R. Drudis Baldrich (eds.), *Wittgenstein y el Circulo de Viena: Wittgenstein und der Wiener Kreis*, Cuenca.

Spanish Doctoral Dissertations about Wittgenstein

Alonso Puelles, Antonio, *Wittgenstein y el arte. El siglo de Wittgenstein.* Universidad del País Vasco, 1995.

Casals Navas, Josep, *La crisis del sujeto en la cultura del finis Austriae.* Universidad de Barcelona, 1990.

Castillo Santos, Ramón José del, *La práctica y los límites de la interpretación (el pragmatismo de Peirce, Dewey y Wittgenstein).* Universidad Complutense de Madrid, 1992.

Cerezo Llana, M. Mar, *El Tractatus Logico-Philosophicus y su interpretación esencialista.* Universidad de Navarra, 1996.

Defez Martín, Antoni, *Wittgenstein i el problema del coneixement: Una exposicio crìtica.* Universidad de Valencia, 1989.

Drudis Baldrich, Raimundo, *La noción de filosofía en Wittgenstein.* Universidad Complutense de Madrid, 1996.

García Selgas, Fernando José, *Aspectos fundamentales de las relaciones entre lenguaje y conocimiento. Lenguaje y realidad: Una investigación a partir de Wittgenstein.* Universidad Complutense de Madrid, 1984.

Gea Izquierdo, Francisco Javier, *Aspectos transcendentales y metatranscendentales en el pensamiento de Wittgenstein.* Universidad de Granada, 1995.

Gil de Pareja Otón, José Luis, *La filosofía de la psicología de Ludwig Wittgenstein.* Universidad de Murcia, 1988.

Izquierdo Martínez, Jesús, *Intenciones y acciones. El problema de la intencionalidad en el contexto de la controversia explicaciones/comprensiones.* Universidad de Salamanca, 1984.

Jareño Alarcón, Joaquín, *Relativismo y lenguaje religioso en la filosofía de Ludwig Wittgenstein.* Universidad de Murcia, 1998.

López de Santa María Delgado, M. Pilar, *El sujeto y la mente en la filosofía de Wittgenstein,* Universidad de Navarra, 1981.

Prades Celma, José Luis, *Filosofía del lenguaje y teoría de la mente en las Investigaciones Filosóficas de Wittgenstein.* Universidad de Valencia, 1986.

Rodríguez Sútil, Carlos, *Wittgenstein y el problema de la mente en la psicología contemporánea,* Universidad Complutense de Madrid, 1989.

Rubio Marco, Salvador, *La estética desde el pensamiento filosófico del segundo Wittgenstein.* Universidad Autónoma de Madrid, 1990.

Vicente Arregui, Jorge Nicolás, *Acción y sentido en el pensamiento de Ludwig Wittgenstein,* Universidad de Navarra, 1981.

Vidal Claramonte, M. Carmen África, *Bajo el signo de Saturno o la apertura posmoderna.* Universidad de Alicante, 1988.

Villarmea Requejo, Stella Gabriela, *El Problema del escepticismo en la epistemología analítica contemporánea.* Universidad Complutense de Madrid, 1997.

Translations

Ayer, A. J. (1986), *Wittgenstein, a life*, [traducción castellana de Joaquim Sempere], Barcelona.

Barret, C. (1994), *Ética y creencia religiosa en Wittgenstein*, [Versión española de Humberto Marraud González], Madrid.

Bartley, W. (1982), *Wittgenstein*, [Traducción (del inglés) de Javier Sádaba] Madrid.

Baum, L. (1988), *Ludwig Wittgenstein: vida y obra*, [traductor, Jordi Ibáñez], Madrid.

Bouveresse, J. (1993), *Wittgenstein y la estética,* [traducción, introducción y notas, José Javier Marzal Felici y Salvador Rubio Marco], València.

Brand, G. (1987), *Los textos fundamentales de Ludwig Wittgenstein*, [versión española de Jacobo Muñoz e Isidoro Reguera], Madrid.

Fann, K. T. (1975), *El concepto de filosofía en Wittgenstein*, [traducción por Miguel Ángel Bertrán], Madrid.

Hanfling, O. (1982), *Filosofía del lenguaje: significado y uso en 'Los Cuadernos azul y marrón' de Wittgenstein*, [Instituto de Ciencias de la Educación de la Universidad de Valencia], Valencia.

Hartnack, J. (1977), *Wittgenstein y la filosofía contemporánea*, [prólogo y traducción de las versiones alemana e inglesa de Jacobo Muñoz], Barcelona

McGuinness, B., *Wittgenstein: el joven Ludwing (1889-1921)*, [Versión española de, Huberto Marraud González], Madrid.

Malcom, N. (1990), *Ludwig Wittgenstein*, [Esbozo biográfico de G.H. von Wright], Madrid.

Monk, R. (1994), *Ludwig Wittgenstein: el deber de un genio*, [traducción de Damián Alou], Barcelona.

Mounce, H. O. (1993), *Introducción al* Tractatus *de Wittgenstein*, [traducción de José Mayoral y Pedro Vicente], Madrid.

Noll, J. (2001), *Ludwig Wittgenstein y David Pinsent*, [traducción de Octavio di Leo], Barcelona.

Pears, D. (1973), *Wittgenstein*, [traducido por José Planells], Barcelona.

Pitkin, H. F. (1984), *Wittgenstein: el lenguaje, la política y la justicia: sobre el significado de Ludwing Wittgenstein para el pensamiento social y político*, [introducción y traducción por Ricardo Montoro Romero], Madrid.

Schulz, W. (1970), *Wittgenstein: la negación de la Filosofía*, [traducción de José Montoya Sáenz], Madrid.

Scruton, R. (1983), *Historia de la filosofía moderna: de Descartes a Wittgenstein* [traducción del inglés de Vicent Raga], Barcelona.

Strathern, P. (1998), *Wittgenstein en 90 minutos*, [traducción de José A. Padilla Villate], Madrid.

Toulmin, A. J. S. (1974), *La Viena de Wittgenstein*, [versión castellana de Ignacio Gómez de Liaño], Madrid.

Wright, G. H. von/Malcolm, N./Poole, D. (1966*), Las filosofías de Ludwig Wittgenstein*, [Traducción, Ricardo Jordana]. Introducción J. Ferrater Mora, Barcelona.

The Work of Ludwig Wittgenstein translated in Spanish, Catalan, Basque

Wittgenstein, L. (1973), *Tractatus lógico-philosophicus*. Introducción de Bertrand Russell, [versión española de Enrique Tierno Galván], Madrid.

Wittgenstein, L. (1979), *Cartas a Russell, Keynes y Moore*. Edición e introducción a cargo de G. von Wright con la colaboración de B. F. McGuinness; [versión del inglés de Néstor Míguez], Madrid.

Wittgenstein, L. (1981), *Tractatus logico-philosophicus*, [traducció i edició a cura de Josep Maria Terricabras], Barcelona.

Wittgenstein, L. (1983), *De la certesa*. [traducció i edició a cura de Jossep Lluís Prades i Vicent Raga ; pròleg de Oswald Hanfling], Barcelona.

Wittgenstein, L. (1986), *Diario filosófico (1914-1916)*, [traducción de Jacobo Muñoz e Isidoro Reguera]. - [1ª ed.], Barcelona.

Wittgenstein, L. (1987), *Observaciones sobre los fundamentos de la matemática*, [edición de G. Henrik von Wright, R. Rhes y G.E.M. Anscombe; versión española de Isidoro Reguera], Madrid.

Wittgenstein, L. (1988), *Investigaciones filosóficas*, [traducción castellana de Alfonso García Suárez y Ulises Moulines. - México: Instituto de Investigaciones Filosóficas], Barcelona.

Wittgenstein, L. (1989*), Conferencia sobre ética: con dos comentarios sobre la teoría del valor*, [Introducción de Manuel Cruz; traducción de Fina Birulés. (Instituto de Ciencias de la Educación de la Universidad Autónoma de Barcelona)], Barcelona.

Wittgenstein, L. (1990), *Conferencia sobre ética: con dos comentarios sobre la teoría del valor*. [Introducción de Manuel Cruz], Barcelona.

Wittgenstein, L. (1991), *Sobre la certeza*, [compilado por G.E.M. Anscombe y G.H. von Wright; traducido por Josep Lluís Prades y Vicent Raga (Ed. Bilingüe)], Barcelona.

Wittgenstein, L. (1992*), Lecciones y conversaciones sobre estética, psicología y creencia religiosa*, [Introducción y traducción de I. Reguera], Barcelona.

Wittgenstein, L. (1994), *Observaciones sobre los colores*, [introducción de Isidoro Reguera; traducción de Alejandro Tomasini Bassols], Barcelona.

Wittgenstein, L. (1994), *Los cuadernos azul y marrón*, [traducción, Francisco Gracia Guillén], Barcelona.

Wittgenstein, L. (1995), *Aforismos, cultura y valor / Vermischte Bemerkungen*. Español. Prólogo de Javier Sádaba; edición de G.H. Von Wright con la colaboración de Heikki Nyman; [traducción Elsa Cecilia Frost], Madrid.

Wittgenstein, L. (1996), *Al voltant del color / Ludwig Wittgenstein i Jacques Bouveresse*. presentació i traducció, Salvador Rubio. Universitat de València, Valencia.

Wittgenstein, L. (1996), *Observaciones a "La rama dorada" de Frazer*, [introducción y traducción de Javier Sábada; edición y notas de José Luis Velázquez], Madrid.

Wittgenstein, L. (1996), *Últimos escritos sobre filosofía de la psicología*, [edición preparada por G.H. von Wright y Heikki Nyman], Madrid.

Wittgenstein, L. (1997), *Investigacions filosòfiques*, [traducció i edició a cura de Josep M. Terricabras], Barcelona.

Wittgenstein, L. (1997), *Ocasiones filosóficas, 1912-1951*, [James C. Klagge y Alfred Nordmann (eds.); traducción de Ángel García Rodríguez], Madrid.

Wittgenstein, L. (1998), *Diarios secretos*, [Edición de Wilhelm Baum; traducción de los textos alemanes, Andrés Sánchez Pascual. *Cuadernos de guerra* / Isidoro Reguera], Madrid.

Wittgenstein, L. (1999), *Tractatus logico-philosophicus*, [versión e introducción de Jacobo Muñoz e Isidoro Reguera], Madrid.

Wittgenstein, L. (2000), *Etika, zientzia eta antropologia*, [sarrera eta itzulpena, Ignacio Ayestaran; Sailaren Arduraduna, Joxe Azurmendi], Donostia.

Wittgenstein, L. (2000), *Movimientos del pensar: diarios 1930-1932/1936-1937*, [edición de Ilse Somavilla; traducción de Isidoro Reguera], Valencia.

Authors and Editors

Prof. Dr. Norberto Abreu-e-Silva Neto

Professor of Clinic Psychology at Institute of Psychology, University of Brasília/UnB. He is Editor of Psicologia: Teoria e Pesquisa [Psychology: Theory and Research], national journal published by the Institute. Previously, he has taught at Institute of Psychology, University of São Paulo/USP, (1972-1992), where also he made his undergraduate and graduate studies. From this university he holds the title of Psychologist (1971), a Master degree (1977) and a PhD (1986) in Psychology, and the title of Associate Professor of Psychology of Personality (1991).

He has published: "Resignation of feelings and will", in: K.S. Johannessen/T. Nordenstam (eds.) (1995), Culture and Value (ÖLWG, Kirchberg am Wechsel, 453-458); "The knowledge of other minds: Wittgenstein and Carnap", in: J.P. Gálvez/R. Drudis Baldrich (eds.) (1998), Wittgenstein y el Círculo de Viena (ed. UCLM, Cuenca, 49-60); "Maurice Drury and the psychiatric vocabulary", in: P. Kampits/K. Kokai/A. Weiberg (eds.) (1998), Applied Ethics (ÖLWG, Kirchberg am Wechsel, 13-20); "Facing the unavoidable metaphysics: Notes on the work of Maurice Drury", in: W. Lütterfelds/A. Roser/R. Raatzsch (eds.) (2001), Wittgenstein-Jahrbuch 2000 (Frankfurt a.M.: Peter Lang, 63-87).

E-mail: norberto.abreu@uol.com.br

Dr. Axel Arturo Barceló Aspeitia

Full Time Associate Researcher (Instituto de Investigaciones Filosóficas) Universidad Nacional Autónoma de México.Studies: Philosophy Ph.D. (2000). Indiana University, Bloomington. Dissertation: "Grammar as Mathematics: 'Grammar' in Wittgenstein's Philosophy of Mathematics during the Middle Period" (UMI Dissertation Publishing, Bell & Howell Information and Learning, Ann Arbor, Michigan. 2000) Directed by Dr. David McCarty. 'Nelson' (1999 – 2000) and DGAPA (1994 – 1999) scholarships. Philosophy B. A. with honors (1994). Mexico's National University. Facultad de Filosofía y Letras. 'Gabino Barreda' Medal. Logic Seminar (1991-1995) Prof. Raúl Orayén. Instituto de Investigaciones Filosóficas, UNAM. Publications: "A Circular Logic for Computational Semantics", in: Carlos Zozaya et. al. (eds.) (2001), Memoria del 3er Encuentro Internacional de Ciencias de la Computación, ENC01. Sociedad Mexicana de Ciencias de la Computación; "Harold Bloom y la Deconstrucción Pragmatista", in: Samuel Cabanchik et. al (eds.), El Giro Pragmatico en la Filosofía Contemporánea, Gedisa (forthcoming); "Porgy, Bess y el Filósofo Crítico", in: Guillermo Hurtado (ed.), Memorias del Encuentro sobre la Naturaleza y el Sentido de la Filosofía, (forthcoming).

E-mail: abarcelo@minerva.filosoficas.unam.mx

Prof. Dr. Alejandro Tomasini Bassols

Full Time Researcher at the Instituto de Investigaciones Filosóficas) Universidad Nacional Autónoma de México (Mexico). He is the author of Los atomismos lógicos de Russell y Wittgenstein (1986); El pensamiento del último Wittgenstein (1988); Lenguaje y Anti-Metafísica. Cavilaciones wittgensteinianas (1994) and Enigmas filosóficos y filosofía wittgensteniana (1995), among others.

E-mail: bassols@servidor.unam.mx

Prof. Dr. Jesús Padilla-Gálvez, MA

Studied Philosophy, History and Mathematics at the University of Cologne (Germany). He took an M.A. (1983) and Dr. phil. (1988) in Philosophy at the University of Cologne (Germany). From 1988 to 1991 he worked as a Research Assistant on research about the Semantical Structure of the Metatheory at the University of Murcia (Spain). From 1992 to 1994 he was Associate Professor for Logic and Philossophy of Language at the University of León (Spain). From 1994 to 1999 Guest-professor at the Johannes Kepler Universität in Linz (Austria). Since 1999 Professor at the University of Castilla-La Mancha in Toledo (Spain). He has been Visiting Professor at the Universities of Erlangen-Nürnberg (Germany), Graz (Austria), Potsdam (Germany) and Cambridge (Great Britain). His publications include Referenz und Theorie der möglichen Welten (1989); Metalógica/ Metalogik. (ed.) (1995); El Círculo de Viena, reconsiderado (ed.) (1996); Wittgenstein y el Círculo de Viena/ Wittgenstein und der Wiener Kreis (ed.) (1998); Metateoría de las teorías científicas (2000).

E-mail: jpadillagalvez@hotmail.com
jpadilla@jur-to.uclm.es

Prof. Dr. Francisco Rodríguez-Consuegra

Philosophy Professor, Department of Logic and Philosophy of Science, Valencia University, since 1994. Former Assistant Professor/Lecturer, Barcelona University, 1991-94. Studies: MA and PhD Barcelona University. Post-doctoral studies: McMaster University, Canada (The Russell Archives, Visiting Scholar) and Harvard University, USA (Visiting Fulbright Scholar). Books: The mathematical philosophy of Bertrand Russell: origins and development (Basel, Boston and Berlin: Birkhäuser 1991, rep.1993); Kurt Gödel, Ensayos inéditos (F.R.-C., ed) (Barcelona: Mondadori 1994; English translation: Kurt Gödel, Unpublished philosophical essays, Basel, Boston and Berlin: Birkhäuser 1995; Japanese translation: Tokyo: Seidosha 1997), Bertrand Russell, Análisis filosófico (F. R.-C., ed., Barcelona, Paidós, 1999); W.V. Quine, Lenguaje, ciencia e indeterminación (F. R.-C., ed., Barcelona: Paidós 2001); Estudios de filosofía del lenguaje (Granada, Comares, forthcoming).
Articles: there is a full list of them here: http://www.uv.es/~rodriguf/publications.html

E-mail: Francisco.Rodriguez@uv.es
WWW: http://www.uv.es/~rodriguf/

Prof. Dr. Josep-Maria Terricabras Nogueras

Full Professor (Catedrático) for Philosophy and Head of the "Cátedra Ferrater Mora de Pensamiento Contemporáneo" at the University of Girona and staff member at the Institut d'Estudis Catalans. He was scholarship holder at the University of Münster (Germany), St. John's College (Cambridge) and at the University of Berkeley (California). His main interests are contemporary philosophy, particular logic, philosophy of language, theory of knowledge and ethics.

Recent publications include: Ludwig Wittgenstein: Kommentar und Interpretation (1978); Ètica i llibertat (1983); Fer filosofia avui (1988); La comunicació (1996); Atrévete a pensar (1999) y Raons i Tòpics (2001). He translated the Tractatus logico-philosophicus (1981) and the Investigacions filosòfiques (1983) into Catalan. He successfully carried out the project Philosophy for Children (1987-1995) and adapted a new version of the Diccionario de Filosofía of J. Ferrater Mora (1994).

E-mail: josepm.terricabras@udg.es

Editors of *Wittgenstein-Studien* – Deutsche Ludwig Wittgenstein Gesellschaft e.V. (DLWG) (German Ludwig Wittgenstein Society)

Prof. Dr. Wilhelm Lütterfelds, President of the DLWG
University of Passau
Institute of Philosophy
Innstr. 51
D-94030 Passau
E-mail: luette01@pers.uni-passau.de

PD Dr. phil. habil. Andreas Roser
University of Passau
Institute of Philosophy
Innstr. 51
D-94030 Passau
E-mail: andreas.roser@uni-passau.de
     roser@aon.at

PD Dr. phil. habil. Richard Raatzsch
University of Leipzig
Institute of Philosophy
Augustusplatz 9
D-04109 Leipzig
E-mail: raatzsch@rz.uni-leipzig.de

Redaction

Dr. Djavid Salehi
DLWG, Redaction of *Wittgenstein-Studien*
University of Passau
Institute of Philosophy
Innstr. 51
D-94030 Passau
Tel.: 0851-5092621, 089-31598562
Fax: 0851-5092622, 089-244367308
E-Mail: dlwg@phil.uni-passau.de
     salehi02@pers.uni-passau.de

Internetperformance (http://www.phil.uni-passau.de/dlwg)

Dr. Frank Börncke
University of Passau
Institute of Philosphy
Innstr. 51
D-94030 Passau
E-Mail: frank.boerncke@web.de

Wittgenstein-Studien

Herausgegeben von Wilhelm Lütterfelds,
Richard Raatzsch und Andreas Roser im Auftrag der DLWG

Band 1 Katalin Neumer (Hrsg.): Das Verstehen des Anderen. 2000.

Band 2 Gianluigi Oliveri (ed.): From the *Tractatus* to the *Tractatus* and Other Essays. 2001.

Band 3 Wilhelm Lütterfelds / Djavid Salehi (Hrsg.): "Wir können uns nicht in sie finden". Probleme interkultureller Verständigung und Kooperation. 2001.

Band 4 Sebastian Lalla: Solipsismus bei Ludwig Wittgenstein. Eine Studie zum Früh- und Spätwerk. 2002.

Band 5 Fritz Breithaupt / Richard Raatzsch / Bettina Kremberg (eds.): Goethe and Wittgenstein. Seeing the World's Unity in its Variety. 2003.

Band 6 Jesús Padilla-Gálvez (ed.): Wittgenstein, from a New Point of View. 2003.

Ludwig Nagl / Chantal Mouffe (eds.)

The Legacy of Wittgenstein: Pragmatism or Deconstruction

Frankfurt/M., Berlin, Bern, Bruxelles, New York, Oxford, Wien, 2001. 164 pp.
ISBN 3-631-36775-9 · pb. € 25.10* / US-$ 26.95 / £ 17.–
US-ISBN 0-8204-4796-X

What is striking in the current reception of Wittgenstein is just how wide-ranging his influence has become among those who are trying to elaborate an alternative to the rationalistic framework dominant today. Pragmatists and deconstructionists are at the forefront of such a movement, of course, and it comes as no surprise that several of them have turned to Wittgenstein and have opened up new perspectives on his work. This joint interest has created a very welcome bridge between post-analytic and continental philosophy which have all but ignored each other for far too long. A promising dialogue is now developing, one to which the contributions to this volume can testify. They were originally presented at a conference organized in November 1999 at the Centre for the Study of Democracy at the University of Westminster in London, sponsored by the Austrian Cultural Institute.
Contributors: Hilary Putnam (Harvard University), Linda Zerilli (Northwestern University), Henry Staten (University of Washington), James Conant (University of Chicago), Stephen Mulhall (Oxford University), Allan Janik (University of Innsbruck), Chantal Mouffe (University of Westminster, London), David Owen (University of Southampton) and Ludwig Nagl (University ov Vienna).

Contents: Hilary Putnam: Wittgenstein's Vision of Language · Linda Zerilli: Wittgenstein - Between Pragmatism and Deconstruction · Henry Staten: Wittgenstein's Deconstructive Legacy · Allan Janik: Wittgenstein's Critical Hermeneutics: From Physics to Aesthetics · Stephen Mulhall: Deconstruction and the Ordinary · James Conant: A Prolegomenon to the Reading of Later Wittgenstein · Chantal Mouffe: Wittgenstein and the Ethos of Democracy · David Owen: Cavell, Derrida and the Ethos of Democracy-to-come · Ludwig Nagl: Wittgenstein's Quest for 'Simplicity' and 'Ordinariness'